LORCA
Living in the Theatre

LORCA

Living in the Theatre

Gwynne Edwards

PETER OWEN
LONDON AND CHESTER SPRINGS

PETER OWEN PUBLISHERS
73 Kenway Road, London SW5 0RE

Peter Owen books are distributed in the USA by
Dufour Editions Inc., Chester Springs, PA 19425-0007

First published in Great Britain 2003 by
Peter Owen Publishers

ISBN 0 7206 1148 2

A catalogue record for this book is available from
the British Library

Printed and bound in Croatia by
Zrinski SA

For Rachel

Preface

Federico García Lorca is, as far as the English-speaking world is concerned, the best-known and most frequently performed Spanish dramatist of the twentieth century. In the last fifteen years, for example, there have been at least ten professional productions of *Blood Wedding* in the United Kingdom, not to mention regular amateur performances, and the reason for the appeal of Lorca's plays is not hard to find. Their plots are enormously powerful and dramatic: in *Blood Wedding* a bride runs off with her lover on the day of her wedding; in *Yerma* a wife longs for a child and murders her husband for his lack of understanding; and in *The House of Bernarda Alba* a widowed mother rules her five spinster daughters with a rod of iron, bringing about in the process the suicide of the youngest girl. Furthermore, Lorca created great and demanding roles, not least for women: Yerma, Bernarda Alba and the Mother in *Blood Wedding*, to mention only three. And, in addition, each of his plays evokes a world that offers marvellous opportunities to theatre directors, stage designers and musicians.

This study of Lorca's theatre sets out to place his plays in the context of his life as a whole: his sexual preoccupations, his social and cultural background and the political circumstances of his time, which led to the Spanish Civil War, and his murder at its outset. His plays were, in effect, the expression of all those things, a knowledge of which will be useful to students, actors and theatre practitioners in general. With the latter in mind, an account is also provided of the major productions of the plays both in Lorca's lifetime and afterwards, in the original Spanish and in English translation.

I wish to express my thanks to Susan Lloyd for her care and patience in preparing the typescript.

Contents

Illustrations

between pages 160 and 161

Introduction

Federico García Lorca's relatively short life (1898–1936) can be divided into a number of clearly defined periods, more or less corresponding to each decade that he was alive, and each in its turn influencing his work profoundly. Some dramatists express political views or deeply felt ideas in their work, which, although it may have a powerful charge, reveals little about their inner lives – Bernard Shaw comes readily to mind as a dramatist of this kind. And then there are those whose plays are metaphors and reflections of the times in which they live but which in a way seem quite divorced from their authors – Samuel Beckett and Harold Pinter are such writers, both clinical observers of the world around them. On the other hand, there are playwrights whose work is essentially the expression of their tortured lives, and of whom it is safe to say that without that anguish, whatever its nature, that work would not exist – Strindberg would not have written the plays he did had his personal life not been marked by sexual and marital conflict, and Tennessee Williams would not have produced such powerful and haunting theatre if his life had not been so beset by personal and family traumas. Lorca, of course, comes into this latter category. His plays are, from beginning to end, the expression of his emotional dilemmas and his sexual anxieties as well as of the pressures exerted on him by the kind of society in which he lived. This, it should be said, does not make the plays any better, for the quality of a piece of theatre depends on other things, but to know something of Lorca's life is certainly to explain the coherent, even obsessive nature of the issues which dominate his work, as well as its powerful emotional charge.

Born on 5 June 1898, Lorca spent the first ten years of his life in the countryside not far from the city of Granada, a factor that would influence much of his later work. Initially the Lorca family lived in the village of Fuente Vaqueros, where Federico's father was a successful farmer, and where he himself delighted in the beauty of nature and the animals that surrounded him. Then, when Lorca was nine years of age, the family moved to the village of Asquerosa (later renamed Valderrubio), three miles away, where they remained for two years and to which they would return for many years during the summer months. In addition to the important influence of the countryside, the future dramatist was also exposed, through the family servants, to the rich vein of traditional songs and ballads that would come to be so characteristic of his theatre. At about the age of eight, moreover, he had received an important present from his parents: a puppet-theatre with which he would entertain the servants and local children – already a dramatist-director in embryo.

A second crucial decade began in 1909 when the Lorca family moved from Asquerosa to Granada, at that time a provincial city of around 75,000 inhabitants. Lorca attended the College of the Sacred Heart of Jesus and, at the age of seventeen, entered the University of Granada where he studied, with no great enthusiasm or success, various arts subjects and Law. But his interests lay elsewhere. This intriguing city, recovered by the Christians from the Moors in 1492 after eight centuries of occupation, and boasting the Alhambra, one of the finest examples of Moorish architecture and craftsmanship, was for Lorca an endless source of fascination and inspiration. There too, under the guidance of Antonio Segura Mesa, Lorca began to develop his musical talents, in particular his abilities as a pianist, which account, of course, for the musical character of his language. At the university the influence of a number of teachers helped broaden his knowledge and interests, and, as a member of the group of intellectuals which met regularly at the back of the Café Alameda, he was constantly exposed to new and stimulating ideas of all kinds. By the age of nineteen he was also beginning to write, and the poems of this time reveal an obsession with sexual love, while a particularly revealing letter to a friend suggests that he was already aware of his homosexuality and of the problems which this would create for him in a narrow-minded, conservative and Catholic society.[1] Already feeling himself to be an outsider, he could identify with the other outsiders of Granada and the surrounding area: the Moors, the Jews and the gypsies who lived in the caves of the Sacromonte, all of them victims of centuries of persecution.

Ten years after the family moved to Granada, Lorca finally flew the nest and in the autumn of 1919 entered the prestigious Residencia de Estudiantes in Madrid, an educational institution based on the Oxbridge college system. As for his studies, he embarked on a Law degree, but, as had been the case in Granada, his interests were non-academic, notably poetry and theatre, both stimulated by his growing appreciation at the Residencia of the new cultural and artistic trends – Symbolism and Surrealism, for example – which were now to the fore in Europe as a whole. Lorca's first play, *The Butterfly's Evil Spell*, was completed and staged in Madrid in 1920. During the next nine years he wrote four more: *The Tragicomedy of Don Cristóbal and Señorita Rosita*, *Mariana Pineda*, *The Shoemaker's Wonderful Wife* and *The Love of Don Perlimplín*. There were collections of poems too: *Book of Poems*, *Songs*, *Poem of Deep Song*, *Suites* and *Gypsy Ballads*. The publication of the latter in 1928 brought Lorca considerable fame. Nevertheless, the end of the decade also brought a period of depression, the causes of which may have been complex but which most likely were a result of Lorca's homosexual involvement with and final estrangement from a young Madrid-based sculptor, Emilio Aladrén, as well as an increasingly strained relationship with Salvador Dalí. At all events, Lorca was persuaded by his family to leave Spain for a while, and in June 1929 he set sail for New York.

New York at the time of the Depression was hardly the place for someone already depressed, not to mention someone who spoke no

English and for whom this concrete jungle was a world away from the calm and tranquil beauty of Granada. It simultaneously horrified and fascinated Lorca. He detested its materialism and felt deeply for the oppressed blacks of Harlem, but he was also amazed by the city's architecture and energy. As far as his writing was concerned, the New York experience seemed to help him to come to terms with his emotional and sexual problems, for it led to three major works: the collection of poems, *Poet in New York* (not published in its entirety until 1940), and the two plays, *The Public* (1930) and *When Five Years Pass* (1931), both as ambitious in technique as they are revealing of their author's inner life.

After spending almost four months in Cuba, where he felt completely at home, Lorca went back to Spain at the end of June 1930. His return more or less coincided with a fundamental shift in Spanish politics and preceded an enormous outburst of creative energy on Lorca's part. The collapse of the seven-year dictatorship of Miguel Primo de Rivera in 1930 led, in 1931, to the creation of the Second Republic and the installation of a left-wing government whose primary aim was to provide greater opportunities in education and to offer the people the kind of freedom they had never previously enjoyed. It was in this context that Lorca became, with Eduardo Ugarte, the director of a touring university theatre company which came to be known as La Barraca and which, from 1932 until 1936, entertained – and thereby educated – the inhabitants of the smaller towns and villages of Spain with performances of the great Spanish plays of the sixteenth and seventeenth centuries.[2] During the whole of this period Lorca increasingly demonstrated his left-wing sympathies. As for his creative writing, over a four-year period he completed *Blood Wedding* (1933), *Yerma* (1934), *Doña Rosita the Spinster* (1935) and *The House of Bernarda Alba* as well as the one-act *Play Without a Title* (1936). He became Spain's most celebrated dramatist and, as far as his poetry was concerned, wrote the moving *Lament for Ignacio Sánchez Mejías* (1935) and the collection of poems, *Diwan of the Tamarit* (completed in 1934 but unpublished in his lifetime).

14

Lorca's increasing success and fame occurred, however, as Spain experienced growing political turmoil. In 1933 the Left had been defeated by the Right, and the next three years witnessed endless Cabinet reshuffles and social unrest, as well as the growth of Fascism in Spain and the rest of Europe. The triumph of the Left in the general election of 1936 made matters even worse, provoking still more bitter confrontations, and so it was that on 18 July the military rose up against the Madrid government in a co-ordinated attempt to save Spain from the Communists. Two days later most of Granada had been occupied and right-wing supporters of the *coup d'état* began to take their revenge on political opponents. Lorca was, of course, a supporter of the Left and a famous man, as well as a homosexual – in short, an affront to right-wing values and someone of whom to make an example. Fearing for his life, he sought refuge in the house of a fellow-poet, Luis Rosales, but he was arrested there on 16 August, held in the city for two more days, and then driven at night to Viznar, a village five miles from Granada. At dawn on the 18 or 19 August he was shot outside the village. His body was never found. In 1939, after the Civil War had ended, the Franco dictatorship declared that Lorca had died in August 1936 'from war wounds'.[3]

The Butterfly's Evil Spell opened on 22 March 1920 at the Teatro Eslava in Madrid. It encountered a hostile and disruptive audience, and was withdrawn after only a handful of performances. Given the staid and conservative nature of Spanish theatre, it is hardly surprising that such a reaction should have occurred, for the characters of Lorca's play are cockroaches, a butterfly, a scorpion and fireflies. The principal character, Boybeetle, falls in love with Butterfly, whose wing has been damaged. Fascinated by her beauty, Boybeetle abandons Sylvia, a female cockroach who loves him deeply, but he is in turn abandoned by Butterfly when she recovers and flies away, leaving him with a broken heart. This, it seems, had been the subject of a poem that Lorca had recited in June 1919 to Gregorio Martínez Sierra, who ran the Teatro Eslava, and his mistress, the actress Catalina Bárcena.

Excited by its possibilities, Martínez Sierra had then suggested to Lorca that, if he could turn the poem into a play, it would be staged in Madrid.

The significance of this first theatrical effort is to be found both in its themes and its style. In the Prologue to the play, directed to the audience, the author speaks of an insect 'who longed to go beyond' ordinary love, who was 'seized by a vision far removed from his normal way of life' (p. 83).[4] From the outset, then, the theme of love, so central to the rest of Lorca's theatre, comes to the fore, and, even though in the play which follows Boybeetle's passion is for a female, there could well be in the lines of the Prologue an allusion to homosexual love, for the point is made that 'love is born with the same intensity at all levels of existence', for in nature 'all things are equal' (p. 84). At all events, love leads to frustration, another Lorca preoccupation, because feelings change, and just as Sylvia is distraught at Boybeetle's change of heart, so he is left in despair by Butterfly's abandonment of him, a situation which anticipates the later work. Again, the fading beauty of the fireflies is linked to the destructive effect of passing time, another Lorca obsession, and the threatening presence of the scorpion carries with it a reminder of death, of which Lorca was always so conscious. *The Butterfly's Evil Spell* contains, in short, all the distinctive preoccupations of the dramatist's subsequent work.

The choice of insect characters may, of course, owe something to Lorca's experience of the countryside in Fuente Vaqueros and Asquerosa, but it was also influenced by avant-garde theatre, as was the play's style in general. Martínez Sierra was himself a dramatist, a translator of foreign plays and an opponent of naturalism in the theatre. Lorca clearly shared his view, and in this respect *The Butterfly's Evil Spell* reveals the influence of the Belgian symbolist playwright, Maurice Maeterlinck, whose work – *The Blue Bird* is an example – emphasized the symbolic and universal resonance of the characters and the stage-action and, in terms of technique, was highly stylized.[5] Lorca's characters are already the archetypal figures we encounter in the later plays – for Boybeetle read Young Man, for Doña Beetle, the Mother. The settings in which we encounter them are, far from being naturalistic, stylized images which reflect the mood of a particular episode, as in the case of the setting for Act One: '*The stage represents a green and humble meadow beneath the deep shade of a great cypress-tree . . . Beyond the meadow is a small pond surrounded by splendid lilies and blue stones. It is the pure hour of daybreak . . .*' (p. 85). This Garden of Eden perfection is an appropriate image for pure, innocent love. On the other hand, Boybeetle's growing anguish is reflected in the later stages of the play, as in the case of characters in the mature work, by the darkening of the stage, and, similarly, the mood of a character at any given moment is underlined by movement or by the absence of movement, anticipating moments in the later plays. For example: '*He [Boybeetle] sits on the stone and weeps, his little head between his hands*' (p. 107). In this particular play the influence of dance is also very important, and in the Eslava production the role of Butterfly was played by the celebrated dancer, Encarnación López Júlvez, 'La Argentinita', dancing to the music of Grieg. In short, regardless of its disastrous première, *The Butterfly's Evil Spell* attempted to put into practice the concept of total theatre – the close integration of setting, costume, movement, lighting and speech – favoured by the avant-garde theatre practitioners of the early part of the twentieth century, and in that particular sense is little different from Lorca's last masterpiece, *The House of Bernarda Alba*.

His second play, *Mariana Pineda*, was completed in 1923, although it was subsequently revised a good deal and did not receive its première until 24 June 1927, when it was performed at the Teatro Goya in Barcelona by the company of Margarita Xirgu. It seems quite possible that the failure of *The Butterfly's Evil Spell* gave Lorca food for thought, at least in terms of subject matter, when it came to writing his second play, for on this occasion he opted for a historical subject with which audiences would be much more familiar. Mariana Pineda, a twenty-seven-year old widow with two young children, had been executed –

in fact garrotted – in 1831 in Granada for her involvement with a liberal group opposed to the tyrannical rule of the then monarch, Ferdinand VII. In 1830 her lover, the liberal agitator Casimiro Brodett, had been deported, and the following March Mariana was accused of embroidering a liberal flag which had been discovered in the Albaicín, the hilly district of the city near the Alhambra. Placed under house arrest on the orders of the Granada Chief of Police, Ramón Pedrosa y Andrade, she was then held in the convent of Santa María Egipcíaca. Her execution followed her refusal to reveal the names of fellow liberals in exchange for a pardon.

What were Lorca's motives in choosing this particular subject, apart from wanting to play safe? Undoubtedly, he was familiar with the stories and the ballads about Mariana, which were part of Granada's folklore. He had heard them as a child, and he was constantly reminded of her by the statue erected in her memory in the Plaza de Mariana Pineda close to the Lorca family home in the city. As well as this, her story contained themes that fascinated Lorca and which he had begun to explore in *The Butterfly's Evil Spell*. For him the story of Mariana was as much about love as about politics, and, when she is eventually abandoned by her lover, about frustration. These were emotions to which Lorca could easily relate. Again, the subject was highly theatrical. What could be more dramatic than the Police Chief's attempt to possess Mariana in exchange for her freedom, her rejection of him, her imprisonment and execution? And thirdly, there was a highly relevant political angle in the sense that the repressive regime portrayed in the play had its counterpart, in the summer of 1923, in the seizure of power by the military, headed by General Miguel Primo de Rivera, who, with the approval of King Alfonso XIII, had seized power and appointed himself president, thereby initiating the dictatorship that would last for seven years. Although he was by no means a political animal, Lorca was throughout his life an advocate of liberal ideas – a point of view bound up, of course, with his own sexuality and his belief that love itself should not be prescribed by a narrow, hide-bound mentality. For him *Mariana Pineda* would be a play about love and freedom in the broadest sense.

In terms of its technique, Lorca's second play again reveals his love of stylization. Its subtitle, *A Popular Ballad in Three Engravings*, suggests that each act, or rather the setting for each act, is in effect a picture, while a closer consideration of Lorca's stage directions reveals the kind of bold simplicity associated with engravings and lithographs, as in the case of the First Engraving (or Act One): '*MARIANA's house. White walls. Upstage small balconies painted in dark colours*' (p. 4). There is here something of the photographic effect which he would achieve in *The House of Bernarda Alba*. And in the changing colours of Mariana's dresses – from mauve to yellow to white – which reflect her movement from hope to despair, there is a clear anticipation, as we shall see, of Doña Rosita. Similarly, from the outset red – in the thread used by Mariana to sew the liberal flag, as well as in the colour of the flag itself – points to the eventual spilling of blood, while the black clothing and cloak of Pedrosa, the Chief of Police, symbolize the evil he represents. The movement of the characters about the stage is also highly stylized, a pointer to the emotions which control the particular moment. So in the First Engraving Mariana's pacing of the stage reveals her agitation, while in the Third Engraving absence of movement – '*She sits on a bench with her head in her hands*' (p. 45) – encapsulates her despair. As for the language, *Mariana Pineda*, like *The Butterfly's Evil Spell*, is entirely in verse. This, of course, creates in this case the sense of a historical period, but at key moments verse also heightens the emotional effect. At all events, it is at the opposite extreme from naturalistic dialogue, and, together with the other stylized elements of the play – settings, costumes, colours, movement – suggests just how much Lorca sought to escape the constraints of the insistence on realism which made so much of the Spanish theatre of his day so tediously repetitive.

The other three plays written during the 1920s – *The Tragicomedy of Don Cristóbal and Señorita Rosita*, *The Shoemaker's Wonderful Wife* and *The Love of Don Perlimplín and Belisa in the Garden* – also represent a desire to escape the stranglehold of the commercial theatre of the time. In articles and interviews Lorca frequently complained of the way in which dramatists were at the beck and call of star actors demanding that plays be written to accommodate them and of theatre impresarios who merely wished to keep their audiences happy. It was partly for this reason, then, that Lorca was attracted by the tradition of the puppet-play, a form over which neither actors nor impresarios had much control.[6] It was also because the puppet tradition was characterized by a lack of inhibition in relation to the behaviour and the language of the puppets, which was in total contrast to the buttoned-up refinement of the drawing-room plays that Lorca so detested. Availing himself of a tradition which, as we shall see later, was much loved in Spain, he sought to write plays which were as fresh as they were innovative.

Although it was later reworked, the first version of *The Tragicomedy of Don Cristóbal and Señorita Rosita* was completed in the summer of 1922, before *Mariana Pineda*, and reveals therefore how Lorca was able to work on very different plays simultaneously. Subtitled a 'guignolesque farce', it is the traditional story of the old man, Don Cristobita, who desires the young girl, Rosita, who in turn loves the young man, Cocoliche. True to the puppet tradition, the play contains much lively knockabout action, including Cristobita's belabouring of the innkeeper and, in the concluding scenes, much dashing in and out and the concealment of two of Rosita's admirers in the wardrobes of her room. Throughout, the emotions of the characters, be they longing or fury, are expressed in a heightened form, and when at the end Cristobita dies of a stab wound and is placed in his coffin, he emits a bassoon-like noise which then becomes the sound of a piccolo.

For all its vigorous action, *The Tragicomedy* is, as its title suggests, the characteristic Lorca mixture of laughter and tears, as well as an exploration of his favourite themes. As to the first point, there is much humour to be found in the passionate declarations of the lovers, in

Cristobita's lustful desire for Rosita, in his preparations for the wedding – including the shaving scene – and in the rough and tumble of the finale. On the other hand, there are elements of sadness, too: in Cocoliche's separation from Rosita and his discovery that she is to marry Cristobita, as well as in the realization of Currito, her other admirer, that she loves Cocoliche more than him. In this respect *The Tragicomedy* dramatizes once more the theme of frustrated passion previously evident in both *The Butterfly's Evil Spell* and *Mariana Pineda*, and in Rosita's arranged marriage to Cristobita – engineered by her father for financial gain – it anticipates a similar situation in *Blood Wedding* and exposes the inability of women to exercise choice in a highly conventional society. In short, Lorca frequently used a traditional comic formula both for the expression of serious issues and the exploration of personal emotional and sexual dilemmas.

The boldness of the characters is, as one would expect in a puppet-play, paralleled in Lorca's instructions for the play's staging. Settings are therefore simply drawn and highly stylized, as in the case of the second scene: '*The small stage represents a square in an Andalusian town. To the right the house of* SEÑORITA ROSITA. *There should be an enormous palm-tree and a bench.*'[7] The characters themselves are boldly and colourfully dressed: Rosita in a long pink dress with a bustle, Cristobita in a green suit, Cocoliche in a dark green cloak and a young girl in a yellow dress. Both stage-settings and costumes reveal how, in the puppet tradition, Lorca encountered a style which was anti-naturalistic and which he would develop in his later and more mature plays. Furthermore, as has been suggested earlier, the use of puppets allowed for the expression of uninhibited and exaggerated emotion – sighing, shouting, cursing, stamping – and bold, spontaneous language, unimpeded by social niceties.

Lorca's fascination with the puppet tradition and the possibilities it offered him as a dramatist are displayed to the full in *The Shoemaker's Wonderful Wife*. He had possibly started work on it as early as 1924 and completed it by early 1928, although it did not have its first performance until 24 December 1930, when it was presented at the Teatro Español in Madrid by the company of Margarita Xirgu, who played the title role. Performed by actors, *The Shoemaker's Wonderful Wife* is not, therefore, a puppet-play, although in terms of style it certainly is, as its subtitle, *A Violent Farce in Two Acts*, suggests. The plot once more concerns the relationship of a young woman and a much older man, in this case the beautiful Wife married to the old Shoemaker. The first act reveals her dissatisfaction with the marriage, her frequent rows with her husband and the scorn poured on both of them by the villagers, not least for their failure to produce children. In Act Two, the Wife, now abandoned by her husband, is regaled by a succession of ridiculous suitors, all of whom she rejects. When the Shoemaker arrives in disguise and publicly relates the story of a disloyal wife, she defends her loyalty and her good name, and when he then reveals his true identity, they resolve to live together and defy malicious tongues.

The Shoemaker's Wonderful Wife anticipates Lorca's later work in the sense that important elements in it are based on personal experience. For example, the '*dress of strident green*' (p. 5) in which the Wife initially appears owes something to a dress worn by the dramatist's cousin, Clotilde García Picossi, in Fuente Vaqueros; the polka which the Wife likes so much was apparently played in the village on a clarinet; the Mayor was modelled on the mayor of the neighbouring village of Chauchina; the sword with which the Boy promises to defend the Wife was something which Lorca recalled from his childhood; and the Wife's colourful and earthy language was influenced by Dolores Cebrián, the maid of Emilia Llanos Medina, whom Lorca first met in Granada when he was twenty.[8] If *Mariana Pineda* reflected the political situation in 1923, *The Shoemaker's Wonderful Wife* drew on people and incidents which had been part of Lorca's personal experience.

The themes of passion and frustration are once again to the fore. The Wife, a passionate young woman, is frustrated by the incompatibility of her marriage to an older man, while he is driven to distraction by her fiery outbursts. Trapped in this unsuitable marriage, she consoles herself in day-dreams of handsome lovers, a world of illusion and fantasy contrasting markedly with the grotesque suitors who pursue her in reality. In this respect the Wife is another form of Boybeetle, dreaming of a future with the Butterfly, and of Mariana Pineda, imagining her lover's imminent return. She is also, no doubt, a form of Lorca himself whose emotional and sexual life had, by the time of the play's completion, become more complicated, not least on account of his relationship with Salvador Dalí. In addition, *The Shoemaker's Wonderful Wife* explores two other issues which would become key preoccupations in the plays of the 1930s. The Wife's affection for the Boy is all to do with the child she longs to have, and it suggests, perhaps, Lorca's growing awareness that, as a gay man, he too would never father a child of his own. Secondly, it is the Wife's failure to conceive which brings on her and the Shoemaker the scorn of the villagers, making them a subject of common and malicious gossip and thereby damaging their name – a theme to which Lorca would repeatedly return, ever conscious of the willingness of people to point the finger at his homosexuality. The exploration of these issues points to the fact that Lorca's comic plays also have an underlying seriousness, on account of which they are also at times extremely touching. The Shoemaker and his shrewish wife may indeed make us laugh, but beneath that laughter we are always aware of the essential sadness of their marriage.

Stylistically *The Shoemaker's Wife* has all the bold simplicity of the puppet tradition, as the setting for Act One suggests: '*The SHOEMAKER's house. A bench and tools. A completely white room. A large window and door. Upstage a white street with some small grey doors and windows*' (p. 5). When the Wife appears, she wears the '*dress of strident green*' (p. 5). At the end of Act One the neighbours are '*dressed in sharp, aggressive colours*' (p. 20). In short, the colours of the costumes are visual images of the nature of the characters, and this is underlined, of course, by gesture and movement, again much of which is firmly in the tradition of the puppet-play. So, the frustrated Shoemaker wallops a shoe with his hammer (p. 7), the Wife storms out in a furious temper (p. 11), and, at the end of the first act, as the neighbours make a great din, the Wife weeps and screams (p. 20). The language, too, is frequently aggressive, as in the opening confrontation between husband and wife: 'Who'd have said you'd treat me like this, you drunk old man? Go on! Hit me if you want to. Hit me with the hammer!' (p. 8). On the other hand, there are moments of great tenderness, as in the Wife's relationship with the Boy, in particular in the episode in Act One where he tries to catch the butterfly and they speak in hushed tones, or when, in lyrical vein, she evokes the men who have courted her: 'But the one I liked best was Emiliano . . . you saw him for yourself . . . the one who rode on a black mare, covered with tassels and tiny bits of glass . . .' (p. 7). Seen from this point of view, *The Shoemaker's Wonderful Wife* is a fine example of Lorca's ability both to breathe new life into traditional forms and to give them a new dimension. It is also another example of his resolve to escape the chains of naturalism.

However, of the plays written in the 1920s, the most intriguing is *The Love of Don Perlimplín and Belisa in the Garden*, which Lorca began in 1925 and had virtually completed by early 1926. Subtitled *An Erotic Print in Four Scenes*, once again it is the story of an older man married to a young and beautiful girl, but although it contains elements of farce and exaggeration, it is not the violent farce that is *The Shoemaker's Wonderful Wife*. It is, rather, a piece of a much gentler kind, distinguished by a note of pathos and, by the end, even of tragedy. In short, this is a highly original play in which, in characteristic style, Lorca revitalized a traditional theatrical form, farce, thus proving once more his capacity as a writer for innovation and experiment.

Perlimplín, fifty years old and completely inexperienced in matters of love, is persuaded by his servant, Marcolfa, to marry the young, beautiful and voluptuous Belisa. Realizing on his wedding-night that he is in fact impotent, Perlimplín falls asleep and, as he sleeps, his sexually precocious wife takes five lovers. Initially distraught by this betrayal, yet aware of Belisa's need for love and of his own inability to meet that need, Perlimplín hits on an ingenious plan. Disguising himself as a young lover, he meets Belisa in the garden and obtains from her declarations of love. When she subsequently finds him dying from a knife wound, the lover is revealed to be Perlimplín himself and Belisa is reduced to tears, her feelings for him finally awakened.

The theme of frustration in love runs like a thread through all Lorca's plays, but in *The Love of Don Perlimplín,* it is linked to the notion of impotence in a way which anticipates the Young Man of *When Five Years Pass,* unable to respond sexually to a woman of flesh and blood. In this sense Don Perlimplín, although fifty years old, is a form of Lorca himself, even though he was only twenty-eight when he completed the play, and the character's anxieties in relation to marriage and its sexual requirements clearly reflect the dramatist's own preoccupations regarding the opposite sex. Lorca's close friendship with Salvador Dalí had begun in 1922, and in the spring of 1925 he visited Dalí and his family in Figueras and Cadaqués on the Costa Brava. While there he was greatly impressed by the beauty of Dalí's sister, Ana María, then seventeen, whom he subsequently described as the most attractive girl he had ever encountered.[9] Nevertheless, Lorca's feelings for Dalí proved to be more intense than those for his friend's sister, strengthening the dramatist's belief that he was indeed impotent as far as women were concerned. In addition, Lorca may well have felt, influenced by his knowledge of the works of Freud, that his homosexuality was somehow related to the influence his mother had exercised over his early life, for Perlimplín's anxieties are certainly linked to his dead mother.[10] When, in the final scenes of the play, he succeeds in obtaining from Belisa an affirmation of her love for him, we should note that it is significant, and tragic, too, that he is able to do this only by employing a disguise, by making her believe that he is someone else. Was it the case, then, that Lorca was able to love a woman only in the realms of fantasy? At all events, *The Love of Don Perlimplín* suggests that, to a greater degree even than in the plays discussed thus far, Lorca was now channelling his emotional life into his work.

The style of *The Love of Don Perlimplín* has much of the simplicity and the exaggeration of farce. Perlimplín's house, for example, has '*Green walls, with chairs and furniture painted black*' (p. 45); in his dining-room '*The perspectives are delightfully wrong. All the objects on the table are painted as in a primitive meal*' (p. 55); and in the final scene we have '*A garden with cypresses and orange trees*' (p. 59). In short, the settings are colourful and stylized picture-frames within which the characters appear, and they too, as in puppetry, are also drawn in bold and colourful strokes. Perlimplín himself wears '*a green dress coat and a white curly wig*' (p. 45); Belisa's mother has '*a large eighteenth-century wig full of birds, ribbons and glass beads*' (p. 47); and when Belisa appears in the garden in Scene Three '*She is magnificently dressed*' (p. 61). On the other hand, the play's broad comic effects are, as the action unfolds, increasingly accompanied by much more delicate and lyrical moments. In the final scene Belisa sings a beautiful song off stage, the stage itself is illuminated by the moon, and later, as Perlimplín dies, it is '*bathed in a magical light*' (p. 64). This is a world away from the techniques of farce, and shows how, in this play in particular, Lorca, identifying himself in various ways with Perlimplín, explored the tragic potential of a comic form.

During the 1920s he also wrote three short plays: *Buster Keaton's Spin* (1925), *The Maiden, the Sailor and the Student* (1928) and *Chimaera*, which was intended for publication in 1928, but did not appear. Influenced by the cinema, *Buster Keaton's Spin* looks forward to Lorca's so-called Surrealist period of the early 1930s but is simultaneously an exploration of Lorca's characteristic preoccupations, for Keaton is the innocent in search of love and of the fulfilment of his dreams, which are always destroyed. Similarly, the Girl in *The Maiden, the Sailor and the Student* indulges in a fantasy of love, in which the Sailor and the Student are a part, but all of them are frustrated in their respective quests. As for *Chimaera*, a husband's departure from his wife and children suggests the passing of time and the way in which things inevitably change – a journey, in effect, in which there is no happy ending. In all three playlets there are situations and characters – Old Man in *Chimaera* and Old Woman in *The Maiden, the Sailor and the Student*, for example – which, inasmuch as they represent old age and unavoidable decay, anticipate *When Five Years Pass, Doña Rosita the Spinster* and *The House of Bernarda Alba*.

The preceding outline of Lorca's life and of the plays written during the 1920s suggests that both were closely interwoven. For the most part the creative work springs in its subject matter from the dramatist's sexual preoccupations, but, as in the case of *Mariana Pineda*, political events informed him, too. In addition, Lorca was strongly influenced by the friendships he formed and by the cultural movements to which he was exposed. He also seems to have been in contact, from the composition of his very first play onwards, with influential individuals – be they producers, directors or actors – in the theatre of his time.[11] It is impossible, therefore, to discuss the theatre of Lorca without reference to all the experiences mentioned above. In *The Public*, the Director, a character based on the playwright himself, boldly declares: 'One must destroy the theatre or live in it!'[12] As the following pages will show, Lorca 'lived' in his plays in a very real sense.

1
The Public:
A Poem to be Booed At

The Public, completed in Granada in 1930, is one of the most extraordinary and powerful plays ever written. Consider its opening scene: its
principal character, the Director, sits in his room, painted blue, on one
wall of which is an enormous hand-print, while the windows are X-ray
plates. A manservant enters, announcing that the public wishes to
speak with the Director. He agrees to the meeting, and four white
horses enter, blowing trumpets. Later, the Director and three men
with black beards and dressed in identical suits are forced to pass
behind a screen, each reappearing in a completely different guise: the
Director as a boy in white satin, played by an actress. In the play's
second scene, two males, one covered with vine leaves, the other with
small bells, play a game which is initially light-hearted but then aggressive and sadistic. In Scene Three we encounter Shakespeare's Juliet in
her tomb in Verona, courted by four white horses. Scene Four involves
a dying red male nude with a crown of thorns and a theatre audience
which rebels when it discovers that in a performance of *Romeo and
Juliet*, Juliet is played by a boy. In the play's final scene, the Director
argues with a magician about the nature of illusion and then dies alone
on an empty stage. As this brief account suggests, *The Public* is a startling
and highly theatrical work, but it is also unique amongst Lorca's plays
in that it is his only overtly homosexual piece. In either late 1930 or
early 1931 he read it to a group of friends. It was greeted with silence
and then with varied reactions, which included shock at both its
violence and its portrayal of homosexual relationships. It is hardly
surprising that in the Spain of the 1930s Lorca's audience, albeit a
sophisticated one, should have been shocked by such lines as 'The arse

is man's failure, his punishment and his death'.[1] The reaction would have been the same anywhere.

There can be no doubt that, as far as the homosexual issue is concerned, *The Public* is an expression of Lorca's anguish at a particular time in his life. His belief that he was different from other men can be traced to his late teens and early twenties, and is as evident in his plays and poetry as in his letters. In a letter written in the spring of 1918 to a young Andalusian poet, Adriano del Valle y Rossi, Lorca compared himself to the French poet Paul Verlaine, who was certainly bisexual if not homosexual, and described his own nature, at the age of twenty, as that of 'a simple youth, passionate and silent, who . . . carries inside him a lily that cannot be watered'.[2] Sensing the reaction of a conventional, narrow-minded and homophobic middle class to someone of his inclinations, he felt that there would be many problems ahead, 'many eyes which will imprison me', and expressed with some anguish the conviction that with 'every day that passes I have another doubt and another cause for dejection, the dejection of the enigma of oneself!' There were, nevertheless, a number of young women who crossed his path and who evidently tested the true nature of his sexuality. When he was nineteen, for example, Lorca met María Luisa Egea González, who was then twenty-three or twenty-four, and the sister of one of the group of creative artists and intellectuals who met regularly at the Café Alameda in Granada and which Lorca had joined sometime earlier. He seems to have been fascinated by the blonde María Luisa, who played the piano with him, but he also described her as 'cold', which appears to imply that she did not reciprocate his feelings. A year later, in the summer of 1918, he encountered Emilia Llanos Medina, a thirty-year-old brunette who was beautiful and also shared many of his interests, not least literature. It has been suggested that these relationships were chaste, although it is far more likely that at this time in his life Lorca was still greatly confused as to where his sexual inclinations really lay. Salvador Dalí was to claim many years later that Lorca hated female breasts, but it is always prudent to take Dalí's statements with a pinch of salt.

Lorca's emotional conflict can be fully appreciated only in the context of the society in which he lived. It was, first of all, a strongly Catholic society, in which sex in general was considered to be solely for the purpose of procreation and homosexuality was not to be countenanced. In addition, Spain has always been a country where machismo has reigned supreme and in which anyone who is seen to be less than a 'normal' man is scornfully dismissed as a *maricón*, a queer. And the Granada society in which Lorca spent his teenage years was characterized by a very conservative middle class. In this respect, the group which met at the Café Alameda was hardly to be approved of. The leader of the regular gathering, Francisco Soriano Lapresa, was a portly, dandyish character, who was suspected by the townspeople of involvement in regular orgies, although he does not seem to have been homosexual. The journalist Constantino Ruiz Carnero undoubtedly was, and so, too, was the quantity surveyor José María García Carrillo, a close friend of Lorca. Most of the group were, on the other hand, straight, but because of their artistic activities and the extravagant dress of some they were undoubtedly considered bohemian and therefore suspect. As for Lorca, his feeling that 'many eyes will imprison me' was less prophetic than based on fact, and the sense of unease created by his ambiguous sexual feelings was, in no small measure, because he belonged to a respectable family, one that he had no wish to become the subject of common gossip.

The desire to seem what he was not followed him to Madrid when, in 1919, he became a student at the by then famous Residencia de Estudiantes. The Residencia resembled the Café Alameda in the sense that those who attended it were exclusively male – and Lorca must have encountered gay men there as well as in the artistic and cultural community of the city in general. In later life, many of Lorca's friends at the Residencia denied all knowledge of his homosexuality, including Luis Buñuel. Indeed, Buñuel has described the occasion when one of the students, Martín Domínguez, spread the rumour that Lorca was gay. Buñuel, completely shocked, at once confronted him with the question: 'Is it true you're a queer?'³ If Buñuel's account of the incident is true, it suggests either that he was not very observant – although he was a well-known homophobe – or that Lorca made every effort to conceal his sexuality. But there were those who were perfectly aware of it and who avoided him as best they could.

Someone who did not avoid him was Salvador Dalí, who arrived at the Residencia in late 1922. Then only eighteen years of age, Dalí cut an extraordinary figure: tall, slim, pale, with shoulder-length dark hair, he wore a broad-brimmed hat, a jacket down to his knees, leather gaiters and a long cloak. Some months later this bohemian image was transformed into another whereby, with neatly cut hair, a small moustache, and wearing a suit, he became much more a young man about town. But despite his outward appearance and his superior air, Dalí was extremely timid and shy, and in that regard the complete opposite of Lorca, who, after several years at the Residencia, was always the centre of attention in any group. Dazzled by Lorca's personality and talent, Dalí would later provide an account of the impression the older man – twenty-four at the time – made on him:

> . . . the personality of Federico García Lorca produced an immense impression on me. The poetic phenomenon in its entirety and 'in the raw' presented itself before me suddenly in flesh and bone, confused, blood-red, viscous and sublime, quivering with a thousand fires of darkness . . .⁴

And there were also occasions when, jealous of Lorca's impact on others, Dalí would run and hide:

> Sometimes we would be walking, the whole group of us, along El Paseo de la Castellana on our way to the café where we held our usual literary meetings and where I knew Lorca would shine like a mad and fiery diamond. Suddenly I would set off at a run, and no one would see me for three days . . .⁵

Prior to 1926 there is no evidence that Lorca was sexually attracted to Dalí, although they were frequently in each other's company and collaborators in various artistic ventures. Indeed, as we have seen, in 1925 Lorca was more taken by Dalí's seventeen-year-old sister, Ana María.[6] After meeting her in Cadaqués, he corresponded with her, often flirtatiously, telling her that his memories of her were unforgettable and referring to her great beauty. Her presence in his life brings to mind the earlier encounters with María Luisa Egea González and Emilia Llanos Medina, but the greater presence increasingly proved to be the brother, not the sister. As a result of the visit to Cadaqués and Figueras, the Dalís' permanent home, Lorca began work on *Ode to Salvador Dalí*, in which his affection and admiration for the painter are very clear, and they wrote to each other constantly. But did they have a sexual relationship?

Dalí was a curious case. Brought up by a doting mother, who was afraid of losing him because she had already lost one child, the young Salvador was certainly immature. He often pretended to be a girl, squeezing his sexual organs between his legs, denying his masculinity in response, no doubt, to a long period of domination by his mother. At the same time he took no interest in women, and in all probability feared a heterosexual relationship. His marriage to Gala was certainly one in which she took care of all practical matters, as he was someone incapable of performing the simplest everyday task. Edward James, a rich Englishman who knew the Dalís well, has suggested that sex played no part in their relationship, in the light of which it is difficult to believe Dalí's boast that 'I possessed my beloved like a brute, I tore her dress, laid bare her breasts, tattered her underclothes, and impaled her on the ferocious stake of my upstretched cock'.[7] It seems quite possible that Dalí, given his aversion to physical contact with women, derived his pleasure from masturbation. Later on, certainly, he was very much a voyeur, hiring couples to perform in front of him. As for Gala, her sexual appetites had always been considerable. In that respect Dalí was hardly the man she needed; their marriage was one of convenience and of minds, not bodies.

Many years after Lorca's death, Dalí claimed that Lorca attempted to sodomize him:

> He was homosexual, as everyone knows, and madly in love with me. He tried to screw me twice . . . I was extremely annoyed, because I wasn't homosexual, and I wasn't interested in giving in. Besides, it hurts. So nothing came of it. But I felt awfully flattered vis-à-vis the prestige. Deep down, I felt that he was a great poet and that I did owe him a tiny bit of the Divine Dalí's asshole . . .[8]

This statement, although characteristic of the great self-publicist, is probably true in certain respects. Dalí was no more homosexual than heterosexual, as fearful of contact with men as with women. He therefore rejected Lorca, and, in so doing, asserted his superiority over someone in whose shadow he had previously lived. Furthermore, that superiority could be sustained if Dalí kept Lorca on a string. In a photograph of Lorca and Dalí at Cadaqués in 1927, both in bathing-costumes, Dalí stands to the right of Lorca and above him, dominant, with a 'come and get me' but superior expression on his face. In another photograph, also at Cadaqués, he stands behind Lorca, holding him by the waist, again looking superior, as if to say 'look what I've got!' These, as well as poses in other photographs of the same period, could reasonably be described as vampish on Dalí's part, even if one allows for an element of calculation: Dalí, in short, as tempter.

Despite his feelings for Dalí, Lorca was by 1928 involved with another young man, Emilio Aladrén Perojo, who was then twenty-two years of age.[9] A sculptor of small talent, he was by all accounts extremely good looking and of a markedly volatile nature. Evidently bisexual, he had been the boyfriend of the painter Maruja Mallo, but he was lured away from her by Lorca. Infatuated by his new conquest, Lorca took Aladrén everywhere, showing him off to his friends. But the friends were not entirely pleased. Many of them saw Aladrén as an undesirable influence, someone who manipulated Lorca for his own ends, and who was also undisciplined, frivolous and lacking in discretion. Not only did he ridicule Lorca's efforts to conceal his homosexuality, he also gossiped about their relationship in public. Even Dalí, perhaps out of jealousy and because he disliked Aladrén, attempted to persuade Lorca of the error of his ways. But Lorca was clearly hooked by this impulsive and handsome young man, whose lack of inhibition was doubtless a reminder of the freer spirit he himself wanted to be. Indeed, from this time on, Lorca became rather more open about his sexuality.

Both relationships played no small part in the depression that Lorca experienced in the latter part of 1928 and well into 1929. In the summer of 1928 his new collection of poems, *Gypsy Ballads*, had achieved a huge success with critics and public alike. Dalí, however, disliked the poems, and in a letter to Lorca berated him for being old-fashioned. Furthermore, Dalí was now drawing away from Lorca and becoming ever closer to Luis Buñuel, both kindred spirits in their love of everything avant-garde and, in particular, of all things Surrealist. Even though Lorca understood and appreciated Dalí's criticism of his poems, the latter's embracing of Buñuel at his expense was, on an emotional level, a betrayal. In January 1929 Buñuel spent a fortnight with Dalí in Figueras, working on ideas which later that year would find their way into their film *Un Chien andalou* (*An Andalusian Dog*). The thought of the two men together in Figueras – a mirror of Lorca's earlier visits to Cadaqués and Figueras – clearly fuelled Lorca's feelings of rejection. In addition to this, by early 1929 Aladrén was becoming involved with a young woman, possibly Eleanor Dove, an English girl from Gosforth, Northumberland, whom he would marry in 1931. And in the spring of the same year, Dalí, who had gone to Paris to join Buñuel, began his relationship with Gala, wife of the poet Paul Eluard, which would dominate the rest of his life. Little wonder, then, that Lorca felt cast aside. Here he was, a famous poet and playwright, but, at the age of thirty-one, facing an empty future. A 'normal' married life would never be his, the world in which he lived despised gay men, and, in any case, the men he loved had abandoned him. There were, in all probability, additional causes for Lorca's depression: the loss of privacy as he became more famous and, perhaps, the feeling that his best work was already behind him. But it cannot be denied that his relationship with Dalí and Aladrén were crucial in causing his depression.

Aware of his state of mind but ignorant of the reasons for it, Lorca's parents felt that a period of time away from Spain might do him good. They arranged that he should accompany a family friend, Fernando de los Ríos, to New York, and so it was that, after first travelling to England, where his companion's niece was to take up a teaching post in Hereford, Lorca and de los Ríos set sail from Southampton on 19 June 1929, arriving in New York six days later. His lack of joy may be gauged from a note he wrote on the ship: 'I don't know why I left. I ask myself that question a hundred times a day. I look at myself in the mirror of the narrow cabin and I don't recognize myself. I seem another Federico.'[10]

He stayed for nine months, until March 1930. Accounts of his emotional state vary, but, as was ever the case, there was the public and the private man. In the company of Spanish friends, of which there were many in New York, he could be cheerful and boisterous; in private, melancholic. Angel del Río, who often met him, sensed a dejection behind the façade, and, in a letter to his close friend Rafael Martínez Nadal, Lorca observed that 'you can see my state of mind'.[11] Dalí and Aladrén were still very much in his thoughts. Although New York often dazzled him, it also depressed him. This was, at bottom, a heartless city where money ruled, where the blacks of Harlem were oppressed by their white masters, where, on Tuesday 29 October 1929, desperate individuals threw themselves from skyscraper windows when the New York Stock Exchange collapsed. The poems written at this time, which would come to form the volume *Poet in New York*, are the true pointer to Lorca's inner state. In the very first poem of the collection he describes himself as 'Assassinated by heaven'. In 'Double Poem of Lake Eden' there are clear allusions to the anguish he experiences 'because I'm not a man, not a poet, not a leaf, / only a wounded pulse . . .' And, in the filmscript *Trip to the Moon*, written in New York in much the same vein as the poems composed there, sex is constantly seen in terms of violence, suffering and death. In one of its seventy-eight brief sequences 'a moon appears, outlined on a white background that fades into a male sex organ and then into a screaming mouth'. Four successive sequences depict: '62 The harlequin boy and the nude woman ascend in the elevator. 63 They embrace. 64 A view of the sensual kiss. 65 The boy bites the girl on the neck and violently pulls her hair'. And in one of the closing sequences two lovers 'are seen kissing over a tomb'.[12] If in public Lorca often seemed bright and cheerful, that façade is contradicted by his writing, the true mirror of his soul.

By the end of his stay, though, there seems to have been a resolution, one source of which was Lorca's admiration for the American poet Walt Whitman. For Lorca, who knew Whitman's *Leaves of Grass* in Spanish translation, the American poet symbolized the ideal of personal freedom and pure, untainted homosexual love, free from its more debased forms and associations. In his own *Ode to Walt Whitman*, on which he may well have started work before he left New York, Lorca depicted Whitman as the perfect example of the gay man, completely lacking effeminacy, and railed against the fairies and the faggots of the world, the 'maricas' who give homosexuality a bad name. In this image of Whitman Lorca was, of course, constructing that form of himself to which he aspired, and by the time he left New York for Cuba in March 1930, he seems to have found more confidence both in his sexuality and his work.

Cuba, where he spent three months, was far less inhibited than Spain or North America, and Lorca clearly delighted in its vibrant atmosphere, its colour, its sensual music and its racial mix. At all events, he became involved with several young men. One was a good-looking twenty-year-old mulatto named Lamadrid; another was Juan Ernesto Pérez de la Riva, whose well-to-do family banned Lorca from their home when they became aware of his sexual inclinations. In photographs Lorca poses with young men, either singly or as a group. When Luis Cardoza y Aragón, a twenty-six-year-old poet, took Lorca to a well-known Havana brothel, the latter wondered why there were no boys, and Cardoza claimed, too, that Lorca had spoken to him of having gone swimming with a number of naked black men.[13] In short, Cuba seems to have continued that process in Lorca that had begun in the latter part of his stay in New York – a kind of catharsis whereby he finally emerged from a tumult of conflicting emotions. In part, the liberation was achieved through his writing and the release which that brings. In this respect, *Poet in New York* was one key element. The other was *The Public*, which he may have started writing in New York, and which was virtually completed during his stay in Cuba.

In this play Lorca transformed personal experience into high art, and in so doing seems to have exorcised at least some of his demons. The play's main character, the Director, is in many ways Lorca himself. We see him initially in his room '*dressed in a morning coat*'.[14] In other words his appearance is entirely conventional and, in that sense, a clear echo of the dramatist, who, in almost every photograph, is seen to be wearing a suit and a tie, and sometimes a bow-tie. Furthermore, when the four white horses enter, reminding the Director of the passionate side of his life, begging him to show compassion, he coldly dismisses them. He is, in effect, 'buttoned-up' both sartorially and emotionally, his outward appearance a façade, a mask adopted for public consumption. He is the Lorca who appeared in public, giving lectures and poetry recitals, the Lorca whom even good friends did not suspect of being anything other than a normal, conventional man. The image is then developed in the three men who arrive as soon as the horses depart: three men identically dressed in morning-suits. Their bourgeois appearance calls to mind the characters in such films as Buñuel's *The Exterminating Angel*, in which the formal attire of dinner-jackets is merely an elegant façade beneath which powerful and often shameful feelings fester.

The reality of their lives soon becomes clear when, in Scene One, the Director's conversation with the three men moves from a discussion of theatre to a process of self-revelation in which all four are seen to be closet homosexuals. The process is initiated by First Man, the most outspoken and courageous of the group, when he suggests that the Director, with whom he has had a sexual relationship, should be more honest. True to form, the Director seeks to avoid the issue, calling on Elena, whom he claims to have been his lover, to vouch for his masculinity. Once again we are reminded of Lorca's relationships with women, as well as of Aladrén's liaison with Eleanor Dove, none of which could ultimately conceal the respective homosexuality and bisexuality of the men in question. Indeed, when Elena appears, she denounces both the Director and Third Man, pointing to a relationship between them and abruptly telling the latter: 'Go with him! Go on, admit the truth you're hiding from me . . . you've kissed him and you've slept in the same bed.' But the truth demanded by Elena is most brilliantly and strikingly revealed by means of the screen behind which each of the four men is obliged to pass, emerging in a completely different form, stripped of their conventional appearance. The Director himself, reluctant to be involved, is pushed behind the screen by Second and Third Man, and is exposed for what he really is. He appears from the other side not as a man in a morning coat but as '*a boy dressed in white satin with a white ruff. He should be played by an actress*'. Similarly, Second Man reappears as a woman wearing black pyjama trousers and a crown of poppies, and holding in her hand a lorgnette with a blond moustache. And when Third Man emerges, he is a smooth-faced, pale individual carrying a whip. Furthermore, the Director is now called Enrique, First Man Gonzalo and Second Man Maximiliana, and, contrary to our first impression that the Director and Third Man have been lovers, they all seem to have had relationships with each other. Nothing, then, is what it seems. Behind the mask, and certainly behind closed doors, there are many secrets. While the play's title refers in part to the public, the audience in a theatre, it also evokes the notion of public image, behind which there is the private man, or woman.

If this parallels Lorca's real-life situation, so too does the play's development, in the course of which the Director begins to acknowledge and accept his sexuality. The need for men to be what they are, to be true to themselves, is voiced by First Man, who observes that no one should be governed by false desires, for 'Can a man cease to be himself?' In *Blood Wedding*, three years later, the same idea would be expressed in a rather different form and context by First Woodcutter: 'You have to follow your instinct . . . You have to follow the blood's path' (p. 74).[15] This was evidently the kind of thing that Lorca repeated to himself endlessly, and whose truth he slowly began to learn. But the journey was, of course, difficult, and for various reasons, not least public attitudes. As we have seen, Spanish society at the time was conventional and easily shocked, the pointed finger quickly raised. In Scene One, First Man describes the public's distaste and revulsion at the sight of a squid being turned inside out, or at the mere mention of the word 'cancer' – he could have added 'homosexual'. An awareness of public attitudes, together with a sense of guilt at being different, can create a mixture of shame, reluctance and cowardice, all feelings that Lorca evidently had. So it is that in Scene Three the Director refers to the mask which we wear in public and which 'fastens our buttons and keeps at bay the unwise blush which sometimes rises to our cheeks'. A few lines later he asks himself why he does not have more courage. And earlier in the same scene, First Man accuses Third Man of being a coward. Nevertheless, First Man's assertion that the mask must be torn off and thrown aside is a point of view which, step by step, the Director accepts. In Scene Five he is said to have gone off with the horses, in other words to have acknowledged the passion which in Scene One he denied. And in Scene Six, in a crucial exchange with the Magician on the nature of truth and deception – the latter the Magician's art – the Director embraces the need to reveal the truth of things, the reality which is so often concealed because it is shameful and uncomfortable. In the course of the play he has travelled far, been subjected to fluctuating and often traumatic emotions, and finally come to terms with his sexuality, as Lorca himself seems to have done in consequence of his difficult time in New York.

Another aspect of *The Public* that reflects Lorca's personal experience concerns the fluctuating relationships between its homosexual characters. Scene Two, for example, depicts an encounter between the Figure with Vine Leaves and the Figure with Bells. Initially, they embark on a light-hearted, teasing, childlike game:

FIGURE WITH BELLS: If I turned into a cloud?
FIGURE WITH VINE LEAVES: I'd turn into an eye.

Soon, though, these teasing exchanges become more menacing and involve an element of domination and cruelty that shifts from one character to the other as the scene unfolds:

FIGURE WITH BELLS: If I turned into a moonfish?
FIGURE WITH VINE LEAVES: I'd turn into a knife.

The mood constantly switches from timidity on the part of one character to intimidation on the part of the other, and, finally, with the arrival of a third character, the Roman Emperor, to the betrayal of the Figure with Bells by the Figure with Vine Leaves. Furthermore, the episode is witnessed by the Director and the three men and is in effect an exteriorization of their own behaviour towards each other. In Scene One, for instance, Third Man, transformed into the pale, clean-shaven youth, whips the Director, accusing him of lying. At the end of Scene Two the Figure with Bells' sense of betrayal is shared by the Director and First Man. At the beginning of Scene Three Third Man abuses First Man, complaining that he turns his stomach, and not long afterwards First Man brutally exposes Third Man as a degenerate homosexual, the kind who frequents the dockside taverns. Still later in the same scene, Third Man observes a struggle between the Director and First Man, and longs for their death, claiming that this would free him from them, while Second Man depends on them entirely and sees their death as his, too. And towards the end of the scene, Second Man is willing to betray his lover by running off with Third Man, although it is not long before he proclaims his love for Juliet. All these relationships, with their elements of tenderness, cruelty, brutality and fickleness, are doubtless based on Lorca's own experiences, both with Dalí and Aladrén and with more casual lovers and pick-ups. In *The Public* Lorca exposes vividly the often vicious relationships of which he had been part behind closed doors.

Given current attitudes towards homosexuals, Lorca undoubtedly experienced both the anguish and the loneliness which find expression in the play in the character of the Red Nude in Scene Five. Here is a suffering Christ-like figure, wearing a crown of blue thorns and close to death. The notion of persecution for behaviour disapproved of by society at large is often to the fore in Lorca's work, his own sense of being 'crucified' channelled into some of his characters, as is the case of Adela in *The House of Bernarda Alba*. She speaks of running away with her sister's fiancé and of having to wear, in consequence of that, 'the crown of thorns that women wear who are loved by a married man' (p. 111).[16] And when the Red Nude refers to the anguish 'of the lonely man, on platforms and on trains', it is not difficult to imagine Lorca in New York. At the end of the scene the same kind of mood and landscape is evoked by the lines 'The solitude of a man in a dream full of elevators and trains where you move at unbelievable speed. The solitude of buildings, street corners, beaches . . .' But the lines are spoken this time by First Man, who is seen to be another form of the Red Nude. In short, if the gay men in the play are different from each other, they are also like each other and like Lorca himself, in the sense that they suffer individually and separately.

In terms of its subject, structure and style, *The Public* is unique in Lorca's theatre, with the possible exception of its successor, *When Five Years Pass*. In response to the shocked reaction of the group to whom he had read it privately, Lorca had observed that 'This is for the theatre years from now',[17] acknowledging the fact that a contemporary Madrid audience would no more tolerate it than the sight of a squid being turned inside out. During the first three decades of the twentieth century, Spanish mainstream theatre was not much different from its British counterpart, Madrid no different from London in the domination of its stages by well-made, uncontroversial plays designed to please a largely unthinking bourgeois audience.[18] The theatre-going public had its favourites: Jacinto Benavente, the author of innumerable drawing-room comedies characterised by well-structured plots, well-to-do characters and polished dialogue; and the brothers Serafín and Joaquín Alvarez Quintero, who specialized in comedies depicting a colourful and idealized Andalusia, complete with handsome young men and beautiful women. There were other writers too, of course: Manuel Linares Rivas and Pedro Muñoz Seca, to name but two, and all of them with one thing in common, the rehashing of a successful formula over and over again. Benavente, having discovered that formula, turned out play after play in almost conveyor-belt fashion, and in so doing contributed to the long-standing stagnation in Spanish theatre. Experimentation, as is always the case, lay in the hands of a few outside the commercial sector. Between 1900 and 1930, Ramón del Valle-Inclán, whose achievement is often compared to Lorca's, produced a body of work that, in its innovation and power to shock, was a world away from the sophistication of the commercial stage. Consider, for instance, the scene in his *Divine Words*, written in 1920, in which the hydrocephalous boy is fed alcohol by the villagers and found dead the following morning, his face eaten away by pigs; or the episode in *Bohemian Lights* (1920) in which the ageing, blind, down-and-out poet, Max Estrella, dies on his doorstep and is peed on by a dog – not the stuff of commercial theatre. There were lesser dramatists, too, who embraced serious issues, be they the condition of Spanish society or the predicament of man in a problematic world. Miguel de Unamuno projected his own dilemmas into plays characterized by stark settings, boldly drawn characters and dialogue stripped to the bone – the very opposite approach to that adopted by Benavente. Carlos Arniches in his best work embodied in his characters the particular vices he observed in Spanish society – ignorance, cruelty, hypocrisy – and developed a style in which an emphasis on caricature and the grotesque is far removed from the cosy 'naturalism' of bourgeois theatre. And Jacinto Grau, in a play such as Mr *Pygmalion*, written in 1921, examined the nature of human freedom and the consequences of human ingenuity when his protagonist creates animated life-size puppets, only to be taken over by them. All these writers were influenced not only by Spanish theatre of the past, in particular that of the seventeenth century, but, more importantly, by those developments in theatre which were taking place in Europe in the early twentieth century and to which the bourgeois commercial theatre closed its eyes.

During his time at the Residencia de Estudiantes, Lorca was constantly exposed to stimulating individuals and progressive ideas. Set up in 1910, just nine years before Lorca arrived there, the Residencia was, as its name suggests, a residential college where talented young men could broaden their education, come into contact with areas of study different from their own and attend lectures given by internationally known speakers, including scientists, writers and musicians. Visitors included Albert Einstein, Marie Curie, John Maynard Keynes, Paul Valéry, Louis Aragon, François Mauriac, Paul Claudel, and the English writers H.G. Wells, G.K. Chesteron and Hilaire Belloc, amongst others. As far as musicians were concerned, the list was impressive indeed: Wanda Landowska, Darius Milhaud, Igor Stravinsky, Francis Poulenc, Maurice Ravel, Manuel de Falla and Andrés Segovia all appeared. Furthermore, the student body contained outstanding talents. Luis Buñuel, although not yet a film-maker, arrived at the Residencia in 1917, two years before Lorca, and Salvador Dalí in 1922, three years after him. Not far away, associated with Madrid's Arts Club, the Ateneo, there were other creative talents, too, such as the poets Guillermo de Torre, Pedro Salinas, Gerardo Diego and, from

1924, Rafael Alberti, who, although not a student at the Residencia, lived close by and frequented it. It goes without saying that to be there was to be exposed to new and stimulating ideas, not least to movements such as Cubism, Dadaism, Futurism and Surrealism, all of which were fundamentally influencing and changing the direction of the creative arts throughout Europe. In the library of the Residencia there were foreign magazines, visiting lecturers informed the students of what was happening elsewhere, and, when individuals such as Buñuel and Dalí left and settled in Paris, they returned frequently with information on cultural developments in the French capital. In 1927, for example, Buñuel screened René Clair's *Entr'acte* at the Residencia, a strikingly avant-garde film full of arresting visual images. Spain was not as cut off from European influence as it is sometimes thought to have been.

Surrealism was an important influence, and consequently *The Public* is often referred to as a Surrealist play, clearly as a result of Lorca's association with Buñuel and Dalí.[19] There can be no doubt, though, that Lorca was familiar with Surrealist ideas from other sources, too. As early as 1924, a critical account of André Breton's key *Manifeste du Surréalisme* had appeared in the Spanish journal *Revista de Occidente*. In April 1925 Louis Aragon, another important figure in the movement, lectured on Surrealism at the Residencia. And, in the following month, there appeared in Madrid Guillermo de Torre's *Literaturas europeas de vanguardia* (*European Literatures of the Avant-Garde*). Around this time Dalí was experimenting with Surrealist techniques – not merely in relation to painting but also to writing – and clearly discussing such matters with Lorca. For both of them, as well as for Buñuel, the workings of the unconscious mind were a source of fascination, and the writings of Sigmund Freud, which had been translated into Spanish, were readily absorbed. In 1928 Lorca himself delivered a lecture, 'Sketch of Modern Painting', in which he spoke of the way in which the Surrealists were freeing themselves from the constraints of the past and learning to express the inexpressible.

Significantly, he illustrated his talk with slides of paintings by Miró in order to show that unconscious desires could be transferred to canvas. *Buster Keaton's Spin*, which he had written three years earlier, was of a markedly dreamlike character in which a parrot flies through a neutral sky, an owl hoots in the middle of the day and Buster encounters a young lady with the head of a nightingale. And in 'Somnambular Ballad', arguably the most evocative poem in *Gypsy Ballads*, there is once again an unreal, dreamlike mood as a girl stands on her balcony waiting for her absent lover, the entire scene bathed in a disquieting green light.

But if Lorca was interested in Surrealism in general, it was without doubt the attacks of Dalí and Buñuel on his more traditional work which by 1929 led him to consider the direction of his writing. In 1926 Dalí had persuaded Lorca to read *The Love of Don Perlimplín* to Buñuel, who, halfway through, had described it as 'a load of shit'. Dalí's adverse reaction to *Gypsy Ballads* was also echoed by Buñuel when he commented that 'between this and anything that has to do with the genuine, exquisite and great poets of the present day, there is a huge gulf'.[20]

Despite his seeking to incorporate modern elements within his work, Lorca himself warned against regarding his work as Surrealist in terms of André Breton's definition of Surrealism: the spontaneous expression, without the control of reason, of everything contained in the unconscious mind. In 1928 Lorca sent some poems to a friend, observing that they corresponded to his new style, 'pure disembodied emotion, free of the control of logic, but, take note!, with absolute poetic logic. This is not surrealism. Beware! A very clear awareness shines through them'.[21] And in the previous year, in a lecture on the work of the great Spanish poet, Luis de Góngora (1561–1627), he had stated that 'I do not believe that any great artist works in a state of frenzy . . . One returns from inspiration as from a foreign land. The poem is the account of the journey'.[22] In some ways this brings to mind Dalí's so-called 'paranoiac-critical method' whereby he claimed he could paint as if in a state of madness while maintaining complete control of what he was painting. As far as *The Public* is concerned, it is certainly a revelation of Lorca's inner, sexual life, but, however bizarre and difficult the play seems, there is without doubt a sense of its author's overriding control.

There were, too, influences other than Surrealism, evidence of Lorca's magpie approach in all his work. His own interest in the visual arts, evidently stimulated by his friendship with Dalí, meant that he took advantage during his time in Madrid of the proximity of the Prado. There he was able to see the paintings of the great Spanish masters, Velázquez, El Greco and, above all, Goya, who proved to be a profound influence on Spanish writers of the nineteenth and twentieth centuries. The frontispiece of Goya's twenty-two drawings known as the *Caprichos*, depicts a sleeping man tormented by flying, bat-like creatures, and bears the caption 'The Sleep of Reason Begets Monsters'. Although the aim of the drawings was largely satirical – to portray a Spain where no enlightened ideas existed – the link between reason's loss of control and the monsters or nightmarish dreams which are then released was one which was bound to appeal to the Surrealists. Furthermore, at the age of seventy-two, Goya projected his own dark visions onto the walls of his house in the fourteen *Black Paintings*, a nightmarish series of murals in which, for example, a procession of madmen wend their way across a Spanish landscape that has all the appearance of hell. Goya, like Lorca, frequently depicted the reality beneath the mask, as in 'The Old Women Gazing into the Looking Glass', in which two hags appear in all their finery. This is a theme which is absolutely central to *The Public*, and Lorca would clearly have responded to the element of dream and nightmare in Goya's work. In the same way the paintings of the fifteenth-century Flemish painter, Hieronymus Bosch, made a powerful impression with their depiction of hell. *The Garden of Earthly Delights*, which has a prominent place in the Prado, shows in its right-hand panel the terrible sufferings of those condemned to eternal damnation: a huge bird devours a man, bodies are pierced by knives and people cry out in anguish. In *The Public*, the episode involving the Red Nude, his wound opened by scalpels, invites comparison.

Scene Two, which begins with the dance of the Figure with Bells, points to Lorca's interest in movement and dance. In Madrid in the early 1920s Diaghilev's famous company performed Manuel de Falla's *The Three-Cornered Hat*, Rimsky-Korsakov's *Scheherazade* and *Tamar* and the Rossini–Respighi *La Boutique fantasque*. A friend of Lorca, Adolfo Salazar, even suggested to him in 1921 that he write two versions of *The Tragicomedy of Don Cristóbal and Señorita Rosita*, one of them 'purely for ballet', and that it might be of interest to Diaghilev.[23] Dance in various forms plays an important part in many Lorca plays – as exemplified by La Argentinita's performance in *The Butterfly's Evil Spell* in 1920 – and in this respect it should not be forgotten that, for innovators in theatre style in the early part of the twentieth century, movement was crucial.

Another influence, to be discussed in more detail in relation to Lorca's next play, *When Five Years Pass*, was the cinema. In the Madrid of the 1920s –as everywhere – the cinema was extremely popular, and cinema audiences loved all kinds of films, from adventure to romance to comedy. The comic films of Charlie Chaplin, Buster Keaton, Harry Langdon, Harold Lloyd and others were much admired by Lorca and his companions, and the madcap antics of those cinematic heroes were regarded by many as truly in the spirit of Surrealism. In addition, Expressionist films such as *The Cabinet of Dr Caligari*, Fritz Lang's *Metropolis* and Eisenstein's *Battleship Potemkin* made a considerable impact, and their influence on the visual aspect of *The Public* should not be dismissed. Consider the stage direction in Scene Four whereby the lighting of the stage takes on '*the silvery tint of a cinema screen*', for example. The Male Nurse and the Thieves exit here '*dancing*', the influence of cinema and dance effectively combined.[24]

Stylistically avant-garde, *The Public* is the opposite of the old-fashioned bourgeois theatre of the time. But Lorca's assault on mainstream theatre also goes far beyond style to the issues with which theatre should be concerned. In 1934, Lorca, in an interview for the newspaper *El Sol*, explained what he thought was wrong with the theatre of the day: '. . . the people who go to the theatre do not want to be made to think about any moral issue'.[25] In the same interview he drew attention to the power of theatre producers and impresarios who, concerned only with profit, gave the public what it wanted and resisted change. And he attacked actors, too, particularly the so-called matinée idols, who wished only to play the same kind of youthful part year after year 'in spite of arteriosclerosis'.

What, then, should the theatre seek to do? Lorca was in no doubt that its aim should be to communicate to people the true reality of human beings, however shocking. Later, in a 1936 interview with Felipe Morales, he expressed this opinion very clearly: 'The Theatre requires that the characters who walk the stage should be dressed in poetry and that simultaneously we should see their bones, their blood.'[26] This notion of seeing the bones, of penetrating beneath the surface, of confronting the audience with uncomfortable truths, is central to Lorca's work, and is expressed in *The Public* with unusual force. At bottom Lorca is the advocate of a revolution in the theatre.

If the Director reflects Lorca's homosexuality, he is initially his opposite in terms of his style of production, described by the phrase 'the theatre of the open air'. This means, in effect, the kind of theatre or production which is on the surface – superficial, entertaining, ultimately lacking in any kind of depth. In Scene One, the three men question the Director about his production of Shakespeare's *Romeo and Juliet*, and we quickly discover that this is a production which sets out simply to please, not to explore the situation and the characters in any depth. If, for example, the Director were concerned with presenting Romeo as a normal, healthy young man rather than a stock character, why not let us see him peeing? But this, of course, would offend the kind of audience on which the Director depends both for income and celebrity. It would, as he puts it, remove 'the handrails from the bridge', in other words, expose his audience to danger, allow them to feel at risk, and this would bring with it untold dangers and retribution, not least to the Director himself. The expectations of a bourgeois audience are set out in Scene Five by some of the women and the students who have just emerged from a performance of the Director's revised staging of *Romeo and Juliet*. First Student, for example, suggests that the audience should always remain at a distance from the play's action, for if we visit an aquarium are we not separated by glass from the creatures on display? And earlier in the scene Second Lady has expressed a similar viewpoint, pointing out that a play need not be more than entertainment: 'The words were alive and the costumes too. Why should we have to lick the skeletons?' But this production of Shakespeare's play is fundamentally different from the Director's first, because the role of Juliet is now played by a boy, with evident homosexual implications. The Director has, in effect, removed 'the handrails from the bridge', and, when the audience discovers this, it is affronted and rises up in protest, as Fourth Student indicates: 'The trouble started when they saw that Romeo and Juliet [played by a boy] were really in love.' Informed that the actress playing Juliet has been removed, hidden away beneath the seats, the women rush out of the theatre in horror.

The Director's 'theatre of the open air' has become in this second production 'the theatre beneath the sand'. This vivid and memorable phrase suggests, of course, the kind of theatre Lorca sought to achieve, and it echoes through *The Public* in all kinds of ways. The opening stage direction describes the windows of the Director's room as X-ray plates, which links up with Lorca's statement six years later that the audience should be able to see the bones of the characters. In visual terms the X-ray plates have their equivalent in Scene One in the portable screen behind which the characters pass, for this is a kind of X-ray machine which allows us to see beneath the surface appearance of things. Similarly, in Scene Three, a wall opens to reveal Juliet's tomb in Verona, and in Scene Six an enormous eye dominates the right-hand side of the stage. Throughout the play, then, there are devices and objects which both suggest the action of seeing through things and which, in the case of the screen and the sliding wall, allow us to do so. These visual elements also have their counterpart in verbal images. In Scene One Third Man suggests the true purpose of the theatre as 'So that the truth of the tombs be known', and the idea is repeated by Second Man: 'Tombs with spotlights, play bills, long rows of seats'. Second Man then asks this question of the Director in relation to his first production of *Romeo and Juliet*: 'Why, at the end, did you not go down the steps of the tomb?' In other words, his presentation has failed to penetrate beneath the surface of the play, when what is required, in the words of First Man, is 'the true theatre, the theatre beneath the sand'. In Scene Three the underground world is revealed to us in Juliet's tomb, where the three men and the Director find themselves, although for him this is still only a first step in the journey and he still champions 'the theatre of the open air'. In Scene Five, however, Third Woman informs us that 'They found the Director inside the tomb', which points to the fact that his new production of *Romeo and Juliet* is no longer merely superficial entertainment. On the contrary, as Second Student observes, 'The skeletons were in love, were yellow in the flame'. And in Scene Six the Director reveals to the Magician that, instead of creating a pleasing illusion, he has opened up the tunnel in order to reveal 'the profile of a hidden force'.

The question of audience involvement was one that preoccupied Lorca greatly throughout his career, both as playwright and director. The theatres of his time, large and small, were of the proscenium arch variety, the audience separated from the on-stage action by the arch and, invariably, by the curtain. To this extent the spectator remained apart from the action of the play, which, when the curtain rose, consisted of a self-contained world, recognizable enough in the case of bourgeois drawing-room plays but still distanced from the auditorium. The existence of the curtain, moreover, is a constant reminder that the on-stage events are something in which the audience is not directly involved. Because of Lorca's desire to confront his audience with the truth of things, he often spoke of destroying the curtain, of emotionally involving the audience in the action of the play. In Scene Six of *The Public* the Director, voicing Lorca's opinion, reveals his new-found aim: '. . . my characters, in contrast, burn the curtain and really die in the presence of the audience'. In short, there should be no distancing between the stage and the auditorium, the characters and their audience. It is not surprising, therefore, that in *The Public* the audience, in the form of the three men, is on stage at the beginning of Scene One:

> SERVANT: The Public.
> DIRECTOR: Let them in.

Furthermore, those who are normally outside the play – in this case the Director and three members of the audience – now become its central characters: 'What play could be more new than ourselves?' And, beyond this, they represent the audience in the theatre as well as the people outside it (the double meaning of the word 'el público': audience and public): 'Come inside with us. You have a place in the play. Everyone has.' What could be more effective in bridging the gap between stage and auditorium than in having an audience watch a play in which they are also the characters? What, indeed, could, in certain cases, be more uncomfortable?

The Public, as well as being Lorca's recognition of his own sexuality, is a stripping away of the layers of untruth behind which the audience conceals its true nature – in particular the 'respectable' audiences of Madrid. The Director may be Lorca himself but, dressed in his morning coat, he is also an image of bourgeois respectability, and in that sense has his equivalent in the three men, each to all appearances a mirror image of the other two, and all of them in turn a mirror image of the audience in the theatre. Reference has been made already to Buñuel's film *The Exterminating Angel* in terms of its characters' elegant dress. In the course of the film a group of sophisticated bourgeois individuals, trapped in a room where they have no food or water, are slowly stripped of clothes and manners, their worst instincts exposed to us and to themselves. This film was premièred in 1962, but Buñuel had, in 1930, also made another film which bears certain similarities, *L'Age d'or*, in which the elegant dinner-jackets of the guests at a dinner-party do nothing to conceal their smugness, superficiality and lack of concern for the suffering of others. Furthermore, the cinema audience who watched these films must have felt that they were seeing themselves on screen. Although *L'Age d'or* was made while Lorca was still in the process of writing *The Public*, it seems more than likely that he and Buñuel had discussed the theme of the reality behind or beneath the appearance. It was, in any case, both a traditional theme in Spanish literature and one which appealed to the Surrealists. And they must have discussed, too, the notion of shocking an audience – one of the principal aims of the Surrealists – by presenting it with the spectacle of its own vices. In this respect, Lorca's emphasis in *The Public* on the homosexuality of his characters is less important than the attitudes which they embody: the element of pretence and denial, their cruelty and hostility towards each other and their deep-seated sense of shame. These are things which all of us, whatever our sexuality, recognize in ourselves, and with which an audience watching *The Public* can easily identify.

That said, *The Public* is not wholly concerned either with the themes of homosexuality or appearance juxtaposed with reality. It is also concerned in part with the nature of love itself, clearly the major preoccupation in the whole of Lorca's work. Shakespeare's *Romeo and Juliet* ends with the tragic death of the two young lovers; Scene Three of *The Public* reveals Juliet, after her death, in her tomb in Verona. She is approached initially by First White Horse, who, as usual in Lorca's work, represents love or passion and here, since it is a white horse, romantic love. First White Horse informs Juliet, in suitably romantic terms, that he has waited for her in the garden, to which she replies: 'You mean the tomb.' In other words, she expresses a disillusionment which springs from her own experience, from the destruction of her hopes and dreams. And, when the horse then speaks to her of 'the perfection of a day . . . with morning and afternoon', she quickly dispels his optimism by emphasizing the existence of night. For Juliet, love is a mere illusion, like a footprint in water, and afterwards there is only despair and, ultimately, death, symbolized here by the entry of Black Horse. In response to the song of love sung by First White Horse and his three companions, Black Horse underlines the inevitability of disillusionment, passing time and death: '. . . things will happen as they have to happen', to which he adds, significantly, 'Oh, love, love, your light must pass through heat that is dark. Oh, sea, resting in shadow, flower in the arse of a dead man!' Significantly, the scene ends with the Director and the three men searching in vain for the men they love. The Director, appearing at first as Enrique, the boy dressed in white satin, is embraced by his lover, First Man, but discards his costume and takes on the form of a female ballet-dancer, Guillermina, only to change again into La Dominga, a figure covered with small bells. Second Man, dressed again as a woman in black pyjama trousers, as in Scene One, is pursued by Third Man, but the latter, adopting a mask, then turns to Juliet, and Second Man is stripped of his black pyjamas and appears once more in the suit he wore in Scene One. Even the discarded costumes take on a life of their own, one seeking the other only to discover that it is not what he or she thinks it is. If Juliet has experienced the disillusionment of love, these other characters discover that their pursuit of it leads only to despair, for nothing is what it seems to be, appearances are deceptive, everything changes. This powerful scene expresses what Lorca had discovered for himself in his own fluctuating relationships with Dalí, Aladrén and others: nothing is certain, people and circumstances change, love is a fragile and ultimately vain pursuit. The scene ends with a highly evocative image: a figure with a face like an egg beats its face with its hands. Lorca's own despair in 1930 could not be clearer, but even more striking is the way in which he has transformed personal feelings into a universal statement, something which is typical of his theatre in general.

In performance, *The Public* has had a difficult time, bearing out Lorca's description of it as 'for the theatre years from now'. In 1933, during a visit to Buenos Aires, he suggested that the play's subject would not be acceptable to a contemporary audience, and that, rather than a play to be performed, it was 'a poem to be booed at'.[27] Indeed, the full text of *The Public* was not published until March 1978. Until that time only Scene Two and Scene Five had ever appeared in print, despite the fact that on 16 July 1936 Lorca had entrusted the entire manuscript to Rafael Martínez Nadal before leaving Madrid on his final, fatal journey to Granada. Lorca's murder by Nationalists meant that the play was unlikely to be published during Franco's dictatorship, but, in addition, the Lorca family clearly resisted attempts to make public a work in which the dramatist's homosexuality was so evident. Tiring eventually of their opposition, Martínez Nadal decided to publish the manuscript version, which, although Scene Four has been lost, has since provided the basis for theatre production.

The first staging of any part of *The Public* occurred in 1972 at the University of Texas, when Rafael Martínez Nadal lectured on the play, and included fragments from it in his lecture. Enthusiastic students then insisted on staging those fragments. Four years later the play as we know it today was performed by a student-theatre company at the University of Puerto Rico as part of that institution's seventy-fifth birthday celebrations. However, both the above were amateur productions, which, however good they might have been, were unlikely to have done justice to such a difficult and complex piece.

The first professional production was a collaboration between the Piccolo Teatro di Milano and Madrid's Teatro María Guerrero, directed by the young Spanish director, Lluís Pascual. It was triumphantly presented in Madrid in the winter of 1987 in a staging worthy of detailed examination.[28] Pascual and his stage-designer, Fabià Puigserver, boldly chose to ignore Lorca's stage directions, seeing them as being, in a sense, old-fashioned, too rooted in the avant-garde of the 1920s, and, because they were conceived with a proscenium stage in mind, too restrictive. For this reason they resolved to open out the whole of the action, and, by removing all but a single row of the María Guerrero's ground-floor seats, created a huge circular space that would suggest the idea of a journey into and through an inner world of dream and imagination. This effect was enhanced by the fact that the surface of this great open space was covered with sand, the colour of which changed with the lighting, evoking a kind of bare, empty moon surface. Upstage, an arrangement of curtains made of solid material, one behind the other, acted as screens from behind which the characters entered and exited.

Because of its length and breadth, the floor area – not unlike a circus ring – allowed for spectacular and expressive movement. When, at the beginning of Scene One, the four white horses appeared, they did so through the theatre entrances normally used by the audience, and, played by extremely athletic actors, ran and leaped across the sand. Rarely can Lorca's vision of a horse as the embodiment of freedom, sexual instinct and power have been so graphically presented as by these actors, bare from the waist up and with flowing white tails attached to their heads. And rarely can the contrast have been so forcefully made between uninhibited passion and the kind of bourgeois restraint personified here in the figure of the Director. Again, expressive and stylized movement caught to perfection the struggle in Scene Three between the white horses and the deathlike, negative character of Black Horse. As Black Horse and First White Horse aggressively confronted each other, Juliet threw herself at their feet, and, when she wished to go off with the white horses, they danced before her, throwing back their heads and gripping phallic sticks, the whole a cleverly choreographed sequence suggestive of a mating ritual. It goes without saying that a similar stylization characterized the encounter of Figure with Bells and Figure with Vine Leaves in Scene Two, as well as the episode at the end of Scene Three in which the characters search in vain for their lovers.

The floor area of the María Guerrero, in contrast to the restrictions of a traditional stage, also allowed for unusual and striking arrangements of the play's characters. On a traditional stage the three men who enter the Director's room in Scene One would do so from a point quite close to him, but in Pascual's production they did so from sixty feet away. And in the final scene, the Director and the Magician held their debate from either side of the great space. The physical distance between the characters evoked a sense of empty landscapes, of unreality, and, in the end, of dream. In addition, it served to emphasize the isolation of the characters from each other, stranded as they were at different points of the circle of sand. Quite often the Director stood alone, and when the Figure with Bells and the Figure with Vine Leaves play their game of alternating submission and domination, the sudden transformation of physical closeness into distance as one of them moves away suggested quite brilliantly both the changing nature of their relationship and their ultimate loneliness.

The lighting of the stage proved to be another telling aspect of Pascual's production. The representation of dreams or the unconscious on stage clearly requires effects which are the opposite of naturalistic, and therefore, in order to suggest the unreality of many of the play's situations, the stage was frequently in shadow or even in darkness, with particular areas in pools or shafts of light. When the Director and the three men meet in Scene One, he was revealed in one pool of light, they in another, separated by an area of unlit stage. In short, the effect was a remarkably ghostlike setting, the characters existing in some disembodied world, and this was further heightened by the angles of lighting, which often illuminated only the sides of faces or created elongated shadows – a mysterious, haunting, inner world, the darkened corners of the mind's recesses.

Narrow areas of light, streaming across the width of the space, were also used to great effect. In Scene Three, when the characters and discarded costumes seek each other out, they advanced along a stream of light some ten feet wide, like moths caught in the headlights of a car.

And when the Figure with Bells and the Figure with Vine Leaves first appeared in Scene Two, they crawled from behind a curtain which, raised a few feet above the level of the stage, allowed light to flood the sand-covered floor. In Scene Five, the students who discuss the nature of theatre were only partly illuminated, their shadows reflected on the curtains behind the figure of Red Nude, and the women who leave the theatre in the same scene did so with the assistance of flashlights. The whole effect was to suggest an interplay of figures and shadows, of the blurring of forms, of the overlapping of appearance and reality which lies at the heart of the play as a whole. And this, of course, was emphasized in the final scene in which the Magician, the master of illusion, held aloft a large fan which was silhouetted on a curtain sixty feet away.

The language of *The Public* is as powerful as any of Lorca's better-known plays. Conflict and confrontation are virtually constant as the various characters argue with each other, more often than not disputing each other's point of view. In addition, the language they use is driven by powerful emotions and is for the most part highly stylized, far from naturalistic. In the large space of the María Guerrero the cut-and-thrust of the verbal exchanges matched the movement and the arrangement of the characters, and the size of the space and the consequent distance between characters demanded that their lines be spoken clearly, with due emphasis on their rhythm and pattern. And when the characters were in closer contact, hurling accusations or voicing their anguish, the effect was just as powerful. In every respect, Pascual's production was a model of what Lorca's theatre should be on stage. Lorca himself would have approved.

A second major production of the play, in French translation, took place at the Théâtre de la Colline in Paris, directed by the Argentinian Jorge Lavelli. Unlike Pascual, Lavelli did not resort to ripping out the stalls. Ronald Hayman, reviewing the production in the *Guardian*, observed that the set reflected in many respects Lorca's original vision, and was, therefore, less experimental than Pascual's staging.[29] He considered that the production was 'full of arresting stage pictures', a point

also emphasized by Michael Coveney in the *Financial Times*: '. . . we witness a procession of diverting surrealist tableaux'.[30] But this point at
once raises the question of the extent to which the audience was
involved in the on-stage action. Hayman evidently believed that it was,
for he concluded that 'though the moral climate has changed, the theatrical shocks are still extremely strong when high camp is fused with
great poetry, verbal and visual'. On the other hand, Michael Coveney
felt that 'M. Lavelli's production does not solve the problem of articulat-
ing its poetic anguish, nor indeed the sense of confused panic arising
from the intermingling of audience and actors, of confession and revelation'. In short, there were brilliant individual visual moments rather
than a sustained emotional impact, and Hayman and Coveney dis-
agreed on the quality of the acting, Coveney concluding that in general
it was 'of a low density of expression', while Hayman felt that the 'general standard of acting is high'. The difference of opinion merely proves
that the reaction of critics to stage performance is as subjective as that of
an audience's, but it seems safe to say that Lavelli's production of *The
Public* was not as original, daring and inclusive as Pascual's.

The British première of the play, and the only British production to
date, opened on 3 October 1988 at the Theatre Royal Stratford East,
directed by David Ultz.[31] It was, unquestionably, a piece which baffled
most of the critics who saw it. Jim Hiley, writing in *The Listener*, bluntly
– and unwisely – described the play as 'a dud, justifying Buñuel's dis-
dain. Adolescent ideas trail behind overwrought images . . . free
association of the most pedestrian kind'.[32] And Jack Tinker, in the
Daily Mail, admitted: 'I'd be hard-pressed myself to apply any adequate
explanation to a great deal of what goes on'.[33] The truth of the matter
is that many British critics are either uninformed about or hostile to
foreign theatre – or both – but, in this particular case, it is also quite
likely that the production team and many of the cast were equally
bemused, for *The Public* is not, after all, the more familiar territory of
Blood Wedding, *Yerma* or *The House of Bernarda Alba*. Given this, the
motto for the production may have been 'If you don't understand it,

tart it up', and so it was that many of the critics responded to the production's visual appeal. Michael Darvell in *What's On* wrote that 'the production is all style and little content', and Gerard Werson in *The Stage* considered that the production was 'visually gorgeous'.[34, 35]

With its proscenium arch, the stage of the Theatre Royal is similar to those for which Lorca wrote his plays, and the director remained largely faithful to Lorca's directions. This said, the need to change the sets from scene to scene proved time consuming and noisy, and disrupted the required dreamlike flow of the action. In addition, the stage was often cluttered, and this, combined with its relative lack of depth – so different from the great space of the Madrid production – meant that the movements of the actors were severely restricted. Other aspects of the production also left much to be desired. The brilliantly athletic horses of the Madrid production here became pantomime horses – actors in body stocking with clumsy horses' heads – almost incapable of movement. The language of the play was often poorly spoken and at other times inappropriately camp. All in all, this first British production did little to suggest that another will follow.

In Lorca's theatre as a whole, *The Public* stands out for many reasons. Although personal experience has been transformed into art, the play is one of extraordinary self-revelation and, therefore, of great emotional impact. In addition to its homosexual preoccupation, it is also a play about theatre – and about Lorca's ideas on theatre – which, far from being a kind of lecture, has an amazing theatricality. Before its composition, Dalí and Buñuel derided Lorca for being old-fashioned. In *The Public* he gave them his response.

2
When Five Years Pass:
A Legend of Time

Completed on 19 August 1931, *When Five Years Pass* is, like *The Public*, an extraordinary play in every sense. In Act One, the Young Man dreams of meeting the Girlfriend in five years' time, and so rejects the Secretary when she reveals her love for him. He and three other characters – the Old Man, the hyperactive Friend and the childlike, nostalgic Second Friend – then witness a violent storm and the appearance of the Dead Child and the Dead Cat, who, despite their protests, are dragged into the darkness by a huge hand. The Girlfriend is introduced in Act Two, and immediately her passion for the strong and energetic Football Player is apparent. When the Young Man then comes to call on her, she rejects him for his lack of passion, a charge which, as the act ends, is also levelled against him by the Manikin clothed in the Girlfriend's bridal gown. In response, the Young Man resolves to seek out the Secretary before it is too late. Act Three presents his quest for her, in the course of which he is thwarted and mocked by the mysterious figures of Harlequin and the Clown. At last he finds her, but only to discover that she no longer loves him, preferring to dream of a handsome young man she will meet in five years' time. In a state of despair, he is visited by the three Card Players, who insist that he play a game of cards. When he is finally forced to reveal his hand – the ace of hearts – one of them shoots him, and he dies alone, listening to the echo of his own voice.

As was his usual practice, Lorca read the play to a group of friends, performing all the parts himself. Their reaction was somewhat different from that which had greeted the reading of *The Public* nine months or so earlier, but it was still less than enthusiastic. Shocked by the overt homosexuality in *The Public*, they were now disconcerted by the modernity and the difficulty of *When Five Years Pass*. Rafael Martínez Nadal suggested later that it was received 'with coldness'.[1] Another friend present at the reading, Carlos Morla Lynch, observed that 'we found ourselves, unexpectedly, outside Spain, in the world of "surrealism", far from *Gypsy Ballads* . . . a great effort is needed to understand the writer's purpose. And here lies the difficulty.'[2] Nevertheless, Morla Lynch was impressed by many aspects of the play. As for Lorca himself, he was well aware of his audience's discomfort and therefore of what the public at large might feel if the play were performed. In an interview with Felipe Morales in 1936, he stated that both *The Public* and *When Five Years Pass* were 'impossible plays', too difficult to stage at that time, even though they contained 'my true intention'.[3] Although there were, in fact, plans to stage *When Five Years Pass* at Madrid's Club Anfistora in the spring of 1936, they were thwarted by the country's increasing political chaos. Indeed, there is a chilling irony in the fact that Lorca completed *When Five Years Pass* on 19 August 1931 and was murdered exactly five years later. The play would not be performed in Spain until forty-two more years had passed.

Lorca finished writing *The Public* on 22 August 1930, *When Five Years Pass* a year later. In other words, he started work on the latter soon after completing the former, and there are clear connections between them, as well as echoes of Lorca's experience of New York. In Act Two, for example, we are introduced to the Football Player, who wears '*knee-pads and football-helmet*' (p. 145), and who is the very epitome of the male athlete.[4] Whether or not Lorca had attended an American football game is not known, but his Football Player is obviously based on real players he had either come across at matches or seen in newspaper photographs. The car in which the Football Player arrives at the Girlfriend's house, furiously blasting the horn, is not described, but the episode as a whole, including the description of the Girlfriend in a '*magnificent dressing-gown covered with lace and large rose-coloured ribbons*', (p. 145) is strongly reminiscent of American films. In Act One, the Secretary, waiting to type the Young Man's letters, is someone Lorca would have encountered in America both in real life and on the screen. And in Act Two, the Manikin, with '*the stiff posture of a dummy in the window of a store*' (p. 159), is something he would often have seen in New York's department-store windows. But in addition to these more or less precise echoes, *When Five Years Pass* belongs to the New York period in more fundamental ways, not least in terms of Lorca's attempt to grapple with his personal problems. If *The Public* is his dramatization of his homosexual anguish, *When Five Years Pass* is, amongst other things, an expression of his failure to respond to women. The problem was one which preoccupied him constantly, but the impulse to write this particular play may well have had something to do with Buñuel and Dalí.

From late 1928, the friendship between Dalí and Buñuel had become ever closer, the two men drawn to each other by their mutual obsession with all things Surrealist, and for that reason scornful of those whom they considered at all traditionalist. Not only had Buñuel called *The Love of Don Perlimplín* 'a load of shit' to Lorca's face, but he had, like Dalí, expressed his dislike of *Gypsy Ballads*. In a letter to José Bello, he described the poems as having only an apparent modernity designed to please the 'homosexual, Cernuda-style poets from Seville'.[5] Buñuel was also fond of describing Lorca as 'asqueroso' ('revolting'), a clever but wounding pun on the name of the village, Asquerosa, where Lorca lived as a child and where the family still owned a house. The film that Buñuel and Dalí worked on in Figueras in January 1929 was originally to be called *Il est dangéreux de se pencher en dedans* (*It is Dangerous to Lean In*) – a pun on the advice given to passengers on French trains – but this was changed to *Un Chien andalou* (*An Andalusian Dog*). Premièred at the Studio des Ursulines in Paris in June 1929, it was a huge success, acclaimed by André Breton, leader of the Paris Surrealist group, as a true Surrealist film. Lorca was convinced that the film's protagonist was, for reasons that we will now consider, closely based on himself, and he was clearly upset by it. In New York, he told Angel del Río: 'Buñuel has made a little shit of a film called *An Andalusian Dog* – and I'm the Dog.'[6] Why would he have thought this?

During their time at the Residencia de Estudiantes, Dalí, Buñuel and others had jokingly described their fellow students from Andalusia as 'Andalusian dogs', and of that group Lorca was clearly the most prominent – the top Andalusian dog, in effect. The film's title would therefore have struck an immediate chord with him. Furthermore, although he did not see the film at the time of its release – he was in Spain and soon on his way to New York – there is no reason to suspect that he did not learn of its content. The Paris première was widely publicized and discussed in the newspapers, both French and Spanish. By the end of 1929 the script of the film had also been published in a number of European literary journals, so it is quite possible that Lorca had read it. And he certainly discussed it in New York with the Mexican artist Emilio Amero, an enthusiastic cinema fan who had also recently completed a short film of his own.[7] Quite apart from the reference to himself that Lorca evidently recognized in the title, the male protagonist of *Un Chien andalou* is a young man whom at first we see riding a bicycle in a listless, mechanical manner. When, shortly afterwards, he falls from the bicycle and is passionately embraced by a young woman, he fails to respond to her. Later he becomes sexually aroused, but then reverts to his former passive state, resisting the efforts of a second, much more active young man to rouse him from his inertia. As for the young woman, she becomes weary of his passivity, mocks him and finally goes off with a lover who is clearly more 'masculine'. The young man of *Un Chien andalou* is an individual who is sexually immature in relation to women, his undeveloped sexuality emphasized by the fact that over his suit he wears baby clothes. He may, of course, be a projection of Dalí himself, but it is not surprising that Lorca, given the film's title and Buñuel's and Dalí's hostility, should have seen their film as a comment on himself. What is more surprising, in the light of Lorca's sense of injury, is that not long afterwards he should have written a play which has clear links with this same 'little shit of a film'.

Lorca's first response to *Un Chien andalou* was possibly the filmscript *Trip to the Moon*, which he wrote in New York in the course of an afternoon.[8] This, as we have seen in the discussion of *The Public*, consisted of seventy-eight short sequences in which the emphasis is very much on sexual violence. Anticipating the disturbing images of the painter Francis Bacon, *Trip to the Moon* vividly reflects Lorca's sexual anguish at the time of writing. But, if it was a response to *Un Chien andalou*, the parallel lies in its style, not in its themes. Like the Buñuel–Dalí film, Lorca's screenplay contains what would have become on screen fade-outs, fade-ins, dislocations of time and place and transpositions and transformations, all of which evoke the illogical and chaotic processes of the unconscious mind. On the other hand, there is little in *Trip to the Moon* that parallels the sexual inhibitions of the protagonist of *Un Chien andalou* or indeed of the various characters whom he encounters. To find such parallels in Lorca's work, we have to turn to *When Five Years Pass*, completed two years after the première of *Un Chien andalou*. It is as if the film provided Lorca, however much he hated its relevance to himself, with a framework for an exploration of his own sexual problems.

Lorca's Young Man is, like the Buñuel–Dalí protagonist, sexually passive in response to women. In the film he lies inert, unmoved by the young woman's kisses, and later he lies on his bed, staring blankly into space, incapable of any kind of activity. The Young Man in *When Five Years Pass* is initially seated, as passive as his cinematic counterpart, unresponsive to the Secretary when, in tears, she openly admits to loving him: 'There's only one explanation . . . I love you' (p. 129). He, in contrast, prefers to indulge in fantasy and day-dream, to keep at bay the reality of a passionate woman in favour of a romantic vision which carries no threat: 'And so I can wait for five years, in the hope of meeting her at night, when the whole world's asleep, and winding her long golden hair around my neck' (p. 127). At the beginning of Act Two the Girlfriend describes his lack of response to her in a vivid image: 'My fiancé had a mouth as cold as ice; he would kiss me, and his lips were covered with small, dead leaves' (p. 146). And later in the act, the Manikin, dressed in the Girlfriend's bridal gown which will never be worn by her, voices the latter's recriminations:

> ... The fault is yours.
> You could have been a horse of lead and foam for me,
> Your bridle rushing air, your haunches sea.
> You could have been a stallion's clarion call.
> Instead you were a stagnant moss-filled pool,
> Where this dress rots and withered leaves now fall. (p. 156)

These powerful allusions to the world of nature in all its energy and life-giving force serve to emphasize the extent to which the Young Man is unnatural, uncreative, outside the normal run of things. It is a damning accusation, and one which Lorca may well have levelled against himself. If, in his work as a whole, the sea is associated with life and creativity, he, a homosexual and therefore unlikely to father a child, was much more the 'stagnant moss-filled pool'. In short, Lorca may well have seen himself at times as a violation of nature and experienced all the despair that this implies. Seen from this point of view, the young man in the Buñuel–Dalí film was merely a point of reference for Lorca, a way in to the creation of a much more complex character, who is also a portrait of the dramatist.

There is, nevertheless, a moment in *Un Chien andalou* when the sexually passive protagonist becomes aroused. From an upstairs window he and the young woman witness a scene in the street below in which another young woman prods an amputated hand with a stick. Excited by what he has seen, the young man advances on his companion, reaching out to squeeze her breasts and buttocks which, in his inflamed imagination, are suddenly divested of their clothing. In Act Two of *When Five Years Pass*, the Young Man undergoes a similar transformation after his encounter with the Manikin. Shaken by her accusations, he suddenly declares: 'I shall bring my naked lover, / Trembling and burning with desire' (p. 159). And in Act Three he passionately addresses the Secretary:

> I'll take you with me naked,
> Crushed flower, flesh so bold,
> There to the place where the silken sheets
> Are trembling with cold. (p. 169)

The contrast between this impassioned lover and the earlier dreamer could not be greater, and the Young Man's vision of naked female flesh is certainly reminiscent of *Un Chien andalou*. In terms of Lorca's personal life, however, this more positive aspect of the Young Man may well have embodied a desire rather than a reality – something that he desperately wanted to do rather than anything he actually did. This being the case, the sense of anguish attached to futile desire must surely have been as acute as that which stemmed from his feeling of being unnatural.

In this context, it is easy to explain the two vibrantly male characters who appear in Lorca's play: the Football Player and the Friend, both based, it would seem, on the energetic young man in *Un Chien andalou*. The character in the film chastises the young man for his passivity, and pulls him to his feet, stripping him of his baby frills; in *When Five Years Pass* the Friend enters the Young Man's house, '*rushing in, causing a great commotion*' (p. 130), and proceeds to pull him up by his lapels. In order to stress the extent to which he is different from the Young Man – 'Ah, well, I'm the complete opposite . . .' (p. 131) – he boasts of his conquests of women: 'Yesterday I made it with three women and the day before two, and today one . . .' (p. 131). But even more striking in this respect is the Football Player who visits the

Girlfriend at the beginning of Act Two. Speaking not a single word – which points to the influence of silent film – he is pure masculinity in action: '*He is a person of enormous vitality and he passionately embraces the* GIRLFRIEND' (p. 145). She describes him as 'a great dragon' (p. 145), his passion for her 'a great flowing torrent' which will sweep her away (p. 146) – the opposite, then, of the stagnant pool. And when she kisses him, she feels the fire within: 'What white heat! And the ivory fire of your mouth!' (p. 146). The Football Player is in many ways an anticipation of the passionate Leonardo in *Blood Wedding*, this episode an earlier form of the more developed relationship with the Bride in the later play. And if the Young Man, in his sexually passive form, is, in essence, Lorca, so the Football Player and Leonardo are figures of his imagination, the vibrant males that he was not. It is no accident that the passionate encounter between the Girlfriend and the Football Player should take place in a setting which is not only romantic but also markedly dreamlike, suggestive of the world of illusion and, in particular, of Lorca's fantasy.

If *When Five Years Pass* is an exploration of Lorca's sexual dilemma, it also voices other significant obsessions. The play's title refers to the passage of time, a point reinforced by its subtitle, *A Legend of Time*. No sooner has Act One commenced than '*A clock strikes six*' (p. 126); at the end of Act Three '*The clock strikes twelve*' (p. 181). Lorca was, for a variety of reasons, highly conscious of the passing of time and the inevitable consequences of this. In the first place, it changes one's appearance, as the Young Man observes of the Girlfriend:

> The last time I saw her face to face, I couldn't bear to look at her really closely because there were two small wrinkles on her forehead. And you know what? If I looked away for a moment, those lines had spread to cover the whole of her face, and they'd changed her into someone old and faded . . . (p. 128)

Similarly, there is a marked difference between photographs of Lorca at twenty years of age – youthful, handsome, quite romantic in appearance – and Lorca in his mid-thirties – podgier and altogether plainer.[9] He was undoubtedly more and more aware and fearful of his fading looks and of his powers of attraction, his future mirrored in the Old Man with his white beard and his faded grey jacket, who pessimistically reminds his younger companions: 'Our clothes wear out, anchors rust and we move on . . . Eyes grow dim and a sharp sickle cuts the reeds on the river bank' (p. 142). At the other extreme from the Old Man is the Second Friend, who – although to be played, according to the stage directions, by a young actor – is, in effect, a child, or at least someone in search of his childhood. His white suit suggests both innocence and unflawed youth. But things are already changing, and, just as the Young Man sees wrinkles on the Girlfriend's face, so the presence of the Old Man reminds the Second Friend that already time is ageing him: 'Once I was young and I used to sing and now there's a man, (*To the* OLD MAN) a gentleman like you, here inside me, with two or three masks at the ready (*He takes out a mirror and looks at himself.*)' (p. 142). Photographs of Lorca in a white suit are certainly reminiscent of the Second Friend, and, like him, the dramatist was always conscious of the magic and innocence of childhood gone for ever, even though its memory was constantly with him:

> My oldest memories of childhood have the flavour of the earth. The meadows, the fields, have been wonderful for me. The wild creatures in the countryside, the livestock, the people who live on the land, they all fascinate me in a way that not many people understand. I recall them now just as I knew them when I was a child . . .[10]

In much the same way, the Dead Cat and the Dead Child recall the games they used to play. The Dead Cat describes them:

> I used to go along the rooftops with my flat nose,
> My little tin-like nose.

> In the morning
> I used to catch fish in the pool;
> And at midday,
> Under the rosebush by the wall I used to sleep and keep cool. (p. 135)

But in both cases their childhood has been taken from them, a loss which, as the Dead Child suggests, is a source of deepest anguish:

> . . . It's not heaven
> We want. It's the earth, with all the
> Crickets singing, the grass swaying,
> The clouds ever so high, slings that
> Shoot stones, the wind as sharp as a
> Sword. I just want to be a little boy! (p. 137)

Thus, an awareness of the remorseless passage of time lies at the heart of the Friend's desperate efforts to savour the pleasures of the moment. No sooner has he rushed in in Act One than he downs one drink after another, hurls himself around the room, talks at top speed, commenting as he does so: 'What's the point of thinking? I'm off. Good God! (*He looks at his watch*). I'm too late. It's frightening. Always the same. No time' (p. 131). But, in spite of his frantic efforts, the moment of pleasure has passed, is already in the past as soon as he has experienced it, and the only future is that evoked by the Old Man's prophecy: 'But in front of us, in four or five years' time, there's a black pit, and we'll all fall into it' (p. 142).

The characters of *When Five Years Pass* are, in effect, the different ages of man – childhood, adulthood, old age – anticipating in that respect the age range, from twenty to eighty, of the women in *The House of Bernarda Alba*. The Second Friend's fear of advancing age finds an echo in the later play in the words of the twenty-year-old Adela to her older sisters: 'I don't want my skin to become like yours. I don't want to lose my whiteness in these rooms!' (p. 39). Lorca himself did not, of course, become the Old Man, for his death at the age of thirty-eight justified, in hindsight, the resolve of the Friend to enjoy life to the full while there is time to do so.

If Lorca dreaded the passing of time, he was also, throughout his life, obsessed by death. As a child he had witnessed the laying out of the corpse of Salvador Cobos Rueda, who worked for his father, an event that he seems never to have forgotten, as in later life he was able to provide his mother with a detailed account of the incident. From the age of twenty Lorca also frequently acted out his own death and his burial, a performance which greatly impressed his friends at the Residencia. Dalí, who witnessed it, wrote in later years:

> I remember his death-like, terrible expression as, stretched on his bed, he parodied the different stages of his own slow decomposition. In this game, the process of putrefaction lasted for five days. Then he would describe his coffin . . . and the progress of the funeral procession through the streets.[11]

At the end of the performance, says Dalí, Lorca would jump up, push his friends out of the room and go to bed 'liberated from his anxiety'. This anxiety is expressed in no uncertain fashion in *When Five Years Pass*, in the episode involving the Dead Child and the Dead Cat. The way in which the Dead Child describes his laying out is strongly reminiscent of Lorca's enactment of his own death:

> They tied my hands together. Such a cruel thing to do!
> The children stared at me through the window.
> And a man came with a hammer.
> And nailed paper stars on my coffin. (p. 134)

But the emotion contained in these lines is as nothing compared with the terror he feels at the thought of being buried:

Oh, wait! They're coming. I'm afraid.

I ran away from the house.

He weeps.

I don't want to be buried!

. . .

I don't want to be buried! Let's go quickly!

He takes her [the cat] by the paw.

CAT: Will they bury us? When will it be?

CHILD: Tomorrow. In two black holes. (p. 136)

As the episode unfolds and the light fades, their sense of panic grows ever greater, and for the Dead Child greater still when his companion is seized and dragged into the blackness by a great hand: 'A great hand's taken her. / It must be the hand of God. / Don't bury me!' (p. 138). Similarly, in Act Three, Scene Two, the Young Man is clearly on edge when he sees his suit laid out on the bed, and then when his servant mentions the shoes with black laces. These omens of death anticipate the agents of death, the Card Players, and the final, despairing words of the Young Man echo the earlier cries of the Dead Child, of whom the Young Man is simply an older form: 'John, John. I want to live' (p. 181). The circumstances of Lorca's own death, described in more detail in Chapter Six, undoubtedly involved the emotions which, five years earlier, he had imagined in his characters. After his arrest by his enemies, he is said to have been in a state of collapse. We can only imagine how he must have felt when he learned of his imminent execution.

Another theme, prominent in this and other plays, is that of childlessness. Spain was, and is, a country in which a great deal of fuss is made of children. In the village of Fuente Vaqueros Lorca had more than forty cousins, yet he knew he would never be a father. The fondness of and a yearning for children which is evident throughout his work clearly derives from the influence of having such a large family around him. When the boy appears in *The Shoemaker's Wonderful*

Wife, the childless wife treats him with affection: 'My dear, sweet child, where are you going?' (p. 18).[12] In *Yerma*, the childless wife's desperation becomes intolerable, driving her almost to madness. In *When Five Years Pass*, quite apart from the touching scene involving the Dead Child, the Manikin – spokeswoman for the Girlfriend – voices in Act Two her burning desire to have a child by the Young Man:

> Fountains of white milk
> Stain with sorrow the silk of my dress,
> And the white pain of a bee
> Implants in my flesh its sharp caress.
> My child! I want my child!
> These ribbons burst at my waist with joy,
> Project the form of an unborn boy.
> And he'll be yours too. (p. 157)

And in Act Three, as he seeks the Secretary, the Young Man seems to hear inside him the voice of an unborn child, while, simultaneously, the Dead Child crosses the stage:

> Yes, my child. Inside me, like a small, solitary ant in a sealed box. (*To the* SECRETARY.) Light for my child, for he's so small, pressing his nose against the glass of my breast, fighting to breathe. (p. 172)

For Lorca, the child or the seed inside him was, in effect, a dead child. This play, more than any other, constantly interweaves those themes and issues which most preoccupied the dramatist in his personal life: his failure with women, the passage of time, childlessness and death. In *The Public* he had grappled with the single issue of his homosexuality; *When Five Years Pass* embraces other concerns, and is, in that regard, Lorca's most autobiographical play.

Stylistically and in terms of its dramatic technique, *When Five Years Pass* is at least as striking as *The Public*, and reveals many of the same cultural influences. The earlier play, as we have seen, owes much to Surrealism in the sense that it lays bare the Director's inner life, and by extension Lorca's. In *When Five Years Pass*, the whole of the action can be seen as the projection of the Young Man's thoughts, dreams and fears; the male characters as facets of himself in the past (Second Friend), the present (Friend) and the future (the Old Man); the women as the creations of his fantasy and imagination. Furthermore, the evocation of a dream-world is, if anything, stronger here than in *The Public*. This is particularly apparent in Act One, when the lighting of the stage, in preparation for the appearance of the Dead Child and the Dead Cat, suddenly changes: '*The light fades and the stage is filled with a blue glow*' (p. 133). The stage immediately assumes the unreality associated with dreams and the unconscious, and the scene as a whole – observed by the Young Man, the Old Man, the Friend and Second Friend – becomes, in effect, their individual nightmare, a projection of their deepest fears rising to the surface in true Surrealist fashion. The element of dream is also very much present at the beginning of Act Two in the presentation of the Girlfriend and her lover, the Football Player. The Girlfriend's bedroom, with its strange furniture, painted clouds and angels on the walls and '*a dressing-table supported by cherubs with branches in their hands that become electric lights*' (p. 145), is, far from being real, a fantasy conjured up in the Young Man's mind. The Girlfriend herself, clothed in '*a magnificent dressing-gown covered with lace and large rose-coloured ribbons*' (p. 145), is his vision of her as he would like her to be when he meets her in five years' time, and the vital and impassioned Football Player, whom she finds irresistible, is, of course, his imagined form of himself – in his wildest dreams, as it were. This encounter takes place, significantly, in the light of the moon, which, therefore, recalls the earlier scene in which the Dead Child and the Dead Cat appear on a stage '*filled with a blue glow*' (p. 133), and a similar effect accompanies the coming to life of the Manikin later in Act Two: '*The light fades. The lights held by the cherubs take on a blue colour. Moonlight pours through the windows, intensifying to the end of the scene . . .'* (p. 155). It is clearly no accident that these three episodes should occur in circumstances which suggest the dark and mysterious world into which we enter as we sleep, when our deepest longings and desires are released by the unconscious mind, and they rise to the surface in the form of dreams.

Furthermore, in Act Three there is a strong sense of those deep-seated fears which unleash nightmares. In the first of the two scenes, with Lorca's stage directions for huge tree-trunks and *'two figures dressed in black . . . their faces and hands white like plaster of Paris'* (p.161), there is a strong sense of the kind of terror associated with childhood dreams, while in the second scene the appearance of the three Card Players in *'dinner-jackets and long capes of white satin that reach to their feet'* (p. 177) has about it an icy inevitability that is decidedly disquieting.

Clearly, *When Five Years Pass* owes something to *Un Chien andalou* in the sense that it abandons traditional plot and story-line in favour of a much more fluid technique intended to suggest the shifting patterns and processes of the unconscious. But, if anything, Lorca's play is much more sophisticated and polished than the Buñuel–Dalí film, however much praise has been lavished on the latter. It illustrates Lorca's notion of a work of art as a journey, in this case a journey from day-dream and fantasy to bitter disillusionment.[13] And in that respect it also has a coherence and a sense of the author's controlling hand which is at odds with Breton's definition of Surrealism as spontaneous expression, free from the control of reason. Lorca's reliance on Surrealist theory and technique was, indeed, only partial.

Quite apart from the direct inspiration of *Un Chien andalou,* the influence of film in general was also extremely important stylistically to *When Five Years Pass,* and particularly the silent films of Charlie Chaplin, Buster Keaton and others, films in which movement in particular tended to be fast and exaggerated. In Act Two, the Football Player, who speaks not a word but who has enormous vitality and who sweeps up the Girlfriend in his arms, owes much to that tradition, while the Girlfriend herself, with her mass of curls and her exotic bed-room with its ornate décor, could well be straight out of one of the more romantic Hollywood films of the 1920s and 1930s. In contrast, there are elements in Lorca's play which have a clear Expressionist tone. Films of this kind, which Lorca would have seen in Madrid, included those classic examples of Expressionism, Robert Wiene's *The Cabinet of Dr Caligari* and Fritz Lang's *Metropolis*, made in 1919 and 1926 respectively. Expressionism was characterized by an emphasis on the nightmarish, on chiaroscuro, on visual distortion and by stark and simplified images.[14] All these elements are to be found in the figures and the settings of *The Cabinet of Dr Caligari*, and they are undoubtedly echoed in *When Five Years Pass* in the two figures who, white-faced and dressed in black, move amongst the great tree-trunks at the beginning of Act Three. Similarly, the three Card Players, with their dinner-jackets (presumably black) and their long white satin capes, have all the starkness of Expressionist images, and so, too, do the Dead Child, dressed in white, its face the colour of wax, and the Dead Cat, '*with two huge bloodstains on its white-grey breast*' (p. 133). In the sense that Expressionism was an anti-realist movement, a means of expressing the creative artist's subjective vision of the world in bold, stylized images, it was as appropriate a method as Surrealism for depicting the inner world that Lorca sought to present in *When Five Years Pass*.

The play also drew heavily on other art forms. Expressionism would have become familiar to him through his interest in painting – Edvard Munch's lithograph *The Scream* immediately comes to mind, but Van Gogh, Kandinsky and Kokoschka, together with many others, were also painters who used violent colours in order to express in their canvases powerful and disturbing emotional experiences. In addition, Lorca would have encountered the figures of both Harlequin and the Clown of his own Act Three in many of the paintings of Picasso – an obsessive theme with the Spanish painter – and both characters figured prominently, of course, in the old Italian theatrical tradition of the *commedia dell'arte* on which Lorca drew heavily in many of his plays.

Traditionally both Harlequin and the Clown were cheerful, happy creatures, part of a European family that also included Pulcinella, or Punch. Later, writers and painters adapted them in their own way, investing them with romantic or sentimental or, especially in the twentieth century, with more disturbing qualities. Lorca's drawings of both Harlequin and the Clown, many of which pre-dated *When Five Years Pass*, express his sadness and anxiety, but in the play itself both figures are presented as cruel and mocking manipulators of human beings, symbolic of those forces which control our lives, and of which Lorca was only too aware. The Clown in particular brings with him an association with the circus, but, far from suggesting a place of entertainment, the circus in *When Five Years Pass* is an image of life itself, in which men and women are merely players at the service of cold and heartless ringmasters, no less helpless than the animals who are made to jump through hoops. The Manikin of Act Two, with her '*golden eyebrows and lips*' (p. 155), and the Mask of Act Three, with her '*yellow silk hair falling like a shawl, and a white plaster of Paris mask*' (p. 165), also point to the influence of *commedia dell'arte* and anticipate characters in the films of Federico Fellini – such as $8\frac{1}{2}$ (1963) and *I clowns* (1970) – no less than the antics of Harlequin and the Clown look forward to particular moments in Samuel Beckett's *Waiting for Godot*.[15]

And then, of course, as in *The Public* and, indeed, many other Lorca plays, the impact of dance is very clear. When Harlequin appears, his '*movements have the visual impact of a dancer*' (p. 161). The Girl who enters shortly afterwards '*leaps around the stage with a garland of flowers*' (p. 162), and when Harlequin and the Clown leave the stage, they '*walk on tiptoe, like dancers, their fingers to their lips*' (p. 169). As the earlier discussion of *The Public* has shown, Lorca had a lifelong interest in movement and dance, and it was, for him – and for other theatre innovators of the 1920s and 1930s – an integral part of dramatic performance. He would have agreed with Rafael Alberti, a fellow poet and dramatist, when the latter described dance as 'the new language, the boldest expression of physical, musical and pictorial rhythms that ushered in the twentieth century.'[16] Dance in a variety of forms would also play a major part in both *Blood Wedding* and *Yerma*.

The language of *When Five Years Pass* is less difficult than that of *The Public*, and there is also a much more extensive use of verse. In the earlier play the language is often very difficult indeed, the meaning of individual phrases frequently obscure, if not incomprehensible. This said, the prose dialogue of *When Five Years Pass* is hardly that of everyday speech, for it often expresses ideas in an intense, heightened and very visual way, as in the case of the Girlfriend's determination to take risks and enjoy life to the full:

> Which is exactly what I want. To be burnt black. Blacker than a young boy. And when I fall, not to bleed; and when I grasp a blackberry bush, not to prick my fingers. Everyone walks along the wire with his eyes closed tight. I want to do so with lead heavy in my shoes . . . (p. 149)

At the same time, as this example suggests, the lines have a force and a rhythm that conveys the emotion of the speaker, something which distinguishes the language of the play in general. Thus, at the beginning of Act Two, the accumulated patterns and repetitions reflect perfectly the ardour felt by the Girlfriend for the Football Player:

> But you, you're even more magnificent. Like a great dragon. (*She embraces him.*) I feel as if I'm going to break in your arms, because I'm so fragile, so tiny, like the morning frost, like a tiny guitar scorched by the sun, and yet you don't break me. (p. 145)

Much of the prose dialogue has, in effect, both the emotional pulse and the patterned structure of poetry. However, when Lorca wanted to express even more heightened emotions, he turned to verse – which anticipates later plays, *Blood Wedding* in particular. Thus, in the pivotal moments of the play – in the episode involving the Dead Child and the Dead Cat; in the scene in which the Manikin accuses the Young Man; in the Harlequin's and the Clown's mocking of the Girl; and in the impassioned encounter between the Young Man and the Secretary – he invariably uses poetry. So we hear the anguish of the Dead Child:

> I don't want to be buried!
> Lilies and glass make my coffin prettier,
> But I'd rather sleep in the reeds by the water.
> I don't want to be buried . . . (p. 136)

It is no accident that at least three of the episodes in which verse replaces prose should consist of dreamlike or nightmarish elements, moments in which the more intense language of poetry seems perfectly placed.

Despite the negative reaction of those to whom Lorca read *When Five Years Pass* in 1931, plans were made to stage it in the spring of 1936. Indeed, the play went into rehearsal in June that year at the Anfistora Club in Madrid, an organization run by the influential Pura Maórtua de Ucelay for the purpose of staging modern works of theatre.[17] The production was then postponed until the following October, when it would be directed by Lorca himself, but the events of July put paid, of course, to any such plans, and the first production in Spanish did not take place until 1954 at the University of Puerto Rico, followed two years later by a Mexican television production. In Spain the circumstances of Lorca's death meant that it did not receive its première there until almost half a century after its composition. When Lorca described *When Five Years Pass* and *The Public* as works for the future, he could not possibly have imagined the reasons for the delay in performing them, nor indeed how far off that future would be.

The Spanish première took place on 19 September 1978, at the Teatro Eslava in Madrid – ironically, the very theatre where Lorca's first play, *The Butterfly's Evil Spell*, had been presented in 1920. The director on this auspicious occasion was the very experienced Miguel

Narros, and the production was, of course, eagerly awaited by both critics and public. It proved to be a great success and was awarded the prize for best play of the year by the theatre journal *El espectador y la crítica*, in which Pablo Corbalán concluded that

> this richness [of the play] has been fused, controlled, structured in all its oneiric brilliance, and every opportunity taken advantage of by Miguel Narros, the actors, the stage- and the lighting-designers of the Teatro Estable Castellano. The beauty of Lorca's text has been translated into a constellation of images. The work undertaken by Miguel Narros, the individual with most responsibility for the staging, has been, perhaps, the most important of his career and one of the most beautiful spectacles the public has been able to see. For this spectacle, he has been able to count on an excellent group of actors, all of whose combined efforts have created a theatrical language rich in its shading . . .[18]

Quite clearly, this production was notable for the visual brilliance of its stage-design and its costumes, and an idea of the former may be gleaned from the review which appeared in the newspaper *Ya*, where the set was described as consisting of

> tall cylinders which are [suggestive of] tombs, chimneys, contortions of the mind, skyscrapers, cypress trees, with men standing like statues on top of them, men who begin to move when it is their turn to do so, men who exist and who do not exist.[19]

At the very opposite extreme from naturalism, the stage-design was evidently evocative of the great empty spaces of the mind and of the transformations which take place within it, whereby a particular object quickly becomes something else in a process of constant movement and change.

But if the set was impressive, the critics were also favourably disposed towards the actors. Effective individually, they also appear to

have worked well together and to have captured both in their movement and in the speaking of the lines the many different moods of the
play. Critically, then, it was a success, although in part, at least, such
generosity is possibly explained by a feeling of relief and gratitude that
at last a major Lorca play could be seen in a lavish and clearly expensive professional production.

Eleven years later Miguel Narros staged the play once more, on
this occasion at the famous Teatro Español in Madrid, which in
Lorca's lifetime witnessed the premières of *The Shoemaker's Wonderful
Wife*, *The Love of Don Perlimplín* and, most famously, *Yerma*. A decade
later, critical reaction to the production, which was different from the
earlier one, was much less favourable. Some of the original cast was
retained but in different roles, and the staging was clearly even more
startling than it had been in 1978. Writing in *El País*, Eduardo Haro
Tecglen commented on the intense colours, the brilliant costumes,
the vivid lighting and the over-use of sound.[20] Lorca, he felt, had been
relegated to a secondary position, the text sacrificed to what was
essentially director's theatre in all its excess. This being the case, the
performances of the actors inevitably suffered, and Lorenzo López
Sancho, reviewing the production in *ABC*, drew attention to the fact
that Lorca's lines, instead of being delivered with appropriate shading,
were spoken at full volume.[21] *When Five Years Pass* is, of course, a play
which invites excess precisely because it contains such startling characters and scenes – a trap into which Narros obviously fell second time
around.

The first British production took place in 1989 at the Edinburgh
Fringe Festival, where *When Five Years Pass* was performed in my own
translation by the National Student Theatre Company, directed by
Maria Delgado and Robert Delamere. Inevitably, the relative simplicity of the staging owed more to the lack of financial resources than
to anything else, but it proved a definite advantage, for it did not
impede the flow of the action or distract attention from the text.
Played with the audience on two sides of the stage, the background

consisted simply of black curtains, but Nick Barnes's design picked out objects that related to given moments in the action – empty trunks, windows and clocks, for example. In short, the design in general suggested the darkened world of dream and the unconscious and those things that are associated with it. Writing in the *Independent*, Sarah Hemmings noted that 'Lorca creates a twilight world where surreal characters arrive to engineer the action', while Lyn Gardner, reviewing the play in *City Limits* a few weeks later on its transfer to the Battersea Arts Centre, London, concluded that the 'surreal, dreamlike quality of the piece is magically evoked'. [22, 23] In creating this dreamlike effect, the lighting by David Stewart played a major part. For Sarah Hemmings, Lyn Gardner and Joseph Farrell in the *Scotsman*, the stage was beautifully and expertly lit, not least in the episode involving the Dead Child and the Dead Cat as well as that with the Manikin.[24] In addition, particular moments in the play were accompanied and underlined by music for violin and flute. For Joseph Farrell it 'adds to the haunting effect', and for Lyn Gardner it was 'measured and effective'. As for the performances of the actors, Jan Fairley observed in the *Guardian* that 'the talented company bring exactly the appropriate vitality and energy to bear to realize the enigmatic core of the play'.[25] Individual performances were picked out, too, by the reviewer writing in the *Festival Times*: 'Particularly good is Marcus Atkinson [as the Old Man], the perfect alter ego to Mark Healy's depressed suitor . . .', while Zareen Hogarth as the Girlfriend and Vernon Douglas as the Football Player created in their particular scene a sensuality that was 'most memorable'.[26]

Perhaps the last word on the production should go to Jan Fairley in the *Guardian*:

In their remarkable British première at the Festival Club the National Student Theatre Company turned an awkward room into the fragmented, inner world of a young man whose intensity is brilliant and palpable. Friends and phantoms intermingle so that there is no distinction between reality and fantasy. We are drawn into a constantly shifting present which re-plays itself through the past . . . Authoritatively directed by Robert Delamere and Maria Delgado . . . this is a Fringe gem which will stay flickering in the mind.

Eight years later, in the winter of 1997, *When Five Years Pass* was produced by the Forbidden Theatre Company at the Chelsea Centre in London, in a translation by Pilar Orti, directed by Phillip Hoffman. Writing in *Time Out*, Charles Godfrey-Faussett referred to the 'bright painterly set', very different, indeed, from that used by the National Student Theatre Company.[27] It clearly aimed at a stylization that was reflected, too, in the performances of the actors, for the same reviewer observed that with 'arch theatricality the six-strong cast assume a dizzying variety of roles . . .' Since Forbidden Theatre Company specializes in the physical aspects of stage performance, *When Five Years Pass* is a play suited in certain respects to the company's style. On the other hand, it is also a piece in which emotion and mood are equally important, and in this particular area the production was less convincing. Charles Godfrey-Faussett concluded: 'What's missing in the headlong rush to hail the fleeting quality of true passion is any subtlety of mood.'

Both British productions, successful in different ways, suggest that effective stagings of *When Five Years Pass* do not depend on huge financial resources. Like many Lorca plays, it can be done simply, for its quality lies in the writing and in the ability of the actors to realize its fluctuating moods. One can imagine it played on a bare stage with a few simple chairs, its effect dependent entirely on lighting and the skill of the performers. Lorca, it is safe to say, would have directed it superbly in just that way.

3
Blood Wedding:
The Force of Destiny

Blood Wedding is one of Lorca's two best-known and most frequently performed plays, the other being *The House of Bernarda Alba*. The wedding takes place between the Bride and the Bridegroom, whose marriage has been arranged by her father and his mother, largely with a view to mutual material gain. The Bride's real love, however, is the passionate and good-looking Leonardo Félix, whom she has loved from the age of fifteen, but who is now married and has a child. Aware of this past relationship, and hating the Félix family for its part in the murder of her husband and eldest son, the Bridegroom's mother views her son's marriage to the Bride with apprehension, not least because Leonardo is a guest at the church and the ensuing reception. The Bride and Leonardo elope in the midst of the celebrations, and they are pursued by the Bridegroom and members of his family. The runaway couple hide in the dark forest where the mysterious figures of Moon and Death conspire to bring about the deaths of the two men, who kill each other in an off-stage confrontation. The Bride, no sooner married, becomes a widow, disgraced for her part in the tragedy, and Leonardo's wife is widowed, too. The Bridegroom's mother is left entirely alone, her one remaining child taken from her. *Blood Wedding* is a powerful tale of illicit passion and revenge, its enduring appeal easily explained.

By the time he completed *When Five Years Pass*, Lorca had written half of *Blood Wedding*, and there are certainly some similarities between the two plays. The great trees and the ominous figures of Harlequin and the Clown in Act Three, Scene One of *When Five Years Pass* have their equivalent in the forest and the woodcutters, as well as in the

Moon and Death, in the final act of *Blood Wedding*. And many other characters in the former have their counterparts in the latter. For example, the rather weak Young Man is echoed in the Bridegroom, the reluctant Girlfriend in the Bride, the Girlfriend's father in the father of the Bride and, most strikingly, the ardent and passionate Football Player in Leonardo, the Bride's lover. Nevertheless, *Blood Wedding* differs significantly from *When Five Years Pass* in the sense that it is less autobiographical, has a clear story-line, and its setting, far from being abstract, is rural Spain. The influence of the avant-garde and of the kind of Surrealism to be found in *The Public* and *When Five Years Pass* is still evident in certain scenes, most obviously in the appearance of the Moon and Death in Act Three, Scene One, but there is also a clear movement away from the two earlier plays. *Blood Wedding* is the first of the plays which are now known as the three rural tragedies, the other two being *Yerma* and *The House of Bernarda Alba*. Undoubtedly, there were several factors which led Lorca in this direction, and one of them was certainly to do with political events in Spain following his return from Cuba.

Less than a year after Lorca had arrived back in Spain in 1930, the country found itself on the verge of democracy, ready to end the dictatorship of Miguel Primo de Rivera. By 1931 both the dictator and King Alfonso XIII, who had approved Primo de Rivera's seizing of power, had gone, and in April of that year, prior to general elections a few months later, a provisional left-wing government was formed and the Second Republic proclaimed. During the course of the next two years, many important reforms were introduced by the Left, all of them intended to transform Spain into a more progressive and enlightened country. Women were given the vote, and divorce became a possibility. The power of the Church and of the highly influential religious orders, such as the Jesuits, was curtailed, not least in relation to their control of education. As a result of the reforms, great advances were made in education: between 1931 and 1933, for example, more than 13,000 new schools were built, thousands of teaching posts were created, and teachers' salaries were doubled. In May 1931, moreover, the Provisional Government set up the organization known as the Misiones Pedagóg-icas (Teaching Missions), the aim of which was to educate those people who lived in the remote, isolated and poor towns and villages of Spain. Public libraries would be created, local teachers would be involved, exhibitions would be arranged, concerts would be organized, and plays would be performed. Lorca took on a significant role in per-forming plays for the Misiones Pedagógicas, and the experience, in turn, fed his own dramatic writing.

The idea of forming a touring theatre company that, in accordance with the plans of the Misiones, would perform plays in rural Spain, seems to have originated amongst the students at the University of Madrid rather than with Lorca himself, but he soon became involved in the project, agreed to become the company's artistic director, and, most importantly, succeeded in obtaining financial backing from the government. A mobile theatre was designed for touring, while plans were made for a permanent building in Madrid, to be known as La Bar-raca. Although the latter was never built, the name came to be applied to the touring company itself. For his right-hand man, Lorca called on the services of Eduardo Ugarte, a highly practical young man and aspir-ing playwright, who would act as stage-manager and general organizer of the company's activities. The members of the company, actors and technicians alike, wore a kind of uniform – blue dungarees for the men, a blue-and-white dress for the women – which symbolized their equal status in a true democracy. To meet the initial cost of purchasing vans, equipment and a portable stage, the government made a substantial contribution of 100,000 pesetas, to be repeated annually thereafter.[1]

The plays which La Barraca would perform to the often uneducated people of rural Spain would be the great plays of the sixteenth and seventeenth centuries, particularly those by Cervantes, Lope de Vega, Tirso de Molina and Calderón. In his presentation of these works, Lorca was concerned that his audiences should be involved, and that the production, in order to achieve that end, should be stripped of all

those unnecessary elements which had, over many years, come to
attend their performance in the commercial theatre, such as elaborate
sets, old-fashioned costumes and a declamatory acting style. The sets
would be extremely simple and practical, capable of being transported
easily and of being erected and dismantled quickly. The set designers
were, in many cases, artist friends of Lorca, and it is interesting to note
that several of them – Santiago Ontañón and José Caballero, for
example – created the sets for Lorca's own plays. (In 1933, the year
after La Barraca undertook its first tour, the sets for *Blood Wedding*
were designed by Santiago Ontañón with Manuel Fontanals.)
Photographs of the costumes used in various productions show them
to be striking but relatively unfussy, and in certain cases contemporary.
Lorca insisted that his actors avoid excessive gesture and the traditional grand style. They were encouraged to speak clearly and
naturally so that the dialogue of these ancient plays should appear
fresh, not stilted. In order that the action moved smoothly and convincingly, Lorca was extremely demanding in relation to timing, be it
in terms of movement, delivery of a line, or an entrance. Having
chosen his actors with great care – at the outset there were thirty
actors and technicians in the company – he then proceeded to
rehearse them thoroughly, paying attention to every detail, as he
informed an interviewer in 1934:

> Long and demanding rehearsal is essential in order to create the
> rhythm that should control the performance of a piece of theatre . . .
> An actor must not be a second late in making his entrance . . . It is as
> if, in the performance of a symphony, the melody or a certain effect is
> not in time . . .[2]

In short, Lorca brought to bear on his productions with La Barraca
his deeply held belief that theatre should combine on stage all the
different aspects of performance: speech, movement, music and design.
This key aspect of his productions for the company, as well as of his

own writing for the theatre, reveals once more the extent to which Lorca was in touch with developments in European theatre. In 1905, the English stage-designer and director Edward Gordon Craig had set out his ideas on stage-production in *The Art of the Theatre*, a book which would prove influential throughout Europe. The following is typical of his approach:

> ... the Art of the Theatre is neither acting nor the play, it is not scene nor dance, but it consists of all the elements of which these things are composed: action, which is the very spirit of acting: words, which are the body of the play; line and colour, which are the very heart of the scene; rhythm, which is the very essence of dance.[3]

This was an approach to performance that was advocated and practised by dramatists and stage-designers as significant as Maurice Maeterlinck, Adolphe Appia and Max Reinhardt, and it was certainly well known in Spain. Cipriano Rivas Cherif, a theatre director and friend of Lorca, had studied the work of Edward Gordon Craig in Italy, and undoubtedly discussed these matters with the dramatist. From his very first play Lorca's commitment to total theatre is quite clear, and this was something that he also brought to his direction of plays with La Barraca.

The first tour began in July 1932. The company visited, in the course of one month, the towns of El Burgo de Osma, San Leonardo, Vinuesa, Soria, Agreda and Almazán, and the repertoire consisted of *The Cave in Salamanca*, *The Two Talkers* and *The Watchful Guard*, all by Cervantes, and Calderón's religious play, *Life Is a Dream*. The three short plays by Cervantes are distinguished by their down-to-earth, colourful language and their boldly drawn characters, and were clearly chosen for their appeal to relatively unsophisticated audiences. The sets were simple, consisting of a number of flats, some of them decorated, at the back of the portable stage. The costumes, although unfussy, were stylized and colourful. *Life Is a Dream*, which can be compared to an

English morality play, gave Lorca an even greater opportunity to put into practice his belief in total theatre. Music, both vocal and instrumental, played an important part. At appropriate moments a chorus sang in the background, an effect which Lorca described as being 'in the style of the chorus in the Greek tragedy' and which he would subsequently use in *Blood Wedding* itself.[4] The musical instruments used by La Barraca were the guitar, the *vihuela* (a larger, more ancient cousin of the modern guitar) and the lute. Lorca himself played the character called Shadow, who is, in effect, death and who, in a way, anticipates Death in *Blood Wedding*. Indeed, whenever Shadow appeared, he was illuminated by a spotlight which suggested the light of the moon and which certainly looked forward to a similar effect in Act Three, Scene One of Lorca's own play, which, as we know, was being written at this time.

While he was writing *Blood Wedding*, Lorca was also, in late 1932, preparing to direct Lope de Vega's famous play, *Fuenteovejuna*, which La Barraca would first present in May 1933. The overlapping of the two plays is significant, for, despite many differences, *Fuenteovejuna* is set in a rural community and contains many colourful and vibrant characters, men and women alike. Above all, Lorca decided to update the play, so that the story of a village under the thumb of a tyrannical feudal overlord became that of a twentieth-century landowner ruthlessly oppressing those who worked on his land. This was an issue that was of particular relevance to the Andalusia of Lorca's time, one which preoccupied the left-wing government of 1931–3, and one which frequently finds an echo in Lorca's work. The audiences that attended the performances of *Fuenteovejuna* would have observed its male characters dressed in a corduroy-like fabric, the village women in typical dresses, and the overlord/landowner in a black business suit, so that the play's contemporary relevance would have been immediate. Lorca's determination to create theatre that was relevant because it was fresh and alive meant, also, that the production of *Fuenteovejuna* included songs, sung by a chorus and based on traditional Spanish melodies, as well as village dances in two of its scenes. Both song and dance are important elements in *Blood Wedding*, especially in the preparations for and the celebrations after the wedding in Act Two, and in this context it is also worth bearing in mind Lope de Vega's play *Peribáñez*, which begins with a village wedding. There can be no doubt that, in the early 1930s, Lorca's activities with La Barraca had a considerable effect on the subject matter and the style of his own writing. *Blood Wedding* seems, in many ways, a continuation of the great tradition of seventeenth-century Spanish drama.

Many of the songs in *Blood Wedding* are also rooted in Lorca's personal experience. As a child in the villages of Fuente Vaqueros and Asquerosa, Lorca had absorbed much in the way of traditional tales, poems, ballads, songs and lullabies from the family servants, not least from Dolores Cuesta, who had been his wet-nurse. Later on, his long-standing interest in folk music and songs was consolidated as the result of his friendship with the great Spanish composer, Manuel de Falla, and, in 1928, at the Residencia, he gave an illuminating lecture on the subject of Spanish lullabies. He noted that 'Spain uses its melodies to colour the moment when its children first fall asleep', and in this respect differs from many other European countries whose lullaby tradition is less dark.[5] Spanish lullabies, according to Lorca, are often

> invented . . . by wretched women whose children are a burden, a cross
> that is frequently too heavy to bear. Each child, instead of being a joy,
> is a sorrow, and, naturally, even though they love him, they cannot
> help singing to him of their own joyless existence.

The setting of such songs is often a 'nocturnal landscape, and [the mother] introduces . . . one or two characters involved in a simple story which almost always has the most melancholy and beautiful effect possible'. The lullaby which begins and ends Act One, Scene Two, falls precisely into this category.

Other traditional songs also greatly influenced him, especially those associated with love, weddings, celebrations and the like, songs which he had heard many times during the years spent in Granada and the surrounding countryside. Particularly important in *Blood Wedding* is the *alboreá*, which, as the word suggests, was a song sung at sunrise (*alba* means dawn), often to newly-weds, and which announced to them the dawn or beginning of their new life together. The following is a good example of the type (the handkerchief was inserted into a bride-to-be to test her virginity):

> On a green meadow
> I laid out my handkerchief.
> Three roses appeared
> Like three morning stars.
> Oh, good father,
> They have crowned your daughter.
> Oh, bridegroom, look at her!
> How pretty she is to the tips of her toes.

It is significant, too, that the *alboreá* was, traditionally, a flamenco song sung at a gypsy wedding, for *Blood Wedding* is suffused with the influence of flamenco.

Lorca's musical gifts, notably as a pianist, proved to be exceptional from an early age. Under the guidance of his music teacher, Antonio Segura Mesa, his talent had developed enormously during his teenage years, and he had also learned a good deal about Spanish folk music. Later he would often dazzle his friends with an impromptu rendition of folk songs on the piano, and, in 1931, he recorded a series of folk songs for HMV with 'La Argentinita', Encarnación López Júlvez. But the most significant moment in Lorca's musical education was undoubtedly the arrival in Granada in 1920 of the composer Manuel de Falla. Lorca had met Falla the year before, but when the he settled in Granada their friendship soon developed, not least because both of them were interested in Spanish folk music. By this time many of Falla's best-known works had acquired an international reputation, particularly his opera *La vida breve*, the ballet *El amor brujo* (*Love the Magician*) and the orchestral work *Noches en los jardines de España* (*Nights in the Gardens of Spain*). All are deeply influenced by Granada, by its gypsy background and by the rhythms of flamenco. *El amor brujo*, in which part of the action is set in a cave, was clearly based on the gypsy cave-dwellings of the Sacromonte, the hilly district near the Alhambra. This is also one source of the cave setting for Act One, Scene Three, of *Blood Wedding*.

The Sacromonte was an area that Lorca knew well. In 1920 he visited both the Sacromonte and its neighbouring district, the Albaicín, when he accompanied the philologist, Ramón Menéndez Pidal, in the course of his investigations into popular Spanish ballads. Furthermore – no doubt through the influence of Falla – the summer of 1921 saw Lorca learning flamenco guitar from two gypsies from Fuente Vaqueros, and claiming to be able to accompany various kinds of flamenco song. And there is also evidence to suggest that, after Falla's arrival in Granada, he and Lorca made several visits to the caves of the Sacromonte in connection with flamenco music and became friends with a number of flamenco singers and guitarists. This was in part in anticipation of the 'Festival of Deep Song', a celebration of flamenco song as well as a competition, which took place in the Alhambra's Plaza de los Aljibes over a period of two days in June 1922.

In conjunction with the festival, in the organization of which he played an important part, Lorca wrote a series of poems inspired by flamenco – particularly by *cante jondo*, or 'deep song', one of the styles of Spanish gypsy music – and also prepared a lecture entitled '*Cante jondo*: Primitive Andalusian Song', which he delivered at the Granada Arts Club. Amongst other things, he drew attention to the emotional nature of these songs, brought to Spain in the fifteenth century by gypsy tribes who had, over several centuries, headed westwards from India, and he emphasized, too, the tragic tone of the oldest forms, of which the most emotional is the *siguiriya*: 'The finest degrees of Sorrow and Pain, which serve the most pure, the most exact expression, beat in the tercets and quatrains of the *siguiriya* and its derivative forms.'[6] The latter, in particular, he noted, is 'like a cautery which burns the heart, the throat, the lips of those who voice it'. The following example, quoted by Lorca in the lecture, encapsulates perfectly the subject matter and the dark tone of the *siguiriya*:

> When I come to die,
> I ask of you one favour,
> That with the braids of your black hair
> They tie my hands.

In the poems that Lorca wrote at this time, and which were published nearly ten years later with the title *Poem of Deep Song*, he attempted to evoke the landscapes and the mood of the *cante jondo* tradition, and he focused on its typical preoccupations of love, unhappiness, death and loneliness. The following example, called 'Sorpresa' ('Surprise'), antici-pates the deaths of the Bridegroom and Leonardo in *Blood Wedding*:

> He lay dead in the street
> With a knife in the heart.
> No one knew him.
> How the street-lamp trembled!
> Mother.
> How the little street-lamp
> Trembled!
> It was early morning. No one
> Could look at his eyes
> Open to the harsh air.
> For he lay dead in the street
> With a knife in the heart
> And no one knew him.[7]

One can well imagine this poem powerfully sung by a good flamenco singer.

Six years later, in 1928, the collection of poems *Gypsy Ballads*, on which he had been working for a number of years, was published. Although these poems, unlike those of *Poem of Deep Song*, are not specifically inspired by flamenco song and its tradition, both collections are linked by the figure of the gypsy and by what, for Lorca, the gypsy symbolized. In a lecture given some years after the publication of *Gypsy Ballads*, Lorca noted:

> Although it is called Gypsy, the book in general is the poem of Andalusia. I called it Gypsy because the Gypsy is the noblest, deepest and most aristocratic element in my country, the most profound representative of its way of life, the keeper of the glowing embers, the blood, the alphabet of Andalusian and universal truth.[8]

For Lorca, the gypsy represented Andalusia through the ages in all its dark and tragic suffering, and the individuals who appear in the poems of *Gypsy Ballads* therefore have a universal resonance: Soledad Montoya, the lonely and frustrated woman burdened by her sexual anguish; the young woman, who, despairing at her lover's non-arrival, drowns herself; Antoñito el Camborio, who, envied and resented by his cousins, dies at their hands; the man, who, told that he will die on a specific day, resigns himself to his fate. But if these are some of the individual characters of the poems, they have in fact one main character, to whom Lorca had also referred in his lecture: 'Anguish, dark and big as the summer sky . . . Andalusian anguish, which is the struggle between the loving intelligence and the impenetrable mystery which surrounds it'. Lorca, of course, identified himself with that anguish. The gypsy appealed to him because he had been, and continued to be in Lorca's Spain, a marginalized, outsider figure, as much an outcast as the homosexual. Thus the oppressed and suffering characters of *Gypsy Ballads* are also Lorca himself, voicing his own anguish, and it is easy to see how he became so attracted to both the flamenco tradition and the history of the gypsies in Andalusia. In many ways *Blood Wedding* is a continuation of *Poem of Deep Song* and *Gypsy Ballads*, for, although its characters may not be gypsies, it possesses all the anguish and the tragic spirit of both collections of poetry.

Blood Wedding also owes something to Lorca's knowledge of classical tragedy. In the spring of 1933, the Ministry of Public Education organized an ambitious artistic festival that would take place in June that year in the town of Mérida. As part of the festival, Seneca's *Medea* was to be performed in the Roman amphitheatre by the company of Margarita Xirgu and Enrique Borrás, directed by Cipriano Rivas Cherif.[9] A spectacular production, it opened there on 18 June, accompanied by choirs and a symphony orchestra, and watched by an audience of 3,000. At the beginning of September it was presented in one of the great squares of the Royal Palace in Madrid before moving on to Salamanca and then to the Greek theatre in the Montjuic park in Barcelona. And on 28 October, a scaled-down version, in which the emphasis was on the acting rather than the spectacle, began the 1933–4 season at the Teatro Español in Madrid. While this production came some months after the première of *Blood Wedding* (8 March 1933), it is important to bear in mind that Lorca was a good friend both of Margarita Xirgu and Cipriano Rivas Cherif. Xirgu, indeed, had starred in Lorca's *The Shoemaker's Wonderful Wife* in 1930 and would do so in *Yerma* in 1934 and in *Blood Wedding* and *Doña Rosita the Spinster* in 1935. As for Rivas Cherif, he was literary adviser to Xirgu's company, as well as someone with whom Lorca frequently discussed theatre matters. It is inconceivable that, while Lorca was writing *Blood Wedding*, he would not have discussed with them particular aspects of *Medea*, including the role of the chorus, of which he would make extensive use in both *Blood Wedding* and *Yerma*. It is worth noting, too, that, in 1931, Margarita Xirgu had presented *Elektra*, a version of the Greek tragedy by the Austrian dramatist Hugo von Hofmannsthal, in an ambitious open-air production in the Retiro Park in Madrid. Later, in the summer of 1934, she would perform both *Medea* and *Elektra* in Mérida's Roman amphitheatre. It is no coincidence, then, that *Blood Wedding* was being written at the same time as the spirit of classical tragedy was very much in the air. Furthermore, like *cante jondo*, this was something that connected the ancient and the modern world, a connection which was very close to Lorca's heart and which transformed particular experience into something much more universal, a process that is the hallmark of his writing.

Given this last point, the direct source for *Blood Wedding* could not have been more local and precise: a newspaper report which Lorca had read in 1928. The Madrid newspaper *ABC* had briefly reported a murder which had occurred near the town of Nijar in the south-eastern province of Almería, and over the next six days the story was told in much greater detail in the *Heraldo de Madrid*, which Lorca often read. It concerned a young woman, Francisca Cañadas Morales, who was engaged to be married to Casimiro Pérez Pino, but who, the night before the wedding, had run away with a former lover, Curro Montes Cañadas. As they escaped, however, they encountered the bridegroom's brother, José Pérez Pino, who was on his way to the wedding, and who, realizing what was happening, shot Curro Montes dead. This dramatic and violent story evidently caught Lorca's imagination both in its broad outline and in terms of many of the details which appeared in the newspaper accounts, although he did, of course, make important changes.[10]

Although there is no indication of the precise setting of *Blood Wedding*, most of its action takes place in a landscape strongly suggestive of Almería. In Act One, Scene Three, the Bridegroom and the Mother visit the home of the Bride and the Father in what the Bridegroom describes as 'the dry lands' (p. 46). This is an isolated place where hardly anyone passes by, where the soil is poor and full of stones, as the Father observes in Act Two, Scene Two: 'You have to wage a constant battle with the weeds, with the thistles, with the stones that come up from who knows where' (p. 65). The dry, dusty, often desert-like terrain is largely due, of course, to the intense heat, inescapable in the summer in Almería, as the Bride and the Servant note in Act Two, Scene One:

> SERVANT: I'll finish combing your hair out here.
> BRIDE: No-one can stay inside there in this heat.
> SERVANT: In these lands it doesn't get cool even at dawn. (p. 52)

The newspaper account in the *Heraldo de Madrid* had referred to 'fields full of stones' and to the barren nature of the landscape 'with barely a tree'. It was a landscape with which Lorca was familiar, for at ten years of age he had spent some months at a boarding school in the town of Almería itself, and been taken on trips into the surrounding area by Antonio Rodríguez Espinosa, the headmaster and a friend of the Lorca family. But, in *Blood Wedding*, Lorca mentioned neither Almería nor Nijar by name. The setting for the events involving the Bride, the Bridegroom and Leonardo is described simply as 'the dry lands'. In other words, the location of the real-life event is made less specific, or, to put it another way, is made more general and so universalized. The hot and inhospitable land is an appropriate place for the unsatisfied longing of the Bride and Leonardo for each other – as much a metaphor as a location, and in that sense typical of Lorca's practice of universalizing the particular.

This kind of transformation may be seen, too, in relation to many other details of the real-life story. The bride-to-be, Francisa Cañadas, lived with her father on a farm near Nijar called 'El Fraile'. In Lorca's play the farm – or rather, the farmhouse – becomes a cave. As we have seen, Lorca was familiar with the gypsy caves of the Sacromonte, and the gypsy was for him a symbolic figure who encapsulated the age-old anguish and suffering of Andalusia. In transforming a farmhouse into a cave, he replaced a man-made building with a natural setting, which, for him, had much more powerful associations and a timeless resonance. As for Francisca Cañadas, she was an extremely plain young woman, lame, with a squint and prominent teeth, desired by the local young men less for her physical charms than for the dowry which her father would give her on her marriage. In Lorca's Bride these physical defects are stripped away, for she is clearly an attractive young woman. When she first appears, the Bridegroom's mother refers to her 'lovely expression' (p. 49), although hers is not a porcelain beauty. In Act Two, Scene Two, her father describes her as 'wide-hipped' (p. 66); in Act One, Scene Three, as hard-working; and at the end of this scene the Servant refers to her as 'stronger than a man' (p. 50). Used to hard work and responsible for running the house in difficult circumstances since her mother's death, she is very much a peasant girl, but, unlike Francisca Cañadas, good looking enough to prove an irresistible attraction to Leonardo.

Leonardo owes rather more to his real-life source. Curro Montes Cañadas was, according to the newspaper reports, rather handsome and something of a womanizer, with a 'girl on every farm'. A cousin of Francisca, he had had a relationship with her previously, when she was much younger and before her engagement to Casimiro Pérez. He was also something of a horseman. In creating Leonardo, Lorca absorbed these details and added others. Leonardo is clearly handsome, for in their dialogue in Act Three, Scene One, the Bride says: 'Oh, I look at you / And your beauty burns me' (p. 83), and, in her final lament, the Wife describes him as 'a handsome horseman' (p. 91). There can be little doubt that Lorca wished to present Leonardo as a kind of Heathcliff figure, physically attractive, virile, dynamic and passionate. His name is carefully chosen, for it is an amalgam of *león* (lion) and *ardo* (from the verb *arder*, which means 'to burn'), and suggests good looks, strength and blazing passion. If Curro Montes had some of these qualities, Leonardo has them in a much more heightened form. In Act One, Scene Two, the Wife observes: 'Yesterday the neighbours told me they'd seen you the other side of the plains' (p. 42). When he and the Wife arrive ahead of the other wedding guests in Act Two, Scene Two, the Servant claims that 'They drove like demons' (p. 64). And later in the scene the Wife describes him as a man who 'likes to fly around too much' (p. 67). In short, he is much larger than life, to be identified with the strength, the speed and the instinct of the horse on which he sweeps across 'the dry lands'. If Lorca transformed Almería into a much more universal setting, he did much the same with the real-life lovers, creating out of them and their earth-bound relationship a passion which, in Leonardo and the Bride, transcends both time and place.

They are a man and a woman destined for each other, their mutual attraction irresistible and ineradicable, as insistent as the forces at work in nature itself. Indeed, Lorca constantly portrays their passion in terms of the natural world. Such is the implication of Leonardo's anguished words as he and the Bride attempt to hide in the wood in Act Three, Scene One: 'Oh, I'm not the one at fault. / The fault belongs to the earth . . .' (p. 82). In the same speech he speaks of his attempts to forget her and of the impossibility of setting aside an instinct which is as natural and uncontrollable as that of his horse:

> And I put a wall of stone
> Between your house and mine
> . . .
> But I'd get on the horse
> And the horse would go to your door . . . (p. 82)

And when, in Act Two, Scene One, he accuses the Bride of betraying their love, he uses an image that suggests both its strength and permanence: 'When the roots of things go deep, no one can pull them up!' (p. 57). As for the girl, her feelings for him are as strong as his for her. In the forest scene referred to above, she reveals her helplessness:

> And there's not a minute of the day
> That I don't want to be with you,
> Because you drag me and I come,
> And you tell me to go back

And I follow you through the air
Like a blade of grass . . . (p. 82)

And in the earlier scene, when she dismisses his accusations of betrayal, she describes his effect on her as one of intoxication:

It's as if I'd drunk a bottle of anise and fallen asleep on a bedspread of roses. And it drags me along, and I know that I'm drowning, but I still go on . . . (p. 57)

Again, in attempting to account for her actions to the Bridegroom's mother in the play's concluding scene, she speaks of Leonardo's irresistible pull:

. . . but the other one's arm [Leonardo's] dragged me like a wave from the sea, like the butt of a mule, and would always have dragged me, always, always . . . (p. 90)

We may, of course, be tempted to see in all these explanations an element of self-justification for actions which both the Bride and Leonardo know to be wrong, but this is set in its proper context by the Woodcutters, objective commentators on events, in Act Three, Scene One:

FIRST WOODCUTTER: In the end the blood was strongest.
. . .
SECOND WOODCUTTER: Her body for him, his body for her . . .
(pp. 74–5)

In the light of their words, the title of Lorca's play, *Bodas de sangre*, which is usually translated into English as *Blood Wedding*, suggesting the bloody outcome, can also be rendered as 'Marriage of Blood', which refers to the instinctive bond between the Bride and Leonardo, as opposed to the arranged marriage of the Bride and the Bridegroom. They are, indeed, lovers on an elemental scale, far removed from their real-life source.

In the newspaper account, Casimiro Pérez, Francisca's husband-to-be, was described as a rather dull and unexciting labourer to whom Francisca was not genuinely attracted. Lorca's Bridegroom is similarly unattractive to the Bride, although the reason seems to be not so much that he is physically unappealing as that he is rather naïve, inexperienced with women and, above all, tied to his mother's apron strings. Praising the boy to the Bride's father in Act One, Scene Three, the Mother observes that 'He's never known a woman' (p. 48). Because of the deaths of her husband and her other son, she has become extremely protective, even wishing that her son were a girl who could stay at home and not be exposed to the dangers men face in the world at large. Although at times he is impatient with her because of this, he does on the whole submit to her authority, rather like an obedient daughter. When, for example, she tells him in Act Two, Scene Two, that in his father's absence she has taken on the paternal role, his reply is revealing: 'I'll always do what you want me to' (p. 72). He is, in short, something of a mummy's boy, his emotional growth rather stunted. Despite the fact that in Act Two, Scene Two, the Servant suggests that, like his grandfather, the Bridegroom has 'the same twinkle' in his eyes (p. 68), we cannot imagine him, as his grandfather did, leaving 'a son on every street corner' (p. 35). At the wedding reception he seems relatively lively, but, even so, his remarks are somewhat gauche, and his embracing of the Bride from behind rather clumsy. The nub of the matter is clearly expressed by the Bride when, in Act Three, Scene Two, following the deaths of Leonardo and the Bridegroom, she explains to the Mother the effect of both men upon her: '. . . your son was a tiny drop of water . . . but the other one was a dark river . . .' (p. 90). Drawing on the source material's suggestion of the basic differences between Curro Montes and Casimiro Pérez, Lorca heightened the contrast, and, in the case of the Bridegroom, linked his character to the influence of the Mother.

In Casimiro's story there was no mother figure, for all the encouragement to marry Francisca was provided by his brother and his sister-in-law. In *Blood Wedding*, on the other hand, the Mother becomes a dominant presence, as much in the play's opening scene as in its final one. What, then, was the reason for this fundamental change in the details? It would be easy to suggest that the introduction of the Mother allowed Lorca to give prominence to the family feud which has long existed between her family and that of Leonardo, but he could equally have done so had the Bridegroom's surviving parent been his father. There may be more than one explanation. In the Spain of Lorca's time, particularly in the harsh environment of rural Spain, there were many widows – women deprived of their husbands and struggling to bring up their children. Lorca knew them well and felt for them. Again, even though women were regarded as inferior both by that society and by the Catholic Church, they were the heartbeat of family life, raising their children, controlling the finances, setting an example. As for Lorca himself, women – the family's servants and, as we shall see later, his own mother – were influential in his early life. From the beginning of his career as a writer, they have a prominent role in his poems and his plays, suggesting an understanding of them. And then, of course, there is the simple fact that in the classical tragedies which probably influenced *Blood Wedding* the protagonists were powerful women, as was also the case in J.M. Synge's *Riders to the Sea* – another probable influence – in which a mother grieves for the death of her loved ones.[11] All these things may have played a part in making Lorca give the Mother such a prominent role. But most important of all, perhaps, was the nature of the bond between the mother and the child she has brought into the world, raised, worried over and feared for. A father–son relationship does not have quite the same emotional closeness, and Lorca, as a dramatist, was well aware that, in a situation where the Mother has seen her husband and a son murdered and fears for her one remaining son, there were tremendous theatrical possibilities. At all events, she proves to be an enormously powerful presence, obsessed with the deaths which have already deeply affected her, constantly apprehensive about the future, driven to seek revenge when her son is betrayed by his wife, and plunged into inconsolable grief when he, too, is killed. She is, indeed, a figure worthy of a place in any classical tragedy.

Lorca also made a number of crucial changes in relation to the events described in the newspaper accounts. First of all, Francisca and Curro Montes ran off together before the wedding, not after it, as do Lorca's characters. It is a fundamental change that transforms an already dramatic situation into a much more dramatic one, not least because the Bride is now also guilty of adultery, with all the implications that this has in a highly traditional and Catholic society. As a result of this shift of emphasis, the Bridegroom and members of his family set out in pursuit of the runaway couple, driven on by the Mother. It is an altogether tighter and more intense situation than that of the source material, in which the fleeing couple encounter Casimiro's brother on the road by pure chance. And, by having the wedding take place, Lorca was also able to introduce the reception in Act Two, Scene Two, which allowed for music and dance and the remorseless building of dramatic tension in the midst of the celebration, right up to the point when the couple make their escape.

Introducing the long-standing feud between the two families represents another significant addition. No sooner is the knife mentioned in Act One, Scene One, than the Mother's obsession with the Félix family, 'the family of murderers' (p. 35), comes to the fore. Although the precise reasons for the feud are not given, it seems to have existed for many years, for in Act Two, Scene Two, the Mother refers to Leonardo's bad blood, which 'comes from his great-grandfather, who started the killing, and it spreads through the whole breed, all of them knife-handlers and smiling hypocrites' (p. 64). In rural communities of the kind in which *Blood Wedding* is set, family feuds and violent crimes were often the result of disputes over land and ownership. Lorca's lack of precision on this point is clearly deliberate. He prefers to avoid the local detail, allowing instead the unexplained family enmity to hang over the play's events like a dark cloud. It is, perhaps, an echo of the dynastic rivalries to be found in many classical tragedies, and it should not be forgotten that, as we have seen in the discussion of *The Public*, Shakespeare's *Romeo and Juliet*, with its feuding families, was a play that Lorca knew well. At all events, the introduction of the family feud could not have been better calculated as a device to heighten the dramatic temperature of the play.

Act Three of *Blood Wedding* bears no relation to the newspaper story, however. In the first of its two scenes, the setting of the forest with its great moist tree trunks is a reworking of a similar scenario in the final act of *When Five Years Pass*, while the characters of Moon and Death (in the form of an old beggar woman), who conspire to bring about the death of Leonardo and the Bridegroom, are reminiscent of Harlequin and the Clown, who, in the earlier play, mock the Young Man. To some extent, too, the three Card Players who pay a final fatal visit to the Young Man in the last scene of *When Five Years Pass* have their counterpart in the three woodcutters of *Blood Wedding*.

In both plays the emphasis is on predetermination and the inability of human beings to change the course of destiny – although in *Blood Wedding* the influence of classical tragedy and gypsy/flamenco culture is much more in evidence. Apart from bringing to mind the Three Fates of classical mythology, the woodcutters intone their lines in a manner strongly suggestive of the chorus in Greek and Roman tragedies. On the other hand, the image of the woodcutter and the tree is frequently to be found in Lorca's poetry, and so indeed is the association of the moon and death. Consider the following poem, 'The Rider's Song':

Córdoba.
Far away and alone.
Black mare, great moon,
And olives in my saddle-bag.
Although I know the roads
I shall never get to Córdoba.
On the plain, in the wind,
Black mare, red moon.
Death is watching me
From the towers of Córdoba.
Oh, how long the road!
Oh, my brave mare!
Oh, death awaits me
Before I get to Córdoba!
Córdoba.
Far away and alone.[12]

And in another poem, 'The Moon and Death', there is a clear anticipation of the conspiracy of the characters Moon and Death in *Blood Wedding*, for in both Death is an old woman:

The river-beds are dry,
The fields no longer green,
And in the withered trees
No nests or leaves.
Doña Death, wrinkled,
Passes amongst the willow-trees,
. . .
The moon has bought
Paintings from Death . . .[13]

In Spanish folklore, and especially in the gypsy culture of Andalusia, fate and destiny are frequently linked to the moon, which, after all, has in its movements and cycles a marked inevitability, and in its colour and appearance a deathly coldness. It is no surprise, then, that these things should acquire such importance in Lorca's work. For example, in one of the most powerful and evocative poems in *Gypsy Ballads*, 'Somnambular Ballad', a young woman drowns herself in the water-tank on the roof of her house:

> On the surface of the water-tank
> The gypsy-girl swayed.
> Green flesh, green hair,
> Her eyes of cold silver.
> An icicle of moonlight
> Holds her on the water.[14]

The moon, reflected in the water, takes on the appearance of an icicle or a knife which seems to connect with the floating body. The visual link between the moon – especially a half or quarter moon – and the ever-present knife of *Blood Wedding* is very clear indeed.

While the play reflects the combined influence of classical tragedy and Andalusian folklore, it also reveals to some extent the imprint of Surrealism. The events of Act Three, Scene One, are, after all, decidedly dreamlike, even nightmarish. Looked at in a certain way, they could be said to be the embodiment of the anxieties and guilt of the Bride and Leonardo: the projection of their unconscious as they lie asleep in each other's arms. Their hiding-place, the forest with great moist tree-trunks, and the events that occur in it could indeed be their nightmare. If *When Five Years Pass* is a play in which, it is possible to argue, the whole of the action takes place in the mind of its main character, the Young Man, so the great wood of *Blood Wedding*, with its eerie atmosphere and its frightening non-human characters, can be seen as the embodiment of the lovers' deepest fears.

In *The Public* and, to a lesser extent, in *When Five Years Pass* Lorca gave dramatic expression to the anguish which was in no small part the consequence of his homosexuality. He would never do so again in such an explicit way, even though he had a number of homosexual relationships after his return to Spain from Cuba. In Madrid he had many gay friends who were writers and painters. In the spring of 1933, the twenty-one-year-old Rafael Rodríguez Rapún, an athletic and passionate man, became secretary to La Barraca, and, although apparently not by nature homosexual, he became Lorca's lover between 1934 and 1936. During a six-month visit to Argentina between October 1933 and March 1934, it seems likely that Lorca had several brief affairs, and there is certainly evidence that he was rejected by a young amateur actor, Maximino Espasande, whom he ardently pursued. Nevertheless, the conflict within him that had previously raged so fiercely – and which obviously continued to exist to some extent – was now expressed in a different way, channelled into characters who were part of a story, which, like the characters themselves, seemed less autobiographical.

Blood Wedding is the first example of this process. Many critics argue, of course, that a work of art has little to do with its creator's life, but the fact cannot be ignored that, as has already been suggested, the work of many dramatists owes its particular emotional charge and its characteristic ideas to their problematic and often intense inner lives. For example, O'Neill's *Long Day's Journey into Night* is essentially a dramatization of his own family history, while many of Tennessee Williams's unstable female characters reflect his sister's mental problems. In channelling personal preoccupations into the more objective story of *Blood Wedding*, Lorca may well have been responding to two things. Firstly, after the anguish of the New York period, he felt more in control of his sexuality and thus more able to objectify his personal feelings. And secondly, he wanted to write not a play 'for the theatre years from now', as he had declared *The Public* to be, but something which would be a success in the Madrid of his time.

It was more than the dramatic possibilites of the events near Nijar that drew Lorca to the story, however: they reflected his own dilemma.

In *When Five Years Pass* he had already created in the Young Man a character who, at least in the first half of the play, is sexually unresponsive to women and who is finally rejected by the Girlfriend. Casimiro Pérez Pino in the Nijar story is a similar individual, a young man incapable of awakening genuine passion in his fiancée and who, it seems, had not even kissed her prior to the wedding-day. This type of man fascinated Lorca precisely because he mirrored his own heterosexual impotence, and so it is that the Bridegroom in *Blood Wedding* is in many ways yet another self-portrait. On the other hand, Leonardo is the man Lorca may well have wanted to be, the male who is attracted to women and whom they cannot resist. He had already appeared in *When Five Years Pass* in the form of the Football Player, who, in Act Two, is described by the Girlfriend as having in his breast 'a great flowing torrent' (p. 146). Leonardo is an extended form of him, the most dynamically sexual male in the whole of Lorca's theatre. But even if he is unlike Lorca in his passionate pursuit of women, he at the same time embodies Lorca's growing belief that one should be true to one's nature, whatever one's sexuality. In *The Public* First Man posed the key question: 'Can a man cease to be himself?' In *Blood Wedding*, as well as in the later plays, the message is even more insistent. Although the relationship of the Bride and Leonardo is heterosexual, the question of following one's instinct would equally have applied had the relationship been homosexual. Leonardo may be Lorca's fantasy, but he is also the embodiment of an important truth which the dramatist had come to embrace.

If *Blood Wedding* has a clear autobiographical resonance, how does the character of the Mother fit into the picture? In the play's opening scene the Bridegroom lifts her in his arms with the words 'You old woman, you old, old woman, you old, old, old woman' (p. 35). This, it appears, was something which Lorca did with his own mother, whose effect on his life was clearly profound. Vicenta Lorca Romero, prior to her marriage, had been a teacher at the primary school in Fuente Vaqueros. She clearly exercised a considerable influence over her eldest son's childhood years, not least because flat feet and a slight limp restricted his ability to take part in physically demanding games. This meant that, while his father attended to the demands of his estate, she encouraged Lorca's already evident artistic talents, in particular his musical abilities. In later life he would say that his mother, more than anyone, had shaped his artistic inclinations. To what extent his closeness to her inhibited his subsequent interest in and attraction to other women is a matter of conjecture, although some of his statements in adult life are extremely suggestive. In 1934, during his visit to Argentina, he was asked if he planned to get married and replied that his brother and sisters were free to do so, but as for himself, '. . . I belong to my mother'.[15] In the following year he spoke of his homosexuality to Cipriano Rivas Cherif, and suggested that his closeness to his mother had made it impossible for him to engage in a heterosexual relationship.

Quite apart from all this, Vicenta Lorca was a woman for whom traditional values were extremely important. She was a practising Catholic whose religious beliefs made their mark on Lorca himself. As a schoolteacher she attached great importance to discipline and hard work, an area in which Lorca, with his lack of application and poor examination results, often disappointed her. And, as the wife of a well-known and prosperous landowner and the mother of two sons and two daughters, she was concerned with the well-being of the family as well as its good name and reputation in the community. Is it surprising, then, that this concern should be reflected by the Mother in *Blood Wedding*? In Act One, Scene One, she expresses the hope that her son's intended bride is good and respectable: 'I know that the girl's good. She is, isn't she? Well-behaved. Hard-working. She makes her bread and sews her skirts' (p. 35). In Act One, Scene Three, she indicates to the Bride's father that the Bridegroom's reputation is unblemished: 'His name's cleaner than a sheet spread in the sun' (p. 48). As for the Bride, she is fully aware that, in running away with Leonardo, she has dishonoured her husband, and the Mother, in urging the Bridegroom to hunt them down, is as much concerned with restoring the family honour as with taking revenge. The point is clearly made when in the play's final scene she confronts the Bride:

> You see her? There, weeping, and me calm, without tearing her eyes out. I don't understand myself. Is it because I didn't love my son? But what about his name? Where is his name? (p. 90)

This preoccupation with family honour was, of course, something that had been deeply embedded in the Spanish psyche over the centuries, as true of Lorca's time as it had been in the seventeenth century, when Spain was at the height of its powers. As for Lorca himself, he was clearly aware that his homosexual activities were precisely the kind of thing to damage the family name, quite apart from causing his parents untold grief. It goes without saying, therefore, that, close to his mother as he was, he would have been anxious not to cause her pain while at the same time he could not resist his true sexual inclinations. The emotional conflict which stemmed from this cannot be underestimated, and it is certainly one explanation for the prominence in *Blood Wedding* of the importance of good name and the extent to which it is endangered by obedience to one's instincts. An appreciation of the anguish which Lorca must have experienced in this respect undoubtedly coloured his view both of himself and of the world around him, and it explains, too, the tragic vision which he set out in his plays.

The principal theme of classical tragedy is that the fates of mortals are determined by the gods; Shakespearean tragedy, on the other hand, is about men and women brought down by some fundamental moral flaw, after whose passing a better future is promised. In more recent times tragic drama is, more often than not, the spectacle of human beings cast adrift in a meaningless universe, and posing questions to which there is no answer. Lorca, given the nature of his life, must often have asked himself such questions. Why, for instance, was he different from most men, not least from his markedly heterosexual brother Francisco? Why, given his difference, must he seek sexual satisfaction in ways which caused him anguish and were also socially unacceptable? And why had the dice been cast in such a manner? Thinking on these things, Lorca must have felt that fate had intervened and that his life was predetermined. Furthermore, the gypsy culture which so interested him believed firmly in the decisive influence of fate on people's lives. The following lines from a *siguiriya* illustrate the point perfectly:

> I looked over the wall,
> The wind answered me:
> 'Why sigh so much
> If there is no solution?'

The unanswerable questions that Lorca must have asked himself echo throughout the serious forms of *cante jondo*, as he himself observed: 'At the heart of all the poems the question is to be found, the terrible question for which there is no answer . . .'[16] It is a question which he often posed in *Poem of Deep Song* and *Gypsy Ballads*, in which the marginalized and persecuted gypsy is simultaneously cast as a suffering individual – a form of Lorca himself – and a symbol of the age-old anguish of Andalusia. In short, Lorca was acutely conscious, through personal experience and cultural background, that the individual finds himself in an uncomprehending universe and at the mercy of a hostile fate in the face of which his deepest aspirations come to nothing and very often prove to be the source of his own downfall. His vision is, of course, pessimistic, suggesting a world without hope, but in that sense it is typical of the twentieth century and places Lorca firmly alongside such dramatists as O'Neill, Arthur Miller and Samuel Beckett.

Blood Wedding, like so much of Lorca's work, has at its very core the essential duality of aspiration and negation, a conflict which gives the play its dramatic tension and leads to its tragic outcome. In the case of Leonardo and the Bride, aspiration takes the form of their sexual longing for each other. For the Bridegroom, it is his desire to marry and enjoy a conventional married life. For the Mother, it is a wish for the Bridegroom's happiness, a long life and children; for the Father, a desire to see his daughter settled and contented. Each of these characters pursues a particular goal, and each of them does so with passion and intensity. But if these aspirations are strong, they are also, for the most part, mutually exclusive, the goals of the Bride and Leonardo completely at odds with those of the Bridegroom, the Mother and the Father. In consequence, the mutually exclusive nature of the characters' aspirations leads inevitably to their final negation.

In addition, the objectives sought by the characters involve passions and desires which are ineradicable, whose course cannot be changed. The attraction of the Bride and Leonardo to each other is, we are told, long-standing, going back to the time when she was only fifteen, seven years before the action of the play. Furthermore, their separation and Leonardo's subsequent marriage have done nothing to change their feelings. The Bride, in Leonardo's presence, is intoxicated by his good looks, is as helpless as a blade of grass in the wind, while he responds instinctively to the scent that comes from her breasts and her hair. But if their feelings cannot be changed, neither can the Mother's concern for her son, the Bridegroom, rooted as it is in her long-standing grief for the husband and son already lost to her. In Act One, Scene One, the Bridegroom takes her to task for endlessly harping on the same subject, and her reply is illuminating: 'If I lived to be a hundred, I wouldn't speak of anything else' (p. 34). Her concern for her surviving son's future is as understandable as it is desperate, as natural as it is single-minded. But, crucially, her objective, as well as her son's, is totally at odds with that of the Bride and Leonardo. In each case the course is set before the events we see unfold on stage, and that sense of inevitability, of the way things are, is underlined by frequent references to fate, as well as by the appearance of characters who are its physical manifestations: the axe-wielding woodcutters, Death and Moon, the girls who, in Act Three, Scene Two, unwind the ball of red wool, suggestive of the thread of life soon to be cut. The fate of the on-stage characters is, indeed, mirrored in advance in the experience of other members of their respective families. Thus, the Bride will suffer as did her mother before her:

> BRIDE: She wasted away here.
> SERVANT: Her fate. (p. 52)

Leonardo's wife will be abandoned, as was her mother: 'It's the way things are. My mother's fate was the same' (p. 62). And, of course, the Bridegroom will die by the knife as did his father and his brother. The knife, indeed, hangs over the action of *Blood Wedding* like the sword of Damocles, as inescapable as the fate which it embodies.

In *Blood Wedding*, as in his other tragic plays, Lorca portrays the predicaments of his characters in all their stark inevitability, and, in so doing, leaves us with a sense of terrible bleakness. If Shakespeare's tragedies, dark as they are, end on a note of hope, evoking the calm which follows the storm, Lorca's, in contrast, provide no such consolation. All aspirations have come to nothing: the Mother's son is dead, the Bride is a widow and Leonardo is dead, too. In the play's final scene, the female mourners can only lament the destruction of beauty by death:

> He was a handsome horseman,
> Now a frozen heap of snow.
> He rode to fairs and mountains
> And the arms of women.
> Now the dark moss of night
> Forms a crown upon his brow. (p. 91)

For none of them is there any relief or escape: the mother's anguish is merely intensified, the Bride is dishonoured and will never re-marry, the Father's life is blighted by his daughter's conduct, and Leonardo's widow is left disgraced and with two small children to bring up. It is, indeed, a depressing spectacle, in which hope for the future has been snuffed out. In *The Public* Lorca drew upon personal experience in relation to the conflicts and the anguish created by his homosexuality; in *Blood Wedding* he gave expression to a view of the world that had its roots both in earlier forms of drama and in the culture of Andalusia, but to which his own life also bore painful witness.[17]

The effect of Lorca's involvement with La Barraca can be seen very clearly in *Blood Wedding*. The sets for their productions were, of necessity, simple and stark, and even if in much of Lorca's earlier work there are examples of this, *Blood Wedding* reveals that kind of economy in almost every aspect. No set in the whole of his theatre is evoked more concisely than that for Act One, Scene One: '*Room painted yellow*' (p. 33). The setting for Act One, Scene Two, is only a little more detailed: '*A room painted pink, with copper ornaments and bunches of common flowers. Centre-stage, a table with a cloth. It is morning*' (p. 39). And that for Act One, Scene Three, is much the same: '*Interior of the cave where the* BRIDE *lives. At the back a cross of big pink flowers. The doors are round with lace curtains and pink ribbon. On the walls, made of a white hard material, are round fans, blue jars and small mirrors*' (p. 45). Lorca creates for all three scenes stage-pictures which are simple and stylized, stripped of unnecessary detail. Furthermore, the figures which are placed against these backgrounds produce an effect which is at once visual and emotional. Against the yellow walls of her house the Mother will be dressed in black, the colour of mourning, and the combination of colours suggests at once the harshness and the bitterness of a life in which she finds no comfort. Indeed, the yellow walls already anticipate the Bridegroom's death and the return of his body to the house with 'lips turned yellow' (p. 93). As for Scene Two, the pink of the walls, the glow of copper, the colour of flowers and the brightness of morning all suggest a calm and tranquil mood, a fitting

115

background for the sleeping baby and the lullaby. The pink of the walls is, indeed, echoed in the lullaby itself – 'Go to sleep, carnation' (p. 40) – but that sense of tranquillity is quickly disrupted by the reference to 'Horsey's hooves are red with blood' (p. 40), and by the end of the scene, after Leonardo's violent altercation with the Wife and the Mother-in-Law, the emphasis on blood is much more anguished and we can well imagine the walls of the room slowly turning from pink to red, the baby's future already threatened by Leonardo's death. In contrast, the pinks, whites and blues of the Bride's home point to optimism, innocence, the wedding to come, a happy future. They form a background to the positive and constructive arrangements made throughout the scene by the Bridegroom's mother and the Bride's father. But, against it, the Bride's final outburst as the scene ends – and, significantly, '*The light begins to fade*' (p. 50) – are jarring, discordant notes, which disrupt the initial mood.

Lorca's use of simple yet careful stylization thus invests the specific with a universality, transforming something Spanish into something with a much wider resonance. The Mother is, at the same time, all grieving and fearful mothers; Leonardo and the Bride, all desperate lovers. It is no accident that the names of most of the characters should be not particular but generic – the Bridegroom, the Bride, the Mother, the Father, the Wife, the Neighbour – and the same universalizing effect is achieved by Lorca's use of music in the play. Although music was used selectively in his earlier work, nowhere was it employed more extensively than in *Blood Wedding*, and this clearly owed something to Lorca's work with La Barraca. Given the use of musical elements in the company's stagings of Calderón's *Life Is a Dream* and Lope de Vega's *Fuenteovejuna*, it is surely no coincidence that in *Blood Wedding* musical effects are created, as in those productions, by instruments, by individual voices and by a sung chorus. The eerie atmosphere of Act Three, Scene One, is underpinned by two violins. Individual voices create the lullaby, the song which opens Act Two, Scene Two – 'Turning, / The wheel was turning' (p. 63) – and the almost operatic soliloquy of the Moon. And choral effects, chanted if not sung, are everywhere: the arrival of the wedding guests, the intonations of the Woodcutters, the three girls' game with the wool and the final lament.

Most important of all, however, is the way in which these episodes work in relation to each other. Act Two, Scene One, for example, begins with the Bride's dejection, but this is soon swept away by the wedding guests' song, 'Let the bride awaken now / On this her wedding day' (p. 55), which comes progressively nearer, and, when the guests finally arrive, becomes a rapturous and infectious outburst of joy and celebration. The way in which the passage is created and constructed is, to use a musical analogy, almost symphonic, words and lines the equivalent of notes and phrases. As the latter pass from instrument to instrument, building to a climax, so here lines pass from one speaker to another, forming a crescendo. And although the words and images are important, the rhythm and tone of their delivery – uplifting, inspiring – are even more important, enveloping not only the characters but the audience. Throughout the play we are moved from one emotion to another: joy, apprehension, despair. It is no coincidence that, while he was writing *Blood Wedding*, Lorca was constantly listening to music – to gramophone records of *cante jondo* and Bach. In many ways, the play itself is a piece of music and, in precisely the same way, its reson-ance is universal. An audience would be moved by it even if it did not know the language in which it was being performed.

Through his work with La Barraca Lorca also honed his skills in other aspects of theatre, particularly movement. Calderón's *Life Is a Dream* is a morality play in which the journey of the characters through life is presented almost as in a ballet, while in Lope de Vega's *Fuenteovejuna* moments of tranquillity are often punctured by dra-matic interventions, in addition to which the rebellion of the villagers against their overlord demands very accomplished choreography.

In *Blood Wedding* the use of movement is as varied as the play's musical effects and is, of course, frequently combined with them. So,

117

for example, the song of the wedding guests in Act Two, Scene One, is performed in the context of constant movement; and Act Two, Scene Two, involves not only the animated movement of the guests at the wedding reception but the agitated coming and going of those searching for the absent Bride, and finally the swift and dramatic entrance of the Wife as she announces that the Bride and Leonardo have escaped together. In total contrast there are moments of great stillness. In Act One, Scene One, the Mother and the Neighbour are both seated, facing each other, the stillness seeming to emphasize even more the former's restless state of mind as she questions the Neighbour about the Bride. And in Act Three, Scene One, Death and the Moon slip in and out of the on-stage action in the most sinister way. In the discussion of *The Public*, mention was made of Lorca's familiarity with the ballets of Manuel de Falla, with the Madrid productions of Diaghilev's ballet company, and the elements of dance in his own early plays. In an interview he gave in Buenos Aires Lorca complained about the neglect of physicality in the theatre, and stated that it was his intention to restore it: 'One must re-evaluate the importance of the body in performance. That is my aim.'[18] This love of movement on stage is everywhere evident in *Blood Wedding*, and Lorca choreographs it with precision in a way which captures the changing rhythms – the movement from sadness to joy, from joy to despair – of life itself.

The première of *Blood Wedding* took place on 8 March 1933 at the Teatro Beatriz in Madrid – and, crucially, the director was Lorca himself. Not surprisingly, he employed individuals who were his collaborators with La Barraca. One of them, Santiago Ontañón, co-designed the sets with Manuel Fontanals, and these, faithful to Lorca's stage directions, had precisely that simplicity which Lorca adopted with the productions of La Barraca. Carlos Morla Lynch attended the première, and subsequently wrote that the setting for Act One, Scene One, comprised a simple room in different tones of yellow; Scene Two a room painted pink; and Act Three, Scene Two, a room painted white.[19] A photograph of Act Two, Scene Two – the wedding reception – portrays the Bride and Bridegroom and their close relatives at stage-level, while other guests stand on steps to the right and the left against a background of white walls. The simplicity and symmetry of the set are very clear. Contemporary reports and photographs of this first production suggest that Lorca staged the play much as we have it in its published form.

His work with La Barraca also revealed his concern with timing and precision when it came to dialogue, movement, entrances and exits. Lorca's brother Francisco wrote subsequently of the problems Lorca had had in this respect with the actors during rehearsals for *Blood Wedding*.[20] As far as the text was concerned, the actors, many of whom were much more used to comedy and the commercial theatre, were bound to have difficulties with a play which, in its combination of poetry and a prose which is itself strongly rhythmic and full of images, was quite different from anything in the mainstream theatre of the 1930s. Furthermore, there are scenes – for example, Act Two, Scene One – in which voices interplay in a very complex manner, and sequences – the intonations of the Woodcutters, the exchanges of the Bride and Leonardo in the wood, the final lament – which have to be performed convincingly if they are not to sound comic. In every case timing, emphasis and rhythm have to be precise, and Lorca evidently drove the actors hard, often losing his temper. Again, these were actors who were simply not used to the variety of movement demanded by the play. Because movement in *Blood Wedding* is so complex, Lorca, according to his brother, demanded mathematical precision, as indeed was the case in his productions with La Barraca.

As we know, Lorca listened to a great deal of music as he wrote the play, and music was used in his own production. He accompanied the entrance of the Woodcutters at the beginning of Act Three with the andante from Bach's second Brandenburg Concerto, played on a gramophone record, the music preparing the audience for the mysterious scene in the wood.[21] And, even if we have no specific information about the music which was used elsewhere in the play, it is clear that many of the scenes were performed as if they were part of a musical score. Josefina Díaz de Artigas, who played the Bride, said of Act Two, Scene One – the arrival of the wedding guests – that

> there was no voice that did not fit with another . . . He [Lorca] har-
> monized voices, their timbre, their resonance, as a musician
> harmonizes sounds. It was an extraordinary exercise. He would call
> out 'Not like that. Your voice is too sharp! Try it again! I need a voice
> with weight . . .' [22]

For the final scene of lamentation, Lorca had originally envisaged a choral chant, although there is no record of how the lines were actually distributed in the production. From the evidence we have it is perfectly clear that, in staging the play, he gave due emphasis to stage design, movement, music and language, thereby achieving that combination of all the different elements of stage-performance that we now call 'total theatre', and which Lorca, along with other leading theatre practitioners of that time, considered essential if the particular work was to transcend time and place and take on a broader, more universal significance. That this is what the production achieved may be gauged from the reaction of M. Fernández Almagro in *El Sol* when he con-cluded that

> There are, in *Blood Wedding*, more than individual characters, general
> states of the human spirit . . . That is precisely what impressed me
> most about *Blood Wedding*: the spirit which energizes it, the common
> breath which comes from far away and from deep down . . .[23]

Critical reaction, in general, was similarly appreciative: the première was a triumph, and Lorca's reputation as a dramatist was firmly established.

During the three remaining years of Lorca's life, there were to be two other highly successful productions of the play in Spain. The first opened at the Madrid Coliseum on 28 February 1935, performed by the company of Lola Membrives, while the second première in Barcelona on 22 November of the same year, presented by the company of Margarita Xirgu. This second production was important for a variety of reasons. Margarita Xirgu and Cipriano Rivas Cherif were, as we have seen, friends of Lorca, and they were also closely associated with his work. In addition to her lead roles in *Mariana Pineda* in 1927 and in *The Shoemaker's Wonderful Wife* in 1930, Xirgu, at the very end of 1934, had appeared as the eponymous heroine in the Madrid production of *Yerma*, which ran for more than a hundred performances, and this production had been directed by Rivas Cherif. Also, the stage-designer was José Caballero, Lorca's colleague from La Barraca. So, even if Lorca was not the director of the Barcelona *Blood Wedding*, it seems clear enough that he would have had considerable influence over the play's staging, and he could be sure that it was in good hands.

An impression of the production may be formed both from the critical reviews which accompanied it and from the photographs available in various archives. Writing in *La Vanguardia*, María Luz Morales spoke of the 'assured stylization' of the piece, and of the way in which 'all the elements in the performance . . . fuse and harmonize: settings, music, visual elements, poetry, delivery, acting . . .'[24] José Caballero's designs, as the photographs indicate, were the very opposite of naturalistic. The wedding reception, for example, reveals his liking for stylized, geometric shapes, for the walls and the stairs are much more like an abstract painting than the stonework of a real building. Particularly striking, too, as far as performance was concerned, was the element of contrast, both within and between scenes. Morales referred to 'colour, song, rhythm, now slow, now quick, now spirited, now vibrant, now slow, as in a symphony . . .' As for the acting, Xirgu, in the role of the Mother, received particular praise, notably for bringing out the inner life of the character, while the performance of the company as a whole was described as highly disciplined. In short, here was a theatre company that was attuned to Lorca's work and which did it justice, paying due attention to its high degree of stylization.

121

Blood Wedding was next staged in Spain in October 1962 at the Teatro Bellas Artes, directed by José Tamayo, with sets once again by Caballero. But on the whole there have been few major Spanish productions, possibly on account of the difficulty of the piece. The one exception, which merits discussion here, is that directed by José Luis Gómez for the Teatro de la Plaza in 1986, in connection with the fiftieth anniversary of Lorca's death, and which in August of that year was staged at the Edinburgh International Festival.

In some respects, this production was far removed from those described above, notably in its initial impression of realism. The actors themselves were both strongly Andalusian in appearance and convincingly rural: Leonardo muscular and unshaven; the Mother dark-skinned and tough; the Bride strong and unglamorous. Their costumes were authentic in every respect, as were the rough, simple furniture and the rustic instruments used to accompany the songs. On the other hand, every other aspect of the production, from the stage-design by Manfred Ditrich to movement on the stage and the speaking of the lines, was distinguished by a clear stylization. The opening setting consisted of a bare, three-walled box, which suggested a room, with a doorway in each of the side walls. Then, as the action of the play began, the back wall of the box rose to reveal two hills and a blue sky, the effect that of a picture-frame to the on-stage action. Within this frame, constant throughout the three acts of the play, the stage remained virtually bare, and changes of location were suggested entirely by lighting and the introduction of small items of furniture. This was a production far removed from Lorca's own but one which retained his stylization, as well as the play's sense of universality.

Stylization was evident, too, in the movement of the actors around the stage. In Act One, Scene One, for example, the Mother's embracing and holding of the Bridegroom emphasized the bond between them and her desire to hold on to him in more than a physical sense. In Act One, Scene Three, the formal arrangement of chairs, as well as the stillness of the actors, suggested the propriety of the occasion. In Act

Two, Scene One, the Bride's intoxication with Leonardo was revealed in her unsteady, almost swooning movement, and in the following scene, the wedding reception, the constant interweaving, entrances and exits of the different characters evoked excitement and, finally, the frantic search for the missing Bride. The mystery of the scene in the wood was, in contrast, suggested by the slow advance of the Wood-cutters across the stage, and by the slow-motion effect of the Moon's entrances and exits. Above all, the careful choreography here created the sense of things beyond this world.

Above all, the production was distinguished by its musicality, both in relation to the speaking of the lines and to the use of music. In Act One, Scene One, for example, the Mother's reference to the knife – 'The knife, the knife . . .' (p. 33) – was more sung than spoken, the almost operatic style vividly expressive of her strong emotions. This was evident, too, when, in Act Two, Scene Two, she recalls how she found her son dead in the road: 'I wet my hands with his blood . . .' (p. 65). In addition, there were many examples of powerful choral effects. In the text of the play, 'Oh let the bride awaken now' (p. 54) is sung initially by the Servant, but here it was sung by a group of men and women, not unlike a chorus. Later, when the wedding guests arrive, their singing of the song was accompanied by a variety of rustic instruments. Again, the opening song of Act Two, Scene Two – 'Turn-ing, / The wheel was turning . . .' (p. 63) – was sung by a group of actors, not by the Servant, and at the end of the scene the escape of the Bride and Leonardo was accompanied by the increasingly urgent rhythm of drums.

Two episodes in Act Three also made use of striking choral effects. The chanting of the girls unwinding the ball of red wool was power-fully performed, pointing to the importance given to language in this production. The final lamentation of the mourning women, from 'He was a handsome horseman' (p. 91) to 'Oh, four handsome boys / Bear death on high' (p. 92), was sung by four of the actors. The next four lines were spoken, the next four chanted by the group of women, and then the remaining lines, from the Mother's 'Neighbours: with a knife . . .' (p. 92) to the end, sung by the Mother and the Bride. Thus, this was a production which, despite its initial impression of realism, was markedly stylized in almost every respect, and one in which that stylization transformed its Andalusian elements into something much more universal.

It is, of course, the universal appeal of *Blood Wedding* that has led to productions and adaptations in different languages all over the world. In Britain the first English-language production was directed by Peter Hall at the Arts Theatre, London, in 1954. Two years later it was produced at the Nottingham Playhouse, and in 1973 at the Leeds Playhouse. In the last fifteen years, the play has been directed by a number of leading British directors: by Anthony Clark at the Contact Theatre, Manchester (1987), Julia Bardsley at the Haymarket Theatre, Leicester (1992) and Sue Lefton, at the Mercury Theatre, Colchester (2001), all in my own translation; other productions have been directed by Jonathan Martin at the Half Moon Theatre, London (1989), Yvonne Brewster at the National Theatre, London (1991), Nigel Jamieson at the Lyric Theatre, Hammersmith, London (1993) and Tim Supple at the Young Vic Theatre, London (1996).

The most successful of these was, in my view, Sue Lefton's Colchester production in 2001. Played on a rectangle of wood, backed by dark walls, it had that austerity and stylization demanded by Lorca himself. Both stage furniture and costumes were extremely simple: a small table, chairs, a tray, jugs, glasses, an upright piano; the Bridegroom and Leonardo in white shirts and dark trousers; the Mother and Leonardo's wife in black dresses; the Servant in grey; the Moon stripped to the waist; the Woodcutters masked. This was a production, moreover, which was, from beginning to end, carefully choreographed by its director, who, as movement director to the Royal Shakespeare Company, has a thorough understanding of that art. At the beginning of Act Three, Scene One, for example, the members of the company used their arms to suggest trees, advanced menacingly towards the front of the stage, and then moved back, making way for the Moon, moving slowly towards the audience with outstretched arms. Furthermore, this was an occasion on which flamenco dance, so often badly performed by British actors unfamiliar with the tradition, enhanced the production in no small measure, linking scenes on the one hand but also underpinning, through the sound of drumming heels, the constant presence of fate. It was a skill in which the actors had been rigorously trained. Again, all the members of the cast spoke their lines with power and clarity, matching phrases to gestures. And music played its part, too: the Moon's soliloquy accompanied, for instance, by eerie electronic music, the winding of the wool by a discordant guitar and a repeated note on the piano. In short, Lefton's production interwove settings, movement, music and speech in just such a way that Lorca would have approved. Reviewing the production in the *Daily Telegraph*, Charles Spencer concluded:

> The Colchester production of Lorca's 1933 masterpiece is one of the finest productions I have ever seen in a regional theatre . . . There are outstanding individual performances, too, especially from Christine Absalom as the grieving, vengeful mother of the jilted groom, from Katy Stephens as the touchingly confused bride and from Victor Gardener as the dangerous, sexy lover who sweeps her off her feet. Throughout, the play's mixture of passion and pain is both intensified and contained by a production of great formal beauty . . . [25]

And Lyn Gardner in *The Guardian* agreed: 'This is an enormously sympathetic production of a big, compassionate play . . .'[26] Quite clearly, *Blood Wedding*, performed in the right way, produces an enormous impact.

4
Yerma:
A Violation of Nature

Although *Yerma* was not first performed until the end of 1934, Lorca had been working on it for several years. During his stay in Cuba in 1930, he apparently read some scenes from the play to the four members of the wealthy Loynaz family, whom he frequently visited, and by the autumn of 1933, some six months after the première of *Blood Wedding*, it seems likely that he had completed two of the play's three acts.[1] By the summer of 1934 he had written the final act, and, as was his custom, on 3 December he read the play to a group of friends at the home of Carlos Morla Lynch. The reading, described by Morla Lynch, took more than two hours and, unlike the earlier readings of *The Public* and *When Five Years Pass*, entranced its audience, all of them overwhelmed by the power and the beauty of the play and by Lorca's dynamic interpretation of its characters.[2] *Yerma*, he had informed José Serna in 1933, would be the second play in a trilogy of the Spanish earth, of which *Blood Wedding* had been the first.

Yerma is the story of the childless wife, who, having been married to the farmer, Juan, for several years, longs to conceive. The marriage, though, is an unhappy one, arranged by Yerma's father, and neither partner truly loves the other. Juan, indeed, prefers to cultivate his fields and tend his sheep, leaving Yerma to spend her time at home in what, for her, are fruitless domestic chores. By now the object of the mockery and scorn of the other women in the village, she slowly becomes more desperate but finds no solution, her situation exacerbated by the fact that other young women are having children. When she seeks the advice of a local woman, Dolores, she is forbidden by Juan to leave the house, for he considers that Yerma's behaviour is increasingly a danger to his reputation. Furthermore, her own sense of honour prevents her from seeking out another man, even though from her teenage years she has been in love with Víctor, another local farmer. In a final act of desperation, she joins the pilgrimage to a shrine where childless women pray to be made fertile, and where, on each occasion, many of them offer themselves to men always eager to fulfil their needs. When Juan appears, drunk and demanding her favours, she rejects him, and finally, in an act of both defiance and despair, strangles him, thereby snuffing out forever the possibility of a child.

Although the source of inspiration for *Yerma* was not as precise as that for *Blood Wedding*, it was still firmly grounded in reality. The theme of the childless woman may, indeed, have had its origin in Lorca's own family, for his father's first wife, Matilde Palacios, had been unable to produce a child in fourteen years of marriage and had then died suddenly from what was described as an intestinal obstruction, although this may well have been a developing gynaecological problem. Lorca seems to have been haunted for years by photographs of the woman who could, in other circumstances, have been his own mother. Again, much of his writing, plays and poetry alike, is centred on the figure of the Spanish spinster, alone, unfulfilled and frequently mocked by others. When he was only twenty Lorca had written a poem entitled 'Elegy', inspired by an unmarried young woman in Granada, Maravillas Pareja:

> In your white hands
> You bear the thread of your illusions,
> Dead forever, and in your soul
> A passion hungry for kisses of fire
> And a love of motherhood that dreams far-off
> Dreams of cradles in quiet places,
> Weaving with your lips the blue of lullaby.[3]

The longing for a child evident here was, as we have seen, powerfully expressed in the words of the Manikin in *When Five Years Pass*, as well as in the character of the Young Man. And even if the theme of child-lessness is not explicitly stated, it is surely implied in many of the spinster characters who appear in Lorca's work. In 'The Gypsy Nun', the young girl, condemned to spend her life in a convent, fantasizes about her lovers:

> Across the eyes of the nun
> Two loping riders move.
> A dull and distant murmur
> Loosens her shift . . .[4]

She will enjoy neither love nor children, and neither will the protag-onist of *Doña Rosita the Spinster*, who, engaged to her cousin, waits vainly for twenty-five years for his return from South America. Her anguish is made even greater by the fact that her friends are married and continue to produce children:

One day a friend gets married, and then another, and yet another, and the next day she has a son, and the son grows up . . . (p. 148)

And then, of course, there are the five spinsters of *The House of Bernarda Alba*, four of whom are left, following Adela's death, to face an empty future. In Act Two, Poncia suggests that, when Augustias marries Pepe el Romano, the other girls can make the clothes for her children. In response, Amelia angrily rejects the possibility of caring or sewing for someone else's offspring: 'Look at the women down the street, martyrs to their little brats' (p. 61). But her and her sisters' bitterness and resentment may well come from the realization that such a prospect is denied them.

Lorca's belief that he would never be a father explains the persis-tence, even the obsession, with which the theme of childlessness runs through his work from beginning to end. Photographs show him with children he encountered in the United States and with the children of his sister Concha, one of them clinging onto his hand. There can be no doubt that, sensitive as he was, Lorca felt for them, and grieved for them, as he does in two poems in the volume *Poet in New York*. In 'The Boy Stanton', he cannot forget the ten-year-old struck down by cancer, while in another poem, 'Little Girl Drowned in the Well', he mourns the extinction of a young life. The fact that he would not have children of his own must have been, in a country where children are cherished, a source of both regret and anguish. In a sense, therefore, Yerma is a projection of himself, and it is very easy indeed to understand the extent of his sympathy for and identification with her.

The theme of childlessness and , in particular, the pilgrimage of the childless women to the shrine in Act Three, Scene Two, was also inspired by an event which took place annually in the village of Moclín not far from Granada.[5] Following the fall of Granada to the Christians in 1492 – the final victory in their eight-hundred-year campaign against the Moors – the Catholic Kings, Ferdinand and Isabella, had donated to the church in Moclín a standard which had figured prominently in the struggle against Islam. Subsequently, the standard, which came to be known as the Christ of the Cloth, was believed to possess miraculous powers, and by the eighteenth century the pilgrimage to Moclín had become established and associated in particular with the cure of male impotence and female infertility. During Lorca's childhood in Fuente Vaqueros and Asquerosa, men and women continued to make their way to the shrine on 5 October, and by this time the activities there had become a good deal less than religious, as local men revealed their eagerness to make the unfortunate women fertile. Although it is unlikely that Lorca visited Moclín during the pilgrimage, he may well have visited the church, and he was certainly well aware of the ritual associated with it. His interest in the event is suggested by the fact that, at least seven years before he completed *Yerma*, he collaborated with Cipriano Rivas Cherif on the scenario for a ballet for which another friend, Gustavo Pittaluga, wrote the music.

Entitled *The Pilgrimage of the Cuckolds*, it was clearly based on the Moclín ceremony, in the course of which the locals shouted 'Cuckolds!' at the impotent husbands in the procession prior to assisting their wives to conceive. In the ballet, the sterile wife, Sierra, eventually gives birth, and the tone of the piece as a whole is far lighter than Lorca's tragedy. But his involvement in it clearly suggests that, from 1927, if not before, he was fascinated by the subject. Furthermore, the ballet had its première in Madrid in November 1933, before Lorca had completed the final act of his play, and it was performed, significantly, by the company of Encarnación López Júlvez, who had danced the part of the butterfly in Lorca's very first play and recorded folk songs with him in 1931, and who remained a good friend and associate. Neither is it a coincidence that the sterile wives in ballet and play have names connected with the landscape: 'Sierra' ('mountain') and 'Yerma' ('barren land').

But if the ballet influenced Lorca directly, it is also worth bearing in mind that during his stay in Cuba in 1930 Lorca had been taken by a woman friend, Lidia Cabrera, to a *ñañigo* ceremony, which involved magic rites and in the course of which he had been terrified by a devil-figure. This, too, may have been in Lorca's mind when he wrote Act Three, Scene Two, of *Yerma*, for the two masked dancers here are announced by the children as the Devil and his wife. Although the source for *Yerma* was, therefore, rather different from that for *Blood Wedding*, the evidence once again points to the fact that Lorca rarely drew his material out of thin air.

Also, in 1933 and 1934 Lorca was working with La Barraca, in frequent contact with the villages and smaller towns in rural Spain. Following the Madrid production of *Blood Wedding* in March 1933, the company set out on a tour that continued through the spring and the summer, while another tour took place the following year. Although the itinerary included cities – Salamanca, Santander, Valladolid – the company often performed in towns with less than six thousand inhabitants, such as Ampuero, Cuéllar, Villercayo and Estella.[6] There, as well as on the journeys through the Spanish countryside, Lorca would have come into contact with the prejudice, the narrow-mindedness, the gossip and the traditional values which are everywhere in *Yerma*, attitudes which would have reinforced in no small measure what he already knew. Act Two, Scene One, in which the women wash their clothes in the stream, is a perfect example of local gossip, of spite and of spying on one's neighbours. When First Woman angrily says: 'Give me a needle, I'd stitch up gossiping tongues', she draws attention to the ingrained habits of small communities which are strongly emphasized, too, in *The House of Bernarda Alba*, when Magdalena alludes to 'spiteful gossip' (p. 33).[7] And just as they gossip about people, so do the villagers constantly watch and even spy on them. These women know precisely what goes on both inside and outside Yerma's house, just as in the later play Poncia spends much of her time 'spying on the neighbours through the cracks to bring her [Bernarda] all the gossip' (p. 7).

Inevitably, gossip is to the detriment of the subject, as Fifth Woman's comment about Yerma suggests: 'These barren women, they're all the same. When they should be making lace or apple jam, they fancy a bit of a rest on the roof or a paddle in the river'. The consequence of all this is, of course, damage to one's reputation, and it is this that so preoccupies Yerma's husband Juan, for, the more defiant Yerma becomes, the more people talk about and denigrate their marriage, destroying his sense of self-esteem: 'I don't like people pointing me out, which is why I want to see this door closed and everyone inside this house.' Subjected to speculation about his virility and Yerma's fidelity, Juan becomes as much the object of mockery as his wife:

> When I come across a group of people, they fall silent; when I go to weigh the flour, they fall silent; even at night in the fields, when I wake up, I think that the branches have suddenly gone quiet . . .

Undoubtedly, Lorca's travels with La Barraca would have exposed him afresh to the kind of things with which he had been familiar in the village of Asquerosa. It is an aspect of the play which is therefore rooted in the reality of rural Spain, as well as something to which Lorca himself was constantly exposed in small towns and large cities alike.

The notion of honour, personal and familial, has already been mentioned in the context of *Blood Wedding*, for the Bride's elopement with Leonardo destroys not only her own good name but also that of her new husband. In the play's final scene the Mother confronts the Bride: 'But what about his name? Where is his name?' (p. 90). The issue is one which is also central, as we shall see, to *The House of Bernarda Alba*, for Bernarda is obsessed by the fear that her reputation may be tarnished, principally by some misdemeanour committed by one of her five daughters. Public image – and how one's honour is defined by it – was, undoubtedly, something deeply rooted in the reality of Spanish life, and as such it is reflected in Spanish literature throughout the ages. In Calderón's seventeenth-century play *The Surgeon of Honour*, an obsessively fearful husband, Gutierre Alfonso Solís, suspects that his wife, Mencía, is unfaithful to him, and, in order to avoid the possibility of public gossip and personal disgrace, arranges her murder.[8] This example, although heightened and exaggerated for theatrical ends, reveals the extent to which a person's honour – Mencía is in fact totally innocent – depended, and still depends, almost entirely on public opinion, which, in Mencía's case, would have proved completely misguided. In precisely the same way Yerma becomes the subject of common gossip and mockery simply because she has not produced a child. In Act Two, Scene One, First Woman defends her: 'It's no fault of hers she's got no kids.' But this does not prevent all kinds of speculation, ranging from Yerma's interest in a man other than her husband to the latter's lack of virility and even the suggestion by Old Woman that, like his ancestors, he is not 'a true man'. Inevitably, to the extent that their relationship is constantly on the lips of others, both Yerma's and Juan's good names are damaged. The effect of this, moreover, is that he attempts to curb her freedom, confining her to the house, while she, increasingly desperate, defies him, damaging his reputation even more.

This concept of honour as public image is, however, sharply contrasted with honour as virtue and integrity, for while Yerma may appear to the villagers to be deserving of their condemnation, she is, throughout the play, steadfastly loyal to her husband and totally resistant to the attractions and temptations placed in her path by others. When, for example, Old Woman suggests in Act Three, Scene Two, that her son could get Yerma pregnant, the latter's reply is unambiguous:

> Stop it! Stop it! I'd never do that. I'd never go looking for someone else. Do you think I could go with another man? What would become of my honour? . . . I look for no one!

And in the previous scene, she spiritedly refutes Juan's suggestion that she might be interested in someone else:

> Don't say another word! Not a word. You and your kind think you are the only ones with a name to protect. You forget my family's never had anything to hide. Come on! Come close to me! Smell my clothes! Closer than that! . . . Do what you like to me but don't soil my heart with another man's name!

In presenting honour as integrity, as an inner quality quite different from its outward manifestation, Lorca was following in the footsteps of, amongst others, the great seventeenth-century dramatist Lope de Vega, who, in his play *Peribáñez* drew a clear distinction between the honour that comes with status and standing, and that of the peasant, Peribáñez, whose honour lies in his qualities of loyalty and honesty. But Lorca also had in mind, no doubt, the Spanish or, more especially, the Granada bourgeoisie, at whose hands he suffered considerably. As one of the regular participants in the literary meetings at the Café Alameda, Lorca had been picked out from an early age as someone different, as someone who did not fit. Later, the matter of his sexuality would be a source of frequent gossip and animosity, and in 1936 he did little to improve the situation when he referred to the Granada bourgeoisie as 'the worst middle class in Spain today'.[9] Even though the gossips of *Yerma* are not middle class, they nevertheless personify the spite, the willingness to criticize and that superficial and shallow concept of honour that Lorca had encountered in his home city, and which took no account of a person's true worth.

By the time he completed *Yerma*, Lorca was thirty-six years old and clearly preoccupied by the fact that the years were passing by. Three years earlier his obsession with time and its destructive effect had been powerfully expressed in *When Five Years Pass*, and in his last three plays he returns to it repeatedly. In *Doña Rosita the Spinster*, the mutable rose, which lasts only twenty-four hours, becomes a metaphor for Rosita herself and the way in which the passage of time erodes both her beauty and her hopes of marriage. In *The House of Bernarda Alba*, the twenty-year-old Adela sees in her sisters and, especially, in her half-mad grandmother, the ravages of time, refusing to accept it for herself: 'No, I shan't get used to it! I don't want to be shut away! I don't want my skin to become like yours. I don't want to lose my whiteness in these rooms!' (p. 39). As for Yerma, she is less concerned with her appearance than with the fact that each passing month is a further confirmation of her childlessness. At the beginning of Act One she reminds her husband that they have been married for twenty-four months, and a little later, in a conversation with the village-girl María, she speaks of the despair her childlessness is beginning to create in her: '. . . but two years and twenty days, like me . . . it's too long to wait . . . If I go on like this, I'll end up bad . . .' At the beginning of Act One, Scene Two, we learn that another year has passed, and in the course of Act Two, Scene Two, a further two years. In addition, there is a strong sense throughout the play of the passing of the seasons and, in conjunction with it, of animals giving birth, of crops ripening – those creative processes of the natural world of which Yerma believes, increasingly, she is not a part.

Yerma's growing conviction that she is a violation of nature echoes the Manikin's accusations against the Young Man in *When Five Years Pass*:

> You could have been a stallion's clarion call.
>
> Instead you were a stagnant moss-filled pool,
>
> Where this dress rots and withered leaves now fall. (p. 156)

In the very first scene Yerma points out that even those things in nature which are despised are productive:

> The rain only has to fall on the stones and they soften and the weeds start to grow . . . and people say that they are good for nothing. The weeds are good for nothing, but I watch them moving their yellow flowers in the breeze!

Later, in Act Two, Scene Two, her awareness of the difference between her own childlessness and the vitality of nature is intense:

> I am hurt, hurt and humbled beyond endurance, when I see the corn ripen, the water running, the sheep giving birth to hundreds of lambs, the bitches pups. It's as if the entire land were rising up to show me its tender, sleeping young, and all I have are these hammer-blows here, instead of my child's mouth.

Furthermore, if the world of nature is distinguished by a clear pattern in which procreation is a central element, Yerma concludes that her own existence has no place in the scheme of things: 'I'll have a child because I must have one. Or the world makes no sense at all.'

How often did Lorca entertain thoughts similar to Yerma's? He was, after all, someone closely attuned to the natural world. The Vega, the fertile plain of Granada in which both Fuente Vaqueros and Asquerosa are situated, figured prominently in Lorca's childhood and in his later years. There he had played in the fields and observed with intense interest the activities of animals and birds, not to mention the ploughing, the sowing of crops and the harvests associated with his father's estate. The family move to Granada itself in 1909, and Lorca's subsequent life in Madrid, did not mean that he lost touch with the countryside. Other than the family's summer retreats to the house in Asquerosa, in 1925 Lorca's father bought the property on the edge of Granada known then as the Huerta de los Mudos and subsequently the Huerta de San Vicente. In the 1920s the Huerta was a fertile paradise, rich in trees and vegetation, from which one could see the Alhambra and the Generalife gardens, as well as the snow-covered Sierra Nevada – today, however, the view is obscured by buildings. It was here that Lorca, surrounded by nature at its most creative, produced much significant work, including *Blood Wedding* and, no doubt, some of *Yerma*. In adult life he spoke of the importance of nature in his work:

I love the countryside. I feel so close to it in all my emotions . . . The meadows, the fields, have done wonderful things for me. The animals in the countryside, the livestock, the people who live on the land, all of them fascinate me in a way few people understand . . . Were this not so, I could not have written *Blood Wedding*. My earliest emotional experiences are connected with the land and with work on the land. This is why there lies at the heart of my life what psychoanalysts would term an 'agrarian complex'.[10]

Given his homosexual leanings, Lorca must at times have seen himself as less than a normal man. Throughout his work there is frequent reference to the traditional, and therefore normal, roles of men and women. In Act Two, Scene Two, Juan states the matter succinctly: 'Sheep in the pen and women at home', while Bernarda Alba's comment to her daughters in Act One of *The House of Bernarda Alba* is much the same: 'A needle and thread for women. A whip and a mule for men' (p. 21). Neither she nor Juan mentions children, but the implication is clear enough: normal men father, normal women give birth. Lorca's homosexual relationships, short- or long-term, must have impressed upon him the extent to which he, like the protagonist of his play, was increasingly estranged from what was then considered to be the normal and natural course of events. And, as in Yerma's case, it was an awareness which must have occasioned considerable anguish.

Yerma is arguably Lorca's most intense and concentrated play. Its action is much tighter than that of *Blood Wedding*, but the sense of concentration and focus is less to do with plot than with the fact that almost everything in the play is related to Yerma's longing for a child. In calling his play *A Tragic Poem* – as opposed to *Blood Wedding* being a *Tragedy in Three Acts* . . . and *The House of Bernarda Alba, A Drama of Women in the Villages of Spain* – Lorca sought in all probability to focus on the inner life of his protagonist, and, in formal terms, to evoke that life in a manner which would possess the austerity, the tightness and concentration of a poem. Yerma herself towers over the play's events like no other character in Lorca's theatre, except perhaps Mariana Pineda. Furthermore, from the very outset, her deep longing for a child is revealed in almost everything she says. The opening conversation with Juan turns quickly to her obsession with her childlessness, and, when he leaves, her sadness flows into the first of the play's songs:

Where will you come from, child of mine?
'From the peaks of the icy mountain'.
And what will you want, oh child of mine?
'The warm feel of your clothing'.

This song is in many ways a pointer to the emotional charge and the focused structure of the play as a whole. In almost every situation in which she finds herself, Yerma's reactions are intense and heightened.

When, after the song, María appears and announces that she is pregnant, Yerma's emotions range from concern for the baby's well-being –
'Don't walk too much, and when you breathe, breathe softly, as if you
are holding a rose between your teeth' – to anger against complaining
mothers-to-be – 'Why do they have them? To have a child isn't like
getting a bunch of flowers' – to her own despair – 'If I go on like this, I'll
end up bad'. It is a display of fluctuating and powerful emotion which
grows even more intense through the course of the action. In Act
One, Scene Two, her anxiety is revealed in the conversation with Old
Woman – 'Why am I dry? Are the best years of my life to be spent feed-
ing the birds . . . ?' – and her impatience with Second Girl who doesn't
want a child. By Act Two, Scene Two, after five years of childless
marriage, the sadness of the play's first song has become a much
deeper anguish, an emotional and even physical pain, the essence of
which is contained in a second song, flamenco-like in its intensity:

> Oh, this field of sorrow!
> This door now closed to loveliness!
> . . .
> Oh, breasts struck blind beneath this dress!
> Oh, doves now black and sightless!

When María appears again, this time with a child in her arms,
Yerma's sense of hurt cannot be contained: 'A woman of the fields who
has no children is as useless as a clump of thorns.' By Act Three, Scene
One, her anguish is that of someone for whom life no longer has any
purpose or meaning:

> . . . it's as if a wave of fire sweeps upward from my feet, and there's an
> emptiness about everything, and the men in the street, and the bulls
> and the stones, everything seems to be made of cotton-wool. And I
> ask myself: 'What's the point of their existence?'

And in the final scene, when Juan tells her that he has never even thought of their having a child, the emptiness and pointlessness of her life is complete: 'Barren, barren! But sure in that knowledge. Now I know it for sure. And now I'm alone . . .'[11] The trajectory of the play, from its beginning to its conclusion, is a kind of graph of Yerma's anguished emotional life, rising without deviation to its highest point in the final scene. In that respect the focus on her feelings is intense, and in the sense that emotion and tightness of structure combine, her experience does indeed have the character of a lyric poem.

The highly concentrated nature of the play also stems from Lorca's handling of the other characters, for all of them, without exception, are spokes in a wheel of which Yerma is the hub. When María first appears, for example, it is to announce that she is pregnant, while later on she carries her child in her arms. In Act One, Scene Two, Old Woman talks to Yerma of her own fertility – nine boys – and later on tries to persuade her to let one of them get her pregnant. In the same scene First Girl speaks of the child she's left at home, while Second Girl has no intention of having one. In Act Two, Scene One, the women at the stream sing of love-making and children, while in Scene Two Yerma is guarded at home by Juan's unmarried and therefore childless sisters. In the first scene of Act Three, Dolores advises Yerma on how to conceive, and, in the final scene, the childless women make their way to the shrine in the hope of having children. There is neither a single character nor a single scene which is not tightly linked to Yerma's need for a child. All these characters have their separate lives and concerns, but in the unfolding of the play's events we are allowed to see only that part of their lives which touches directly on Yerma's problem. In no other play does Lorca focus his material with such single-mindedness. Indeed, the plot of the play lacks the narrative structure of *Blood Wedding* and *The House of Bernarda Alba*, for it consists of what in effect are a number of individual scenes separated by significant periods of time. Each of these scenes, moreover, highlights very selectively a key moment in Yerma's experience, ignoring the gaps in between. Nowhere else in Lorca's theatre is the effect so unremitting.

As far as theatrical influences are concerned, *Yerma* owes little to the rural plays of Lorca's time.[12] Serafín and Joaquín Alvarez Quintero and Jacinto Benavente had written some plays with rural settings, but none of them caught the true flavour of life in the Spanish country-side. The one Spanish dramatist who may well have influenced Lorca – and who, like him, detested the largely bourgeois commercial the-atre of Benavente and the Quintero brothers – was Ramón del Valle-Inclán, who was born in north-west Spain in the fishing port of Villanueva de Arosa in the province of Pontevedra. The rural back-ground of Galicia figures in many of his plays, and in *Divine Words*, published in 1920 and first performed in 1933, he created a vision of life in Spanish villages which is uncompromising in its portrayal of greed, selfishness, viciousness and physical and moral deformity. Nevertheless, *Divine Words*, for all its power, is a sprawling play, quite unlike *Yerma* in that respect, and it seems far more likely that Lorca turned again for his inspiration to those Greek and Roman plays that were performed in Spain in the early 1930s. It is surely no coincidence that in *Medea* and *Elektra* a single woman dominates the action and gives the play its title. Even if he had not seen the contemporary pro-ductions, Lorca would have been well aware of other classical plays in which a female figure is predominant, such as *Antigone*, *Hecuba* and *Iphigenia in Aulis*. Many of these women are, of course, put upon by husbands, uncles, not to mention the gods, and are as much victims as is Yerma. And again, these plays have precisely that emotional and structural concentration that is the very essence of Lorca's play. Every-thing is focused on the protagonist's situation and ultimate fate, and all the characters are seen in relation to it.

The tragic vision expressed by Lorca in *Blood Wedding* is also true of *Yerma*. In the earlier play Leonardo and the Bride yearn to be together, while the Mother and the Bridegroom have quite different aspirations: the former, her son's happiness and grandchildren for herself;

the latter, a settled marriage. Yerma's aspiration is to have a child, Juan's to work on his farm and lead a quiet life, unencumbered by children. As in *Blood Wedding*, they are aspirations pursued with great intensity and single-mindedness. In Yerma's case, her longing for a child goes back at least as far as the very first day of her engagement to Juan: 'Because the very first day that I was engaged, I thought about . . . children . . .' As for Juan, his lack of interest in them and his obsession with his farm is constantly expressed. In the very first scene he makes the point that 'The work's going well . . . and no children to waste our money on', and it is one which is repeated many times afterwards. Clearly, then, Yerma and Juan pursue objectives which are incompatible and mutually exclusive, which means that there can be no resolution of their differences. Indeed, if these differences are already marked at the beginning of the play, they become much greater as its action unfolds. Yerma's obsession with producing a child, far from awakening Juan's sympathy, alienates him even more, driving him to seek both escape and consolation in his work on the land. Having spent all day pruning the apple-trees, he comes home only to eat, seeking an excuse to go out again as soon as he can: 'I've got to see to the sheep. You know it's something that has to be done.' This, in its turn, increases Yerma's desperation to the point where she seeks the advice of Dolores, as a consequence of which Juan becomes more concerned about the effect of her behaviour on his reputation:

> What are you doing in this place? I'd shout it from the rooftops if I could, I'd get the whole village out of bed to see what's become of my good name. But I have to choke on it and keep quiet . . .

There is no escape for either Yerma or Juan from the unavoidable fact of their mutually exclusive desires. In Act Two, Scene Two, Juan sums up the impossibility of Yerma's aspiration in a telling phrase: 'You persist in banging your head against a wall of stone.' This is a notion echoed later by Yerma herself: 'I went out to look for carnations and instead I found this wall. Oh! I am forced to beat my head against this wall!' The sense of inevitable catastrophe is, consequently, very strong, although the suggestion of an overriding destiny is neither as explicit nor as theatrical as it is in *Blood Wedding*, embodied in the figures of the Woodcutters, Death and the Moon. Instead, the actual references to fate are few and far between. In Act Two, Scene One, Second Woman refers to Yerma and Juan's lack of children: 'All that's a matter for people who can't accept their fate.' She may, of course, be wrong in her conclusion that Yerma is destined to be childless, but Yerma herself later speaks of being born in this 'God-forsaken wilderness', implying that she, too, believes herself to have been forsaken, abandoned to her fate. In the last scene of the play María suggests that 'Women have children if they are meant to have them', and Juan, later in the same scene, points to the inability of Yerma and himself to change the course of events: 'Things that haven't happened and that neither you nor me can make happen'.

As in *Blood Wedding*, there is a strong sense of Yerma and Juan's fate being presaged by the experiences of other members of their families.[13] Yerma is the daughter of Enrique the shepherd, who, in Yerma's own words in Act Three, Scene One, 'gave me blood for a hundred children'. In contrast, the male members of Juan's family, in the words of Old Woman in Act Three, Scene Two, had the utmost difficulty in fathering children:

> You can cut my hands off if I tell a lie, but neither his father, nor his grandfather, nor his great-grandfather . . . not a single one of them was a true man. They had to move heaven and earth to father a son . . . Not like your [Yerma's] people. You've got brothers and cousins for hundreds of miles. Do you see what a curse has been put on your beauty?

This last sentence suggests, then, that the fate of this couple, in terms of their childlessness, is determined in advance, and that Lorca, in

143

dramatizing their situation, as well as pondering on his own, was again asking the questions: why must this be, and why is the world like this?

The ending of *Yerma* is, if anything, the bleakest out of all three rural tragedies. Yerma murders Juan and thus destroys for ever her hope of having a child. While *Blood Wedding* and *The House of Bernarda Alba* also end on dark and depressing notes, Yerma's fate seems harsher still, perhaps because throughout the play she invites such sympathy. She is, after all, an attractive woman – described by Old Woman in Act One, Scene Two, as 'a beautiful creature' – she is also warm-hearted and caring, reminding Juan in Act One, Scene One, of how she would look after him if he were ill, and her concern for the pregnant María is equally evident. In addition, she is a woman of principle and virtue who utterly rejects the possibility of giving herself to another man in the hope of becoming pregnant. Yerma is a woman who invites admiration and who, in different circumstances, would have flourished. It is hardly surprising, then, that the slow erosion of all these qualities and, above all, the destruction of her hope of a child should invite our compassion. But there is more to it than that, for the relentless stifling of her dream means that in the course of the play Yerma is transformed from the woman she once was into someone cast into the depths of despair. She changes into a desperate and depressed woman, one whose once positive qualities are lost, turned into someone finally driven to murder, and the spectacle invites, in the end, not so much sympathy as terror. As for Juan, he is far less sympathetic than Yerma, but we can understand his annoyance with her, his concern for his name, his longing for a quiet life. He is, in the end, as much a victim of circumstance as she is, and when he is killed, the event is both tragic and terrible. Lorca's achievement in this respect is to have fused the tragic nature of Greek tragedy, which also evokes admiration and terror, with his own deeply personal vision of the world.

In the summer of 1934, after his return from Buenos Aires, Lorca prepared for La Barraca's next production, Tirso de Molina's Don Juan play, *The Trickster of Seville*, which was first presented in August in Santander and then at other venues. The important point about this production is that it once again revealed Lorca's love both of stylization and of total theatre. The backdrop consisted simply of black curtains, partly because of economic necessity, partly because Lorca considered that the interaction of the characters was strong enough not to require sets. The actors wore costumes in the style of the Italian Renaissance, designed by Alfonso Ponce de León, and at key moments music was used to heighten the emotion. In the wedding scene involving Aminta and Batricio and set in the countryside, Lorca introduced traditional ballads and dances, the former sung by a choir and both accompanied by violins.[14] Quite clearly, this performance style was far removed from the tradition of bourgeois drawing-room plays which filled the Madrid theatres, as well as from the heavy, unimaginative and dull manner in which the 'classics' of the seventeenth century were so often presented. Summing up La Barraca's productions at this time, Ezio Levy, a professor at the University of Naples, wrote:

> The ballads, the poetry of Machado, the short plays of Cervantes and the dramas of Lope de Vega are interspersed with music. The music of ballet accompanies the wedding scene in *Fuenteovejuna*, the music of the Galician bagpipe, the music of folk song. García Lorca . . . has rediscovered the ancient music, or he has made use of the rhythm of popular contemporary songs. And the liveliness of the poetry goes well with the bounce of the joyful little folktunes, or the sadness of the ancient tragedy is underlined by the nostalgic song of the rustic choristers.[15]

In many respects, Levy could have been describing the style of *Yerma*, sufficient proof that Lorca's direction of La Barraca and the composition of his own plays had so much in common.

Lorca's brother Francisco has suggested that 'Of the trilogy . . . *Yerma* is the play which has the smallest number of elements directly inspired by reality' – a pointer, in effect, to its non-naturalistic empha-sis.[16] The stage-settings, for example, are distinguished not by their realistic detail but by their stark simplicity. For Act One, Scene One, what could be simpler than '*When the curtain rises* YERMA *is asleep, a sewing-basket at her feet*'? For the following scene the stage direction reads: '*The fields.* YERMA *enters. She is carrying a basket . . .*' Act Two, Scene One, continues in the same vein: '*Sound of singing. A rushing stream where the village women wash their clothes. The women are on dif-ferent levels.*' Scene Two is simply 'YERMA's *house . . .*' The first scene of Act Three is set in '*The house of* DOLORES *the healer*', while Scene Two has for the stage direction: '*A shrine in the mountains. Downstage some cartwheels and some blankets which form a rough tent.*' These are, quite clearly, directions stripped of detail, reduced to a bare minimum, and they clearly have the simplicity of Lorca's productions with La Barraca. Indeed, it is almost the case that, if his suggestions were fol-lowed closely, *Yerma* could be performed, as in the case of *The Trickster of Seville*, against a background of black curtains. With reference to the two houses – Yerma's and Dolores's – there is no indication of which room the action takes place in, nor any allusion to the furnishing or decoration of that room. Instead, Lorca picks out only those things which are important in the context of individual lives, and most of these can be suggested not by the backdrop but by the use of the stage area itself. Thus, the sewing-basket is picked out because it emphasizes both the domestic drudgery and the frustration of Yerma's life, and in Scene Two, the fields – which could easily be evoked by objects placed on the stage – are important because the fertility of nature is a telling contrast to and reminder of her barren state. Again, in Yerma's house, Act Two, Scene Two, the only household objects mentioned, precisely because of their importance, are the two pitchers full of water which Yerma brings from the stream, another cruel reminder of her own dryness. It could be argued, of course, that Lorca pared his stage directions to the bone in order to allow more scope to the directors of his plays, although it is far more likely that he did so because he knew exactly the effect he wanted.

Again, as with his work with La Barraca and his own plays, *Yerma* contains a number of songs, the majority sung by Yerma herself, the others of a choral nature. Yerma's first song, following Juan's departure in Act One, Scene One, reveals to the full both her longing for a child and her sense of isolation:

> Where will you come from, child of mine?
> 'From the peaks of the icy mountain'.
> And what will you want, oh child of mine?
> 'The warm feel of your clothing'.

Later, in Act One, Scene Two, she listens to a song which is being sung off stage by Víctor, her true love, and, although she does not sing it herself, its words reflect precisely her own feelings:

> Why do you sleep alone, shepherd?
> Why do you sleep alone, shepherd?
> On my thick quilt you'd sleep better.

Later still, in Act Two, Scene Two, another song encapsulates Yerma's desperation:

> Oh, this field of sorrow!
> This door now closed to loveliness!

Of the two lengthy choral passages, the first, sung by the village women at the stream, itself a symbol of fertility, is a vigorous celebration of love-making, marriage and children, a complete contrast to Yerma's situation:

> SECOND WOMAN: From the hill my man
>   Comes for his tea,
>   Gives me a rose,

I give him three.

FIFTH WOMAN: From the plain my man

Comes hungry and tired,

My myrtle cools

His red-hot fires.

The vigour of the women's song then finds its parallel in Act Three, Scene Two, when the symbolic figures of Male and Female appear at the shrine and enact what amounts to sexual intercourse:

FEMALE: Oh, love, how it offers her

Its crowns and flowers fresh!

Oh, love, how its arrows pierce

Her white and eager flesh!

MALE: Nine times she rose,

Seven times she moans,

And fifteen times in all,

Jasmine with orange joins.

In every case the songs are expressive of the mood and emotion of a given character or situation, thus becoming a more concentrated form of the dialogue. And, as in *Blood Wedding*, they acquire a strong sense of universality.

In the final scene the songs sung by Male and Female are preceded by girls who enter running, and the scene as a whole is full of vigorous movement and activity. Lorca's belief in the dramatic possibilities of movement or its opposite is well illustrated throughout, for vigorous action has its counterpart in slower movement, as well as in its total absence. At the beginning of Act One: '*A shepherd enters, walking on tiptoe . . . He leads by the hand a small child dressed in white.*' The slow movement of the shepherd across the stage immediately suggests that this is not reality but Yerma's dream, and it clearly looks back in this respect to certain moments in *When Five Years Pass* – notably the appearance of Dead Cat and Dead Child. Again, the lifelessness of Juan's two sisters in Act Two, Scene Two, is suggested by their slow movement around the house: '*The first sister-in-law enters slowly and goes to a cupboard.*' And again: '*The sister-in-law goes out with the jug, slowly.*' This, however, comes immediately after the scene in which the village women at the stream vigorously pound their clothes, their strong and powerful movements reflecting their healthy enjoyment of life as a whole: '*They move the washing rhythmically, pounding away at it.*' And then there are moments of stillness, as at the end of Act One, where Yerma and Victor meet, and their lack of movement as they face each other suggests their inner struggle with their feelings: '*Pause. The silence is intense. Both of them are quite still. A struggle develops between them.*' The play has a clear rhythm, which is important to the overall effect, and this owes much to Lorca's interest in ballet and dance as well as to his knowledge of Edward Gordon Craig's theories on dance in drama.[17]

Lighting effects are crucial to the play, and they highlight Yerma's journey from hope to despair. Her initial optimism is thus suggested in the dream sequence at the beginning of Act One, when the stage is '*lit in a strange, dream-like manner*', and then, as she awakens, '*the lighting changes to suggest a bright morning in spring*'. By the end of the second act, however, her situation has fundamentally changed: she is watched over by Juan's two sisters, and Víctor, her true love, is on the point of leaving the area. Yerma's increasing despair is mirrored in the darkness which now engulfs the stage: '*The sound of sheep-bells and shepherds' horns. The stage is in darkness.*' Act Three, in which Yerma visits Dolores and then takes part in the procession to the shrine, is set at night, its overall darkness an image of Yerma's hope finally being extinguished. On the other hand, just as the vigorous song and physical movements of the village women at the stream embody their love of life, so this particular scene takes place in bright daylight, a vivid contrast to Yerma's descent into darkness. The combination of the different elements of dramatic performance here, as well as elsewhere in the play, once again proves Lorca's dedication to total theatre, as well as to stylization.

Yerma was premièred at the Teatro Español in Madrid on 29 December 1934, directed by Cipriano Rivas Cherif and with Margarita Xirgu in the title role.[18] It was an auspicious occasion, attended by the leading lights of the theatre world. However, in protest at Xirgu's friendship with Manuel Azaña, the left-wing politician who had recently been jailed by the government for his suspected involvement in the miners' revolt in Asturias two months earlier, as well as Lorca's Republican leanings and his sexuality, right-wing elements in the audience attempted to disrupt the performance. Indeed, the kind of intolerance displayed by these individuals had its equivalent on stage in the lack of understanding shown by many of the villagers in relation to Yerma. But after the unruly protestors had been thrown out, the performance continued smoothly and proved to be an enormous success, greeted with acclaim by a wildly enthusiastic public and, in the following day's papers, by most of the theatre critics.

Rivas Cherif and Xirgu were not the only people on this production with whom Lorca had worked before. The sets for *Yerma* were designed by Manuel Fontanals, who had worked on the 1933 Madrid and Buenos Aires productions of *Blood Wedding* as well as on the Buenos Aires *The Shoemaker's Wonderful Wife*, *Mariana Pineda* and Lorca's adaptation of Lope de Vega's *The Foolish Lady* in 1933 and 1934. Quite clearly, Fontanals' sets for *Yerma* captured the stylization that Lorca demanded and which his own stage directions suggest. Writing in *La Voz*, the leading theatre critic, Enrique Díez-Canedo, referred to 'Fontanals' magnificent design. Visually arresting but without fussy detail, it has a striking and austere boldness . . .' Photographs of the production illustrate the point well, for in one of them Yerma is seen with Juan against a painted background of hills, while in another the hermitage of the play's final scene is painted on a flat or possibly a curtain at the back of the stage, and this is, as it were, framed by vertical flats to either side and at an angle, the whole contained within the larger frame of the proscenium. Old-fashioned, no doubt, by present-day standards, the sets nevertheless had that bold simplicity which Lorca demanded.

José Caballero, who designed the poster for the play, noted fifty years later that in rehearsals Lorca insisted on precise timing by the actors, even though he was not the director.[19] This would, of course, have applied both to movement and to the delivery of the text, and the reviews suggest that in this respect the standard was indeed high. Enrique Díez-Canedo drew attention to the precision of the choral scenes and to how well Lorca and Rivas Cherif had worked together – a significant pointer to the author's hand in the production – while the reviewer for *ABC* praised the staging of the scene involving the women at the stream and the fertility rite.[20, 21] Rivas Cherif was himself, like Lorca, a lover of the Greek chorus and would have drilled the actors in this respect. As for the performances of the major roles, Fernández Almagro in *El Sol* emphasized how expressive Xirgu was speaking her lines, and using gesture and movement, as well as her capacity for suggesting Yerma's changes of mood, from sadness to anguish to rage. And many of the other actors – López Lagar and Alvarez Diosdado in particular – were also praised, sufficient proof of the quality of this first production.[22]

As with Lorca's other plays, *Yerma* was not staged again in Spain for many years. A second production opened on 3 October 1961 at the Teatro Eslava in Madrid, directed by Luis Escobar and designed by Lorca's old colleague José Caballero. The dramatist's influence on some of the earlier productions of his plays continued to be felt, therefore, long after his death, and in the Teatro Eslava staging it was very evident indeed. Once more the sets were characterized by their boldness and simplicity. A photograph of the village women at the stream reveals, behind them, a great slab of dark-coloured rock, and another, showing one of the final moments of the play, has Yerma, with her dead husband at her feet, set against a background consisting of great slabs of stone. Both settings are, however, stripped of realistic detail, for they suggest not so much real rocks as geometric shapes that create the impression of rocks. Fussy realism is replaced by abstraction, and this brings to the play a sense of universality which naturalism would not provide to the same extent. In addition, Caballero's use of red, black and white, as well as being visually arresting, matched the play's emphasis on passion, death and despair, and emotional coldness.

Reviews of the production also point to the close attention paid to speech and movement. According to J.L. Pérez Cebrián, writing in *ABC*, Aurora Bautista in the title-role revealed 'all the varied and rich registers of voice and expression, of posture and movement', while Enrique Diosdado brought to the role of Juan an appropriate austerity.[23] The same critic praised, too, the work of most of the other actors and concluded that the director, Luis Escobar, had succeeded in integrating into a moving and convincing whole all the different elements of performance that Lorca valued so much, as well as the difficult contrasts and changes of rhythm inherent in the play.

While the two productions described above put into practice Lorca's stated intentions, the third major production in Spain ignored them, particularly when it came to stage design, and has proved to be the most controversial to date. The director in this instance was the Argentinian Victor García, the role of Yerma was played by the famous Spanish actress Nuria Espert, and the play opened at the Teatro de la Comedia in Madrid on 29 December 1971, exactly thirty-seven years after its première. The set, designed by García and Fabià Puigserver, could not have been more different from those of the earlier productions, for it consisted of a huge five-sided metal frame on the stage itself, tilted towards and projecting a little into the auditorium. The rigid frame was sufficiently wide to allow the actors to walk on it, as well as around its circumference, while across it was stretched a huge canvas, a kind of trampoline on whose surface there were numerous metal locking points to which cables could be attached, allowing the canvas to be hauled up or lowered in order to assume a variety of shapes. When the actors walked on the outer frame their movements were, of course, normal, but when they stepped off it onto the canvas, they acquired a bobbing character, as on a trampoline.

Well aware that his staging departed markedly from that of pre-vious productions, García suggested that his intention was, above all, to reveal the inner life of Yerma, and that, in order to achieve his aim, it was necessary to remove the action from an earth-bound setting, to evoke a kind of landscape of the mind, of dreams and desires, while at the same time, the solid outer frame of the set was a constant reminder of the real world in which Yerma lives and from which in the end she cannot escape. Despite its differences, García's approach nevertheless echoed the earlier ones in its avoidance of naturalistic detail, a point picked up by the theatre critic, José Monleón: 'He [García] has refused . . . to tie the play to any preconception in terms of staging that is remotely naturalistic.'[24] Instead, García sought to create on stage the 'poem' of Lorca's subtitle, to suggest inner rather than outer states, to evoke rather than to describe. A photograph from the production shows Yerma and Juan face to face on the bare canvas raised at one corner to form a small hill. While the canvas may well suggest a barren landscape, it evokes, much more importantly, those things that are not physical: the emptiness of Yerma's marriage to Juan, her barren state and her equally empty future. Similarly, another photograph shows Old Woman sitting on the solid outer frame, Yerma on the canvas. Thus, Old Woman with her many children is separated from Yerma's bare and barren world, as represented by the canvas. The capacity of the design to suggest these things was, then, considerable, its effect upon the imagination of the spectator much greater than in more traditional productions.

Needless to say, the trampoline also had a marked effect on move-ment, normal walking or running rendered impossible. Suggestive of spacemen walking on the surface of the moon, the floating movements of the actors, in particular of Yerma, underlined the insubstantiality of her dreams, thus bringing out particular allusions in Lorca's own stage directions, as well as in the text. Thus, the opening stage direction:

'The stage is lit in a strange, dream-like manner. A shepherd enters, walking on tiptoe.' Lorca's suggestion for the movement of the shepherd is decidedly balletic and well on the way to the floating demanded by García. In the text itself Yerma is constantly dreaming and fantasizing, as in the encounter with Víctor towards the end of Act One, Scene Two, when she thinks she hears the cry of a child but then decides: 'I must have imagined it.' In the sense that she is cut off from reality by her self-absorption, her floating, dreamlike movement across the canvas was, then, highly expressive, and, as the action of the play unfolded, it suggested too the extent to which she is increasingly a woman adrift, vividly described by herself as 'the moon looking for itself in an empty sky'.

A production as innovative as this was never going to be to the taste of many theatre critics. When, for example, García's production was revived by Nuria Espert and presented at the Edinburgh Festival in 1986, Nicholas de Jongh in the *Guardian* noted: 'I doubt whether the trampoline works except as an incitement to spectacular athletic performances, and as a source for brief flurries of physical excitement.'[25] There were, however, a number of approving voices, such as that of John Barber in the *Daily Telegraph*, who suggested that 'the trampoline evokes the earth better than bare boards ever could'.[26] And the performance of Nuria Espert as Yerma was in general greatly admired. Rosemary Say in the *Sunday Telegraph* summed up the performance very neatly:

> Miss Espert, as her despair and panic increase, gives a display of physical hunger for a child that has the Edinburgh audience stirring uneasily in its seat at such total demonstrations of failure. But always there is, running alongside, a delicacy of feeling . . . We are lucky to see such acting: few would dare expose so completely the whole range of female emotion.[27]

García's unique production, a landmark in the staging of this play, revealed, nevertheless, the extent to which Lorca's theatre lends itself to different directional approaches, provided that they avoid naturalism. Not doing so was one of the sins committed by the production, in English, presented at the Cottesloe Theatre on London's South Bank in March 1987, directed by Di Trevis and with Juliet Stevenson in the title role. Because the action of the play took place in a bare rectangular space with the audience on two sides of it, it had that simplicity suggested by earlier productions, but this was strangely offset by the washing – sheets and blankets – draped on the balconies above the spectators and which was strongly reminiscent of the Italian Neo-Realist films of the 1940s and 1950s, such as De Sica's *Bicycle Thieves* (1948) and Rossellini's *Open City* (1945). The clash of styles was noted by Michael Billington in the *Guardian*: 'Lorca's *Yerma* is as much a poem as a play. For that reason Di Trevis's new production at the Cottesloe, played for the most part with quiet, naturalistic intensity, seems far less urgent and expressive than Victor García's legendary 1972 version staged on a canvas trampoline that symbolically became desert, mountain or barren womb!'[28] Similarly, Billington criticized the company's performance of the fertility rite, which sought to introduce flamenco dance elements, but which for him was 'about as far from pagan sexuality as a night in an ethnic Spanish eaterie in west London'. Furthermore, although some critics were convinced of the quality of Juliet Stevenson's acting, others were not, notably Milton Schulman in the London *Evening Standard*, who wrote that: '. . . in spite of . . . technically adroit representations of passion, I felt something clinical and detached about her performance . . .'[29]

Yerma, like all Lorca's major plays, is extremely difficult to stage convincingly, for it requires not only an actress who is capable of communicating all the changing moods and emotion of its central character, but also a director who understands and is capable of bringing to his or her production that close integration of elements – setting, music, lighting, movement and speech – which Lorca himself insisted on, and which he so effectively brought to his own work in the theatre.

5
Doña Rosita the Spinster: A Poem of Granada

Although it is less well known than the three rural tragedies, *Doña Rosita the Spinster* is unquestionably one of Lorca's major plays. Completed in the early summer of 1935, one year after *Yerma* and a year before he finished work on *The House of Bernarda Alba*, *Doña Rosita* is a very different play. Its setting is not the countryside but Granada, Lorca's home town, and its characters are not farmers but middle-class *granadinos*. Furthermore, this play is not a tragedy but a bitter-sweet comedy, somewhat reminiscent of Chekhov. Lorca gave it the subtitle *A Poem of 1900 Granada, Divided into Various Gardens, with Scenes of Song and Dance* (p. 97).[1] The play does not contain the turbulent passions or the violent and fatal confrontations of the three tragedies. But this is not to say that the story of Rosita is not in any way sad. On the contrary, it is extremely moving. As in the case of *Yerma*, Lorca called his play a poem, although not a tragic poem on this occasion. In reality, even though its action evokes the mood of Granada over a period of time, Lorca's principal focus is Rosita herself, and the play is a poem inasmuch as it lays bare, as did *Yerma*, the inner life of its protagonist.

After her parents' deaths, the orphaned Rosita has been raised by her aunt and uncle, and at twenty years of age she is engaged to be married to her cousin. However, before the marriage can take place he is obliged to return to South America. Although he vows to return, fifteen years later Rosita is still waiting, her only consolation her fiancé's letters.[2] But she is overjoyed when he informs her that they can be married by proxy, after which he will soon be with her once more. Ten more years elapse, Rosita's kindly uncle is dead, and for financial reasons her aunt is obliged to move to a smaller house. By this stage Rosita has

157

abandoned all hope of her fiancé's return. Indeed, she has discovered that he is already married. As she and her aunt prepare to leave the house where they have lived for many years, Rosita faces a bleak future, made worse by the knowledge that her friends are married and have children.

Doña Rosita the Spinster is in many respects Lorca's most personal play, or at least the play in which there are most personal reminiscences. While he was working on it in 1934, he spoke of his intentions to Alardo Prats, a journalist for *El Sol*:

> It will be a piece with many gentle ironies and examples of tender caricature; a comedy of middle-class manners, with soft tones, containing the charm and delicacy of moments and times past. I believe that people will be surprised by this recreation of past times, when nightingales genuinely sang and gardens and flowers appeared as subjects in novels. That marvellous period when our parents were young. First, the time of the hooped skirt; then the bell-shaped skirt and the hobble; 1890, 1900, 1910.[3]

But if this statement suggests an evocation of the past, he also observed in 1935 that the play's principal concern was 'the tragic aspect of our social life: all those Spanish women who never found a husband'.[4] It was a theme that he had explored in earlier poems and plays, would do so again in *The House of Bernarda Alba*, and which, in the end, paralleled his own situation. Rosita the Spinster is to a large extent the female equivalent of Lorca the single man. But she is also the centrepiece of a play in which Lorca drew heavily on other aspects of his life, including people he knew or had known.

The Housekeeper, a brilliantly drawn character, is based on many servants who had worked for the Lorca family over the years, but in particular on Dolores Cuesta, of whom Lorca himself was particularly fond. Don Martín, the teacher of Act Three, is an amalgam of two teachers who had taught him in Granada.[5] The first, Antonio Segura Mesa, had been his music teacher, the composer of a failed one-act opera called *The Daughters of Jephthah*, which in *Doña Rosita* becomes Don Martín's unsuccessful play, *The Daughter of Jephthah*. The second, Martín Scheroff y Aví, taught Literature and Rhetoric at the College of the Sacred Heart of Jesus, which Lorca attended from 1909 to 1915. Like Lorca's Don Martín, the real-life teacher lived alone, wrote stories and poems in an old-fashioned, high-flown style, and was the constant butt of his pupils' practical jokes. Mr Consuegra, another teacher mentioned by Don Martín as having had cat droppings smeared on his class register (p. 142), was also based on a teacher at the college; Mr X, the eccentric Professor of Economics of Act Two, was modelled on the real-life Ramón Guixé y Mexía; the father of the Ayola girls, described in Act Two as being 'photographer to his Majesty the King', did in fact hold that position; and the two well-to-do families, the Ponce de Leóns and the Herrastis, mentioned by the three spinsters as being friends of theirs (p. 126), were well known in Granada society. As well as this, the three *manolas*, who appear in Act One, and who are described by Rosita as going to the Alhambra in search of love, had their origin in three girls whom Lorca knew. These three were always together and they lived on the hill, the Cuesta de Gomérez, which leads to the Alhambra Wood.

Rosita herself is a composite of several women known to Lorca, one of whom was Emilia Llanos, whom he had met when he was only twenty and who at that time lived in a house near the Alhambra. Although he was impressed by her beauty and attractive personality, Lorca had presumably been unable to respond to her sexually, while she, attracted to him, subsequently saw him as her lost love and became more and more like Rosita. In other ways there are echoes, too, of Lorca's mother, Vicenta. At the beginning of the play, set in 1890, Rosita is twenty, the same age as Vicenta would then have been.[6] Before her marriage, Vicenta's life was difficult, she and her widowed mother often had to move house for financial reasons, and on one occasion, like Rosita at the end of Act Three, were obliged to abandon a villa for a less expensive property.

As for the location of the house in which Rosita lives with her aunt and uncle, it is a place which Lorca knew and loved: the district of Granada opposite the Alhambra known as the Albaicín.[7] The house itself is a *carmen*, a villa with an enclosed garden, of which there were many in that hilly area. Indeed, Lorca was a frequent visitor from 1920 onwards to the *carmen* owned by Manuel de Falla near the Alhambra itself. Such houses were for him places of enchantment. On the other hand, he felt, too, that to live there alone, without the person one loves, would be a kind of physical and emotional imprisonment, exacerbated by the beauty of the flowers and vegetation surrounding these lovely, whitewashed houses. In a way the *carmen* was for Lorca a symbol of Granada itself, a town whose beauty inspired him but where he also often felt imprisoned both by his own sexuality and the narrow-mindedness of the people.

One other source remains to be considered, that of the origin of the mutable rose, which lasts for only one day – red in the morning, white by evening, withered away during the night – and with which Rosita herself is compared throughout the play. Lorca was quite specific on this point:

> I had the idea for my latest play, *Doña Rosita la soltera*, in 1924. My friend Moreno Villa said to me one day: 'I am going to tell you the charming story of the life of a flower – the mutable rose – from a seventeenth-century book about roses.' And so he began: 'Once upon a time there was a rose . . .' And by the time he had finished the wonderful tale of the rose, I had written my play. It came to me already completed, unique, impossible to change.[8]

This was, of course, a typical exaggeration, but, as in the case of the newspaper reports that inspired *Blood Wedding*, a seed was sown in Lorca's imagination that would grow over the next ten years. In addition to the central image of the rose, Act Two contains a song, 'What the Flowers Say', which is sung by all those on stage to a piano

Lorca in Granada in 1919, aged twenty-one

By permission of the Fundación Federico García Lorca

Lorca (left) and Salvador Dalí in Cadaqués, 1927
By permission of the Fundación Federico García Lorca

Lorca (far right) in New York in the Autumn of 1929, accompanied by, from left to right, a pianist from Hawaii, a Hindu dancer and Maria Antonia Rivas Blair

Lorca (left) and Luis Buñuel at the Residencia de Estudiantes, Madrid, 1922

Lorca (right) and Emilio Aladrén, c. 1928

The production by La Barraca of Calderón's religious play *Life Is a Dream* in 1932

The production of *Blood Wedding*, directed by José Tamayo, at the Teatro
Bellas Artes, Madrid, 1962: Act Two, Scene One

The production of *Blood Wedding*, directed by José Tamayo, at the Teatro Bellas Artes, Madrid, 1962: end of Act Two

By permission of the Centro de Documentación Teatral, Madrid

The production of *Yerma*, directed by Cipriano Rivas Cherif, at the Teatro Español, Madrid, 1934: the fertility rite

By permission of the Fundación Federico García Lorca

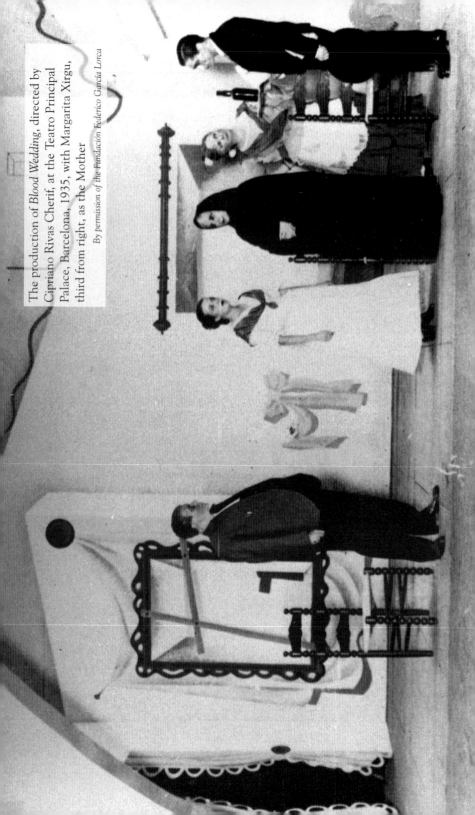

The production of *Blood Wedding*, directed by Cipriano Rivas Cherif, at the Teatro Principal Palace, Barcelona, 1935, with Margarita Xirgu, third from right, as the Mother

By permission of the Fundación Federico García Lorca

The production of *The House of Bernarda Alba*, directed by Juan Antonio Bardem, at the Teatro Goya, Madrid, 1964: the mourners in Act One

By permission of the Centro de Documentación Teatral, Madrid

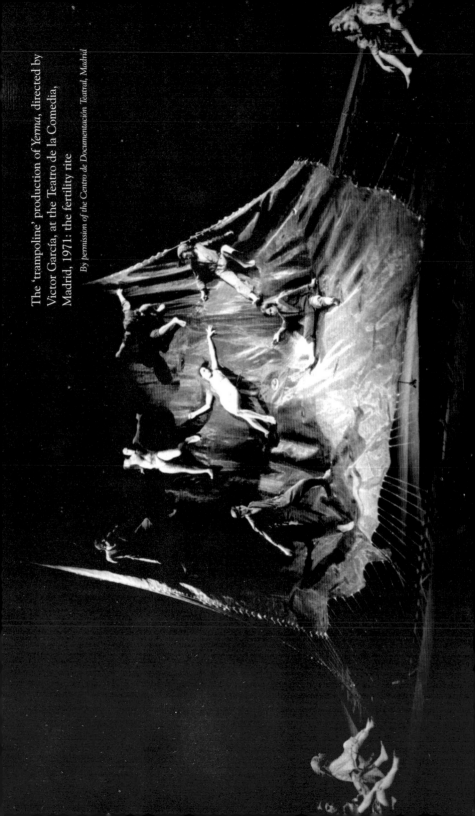

The 'trampoline' production of *Yerma*, directed by Victor García, at the Teatro de la Comedia, Madrid, 1971: the fertility rite

By permission of the Centro de Documentación Teatral, Madrid

The production of *Blood Wedding*, directed by Anthony Clark, at the Contact Theatre, Manchester, 1987: the wedding guests

The production of *When Five Years Pass*, directed by
Robert Delamere and Maria Delgado at the Edinburgh
Fringe Festival, 1989: the Girlfriend and the Father,
Act Two

The production of *Doña Rosita the Spinster*, directed by
Phyllida Lloyd, at the Theatre Royal, Bristol, 1989

The production of *Blood Wedding*, directed by
Sue Lefton, at the Mercury Theatre, Colchester,
2001: the Mother and the Bridegroom

The production of *Blood Wedding*, directed by
Julia Bardsley, at the Haymarket Theatre,
Leicester, 1992: the Moon

The Lorca family house in the village of Valderrubio (formerly Asquerosa) near Granada, one source of inspiration for *The House of Bernarda Alba*

The house in Valderrubio once occupied by Frasquita Alba

accompaniment, and which associates different flowers with the different emotions connected with love. Lorca's brother has suggested that its source was a small book that also contained the language of fans, stamps and various other things.[9] Flowers play an important part in Lorca's work, for the most part in a symbolic sense, but in *Doña Rosita* they appear in profusion. In Granada and the surrounding area he was, of course, surrounded by flowers of all kinds, and in particular he was a frequent visitor to the gardens of the Generalife in the Alhambra. But in Easter week of 1935 Lorca had also visited Seville, where he stayed with Joaquín Romero Murube, keeper of the Arab palace known as the Alcázar. It, too, had wonderful gardens, as it still does, and Lorca evidently had ample opportunity to discuss with the gardeners the nature and variety of flowers cultivated there.

In addition to drawing to a large extent on his own memories when writing *Doña Rosita*, Lorca also explored those personal preoccupations that are to be found in his other plays. Over the two decades or so of the action of the play Rosita's beauty, like that of the rose, begins to fade. One of the play's major themes, therefore, is the theme of passing time, which Lorca had previously made one of the principal themes of *When Five Years Pass*. In the earlier play the Young Man had dreamt of meeting the Girlfriend in five years' time, while here Rosita dreams of her fiancé's return from South America. Her comment in Act Three – '. . . my back will become more bent with every passing day' (p. 150) – is a variation on the Second Friend's remark to the Old Man in the earlier play: '. . . I don't want to be all wrinkles and aches like you' (p. 142). And earlier in the play, when she is only twenty, the Housekeeper describes Rosita's zest for life – 'She wants everything at top speed' (p. 101) – in terms which are strongly reminiscent of the Friend of *When Five Years Pass*: 'I've no time. No time for anything. Everything's rushing by' (p. 131). Furthermore, in Act Three Rosita is conscious not only of the change in her physical appearance but of the way the world is changing around her:

One day a friend gets married, and then another, and yet another, and the next day she has a son, and the son grows up and comes to show me his examination marks. Or there are new houses and new songs . . . And then one day I'm out walking, and I suddenly realize I don't know anyone. (pp. 148–9)

This recalls the Old Man's ominous statement in Act One of *When Five Years Pass*: 'Our clothes wear out, anchors rust and we move on . . . Houses crumble to dust' (p. 142). The theme of passing time is, to a greater or lesser extent, present throughout Lorca's work, but as he himself grew older – he completed *Doña Rosita* at the age of thirty-seven – it seems to acquire a greater poignancy, almost as though Lorca felt that he did not have much time left.

The theme of love is also, as in his other plays, central to *Doña Rosita*, but it is presented somewhat differently. There is none of the blazing passion that drives the Bride of *Blood Wedding* to abandon her husband in favour of Leonardo, or Adela to risk all for the experience of physical pleasure with Pepe el Romano in *The House of Bernarda Alba*. On the contrary, when the Nephew says goodbye to Rosita in Act One, it is to the accompaniment of a Czerny *étude*, the mood one of romantic sentimentality in which physical passion seems to have no place.[10] Subsequently, Rosita's feelings for her cousin are sustained by the exchange of letters and are less to do with reality than with hopes and illusions. Indeed, fifteen years after his departure, Rosita has forgotten what he looks like, and her vision of him has supplanted the reality, as the Housekeeper observes in Act Two: 'Yesterday she had me with her all day long at the entrance to the circus. She insisted that one of the puppeteers looked like her cousin . . . He wasn't a bit like him' (p. 118). In this respect she parallels the Young Man of *When Five Years Pass*, who, in Act One, imagines the Girlfriend, 'her long golden hair around my neck', but is at once reminded by the Old Man that she does not have long hair (p. 127). And Rosita is also reminiscent in many ways of Mariana Pineda, who, in Act Three, clings to the hope that her beloved Pedro will soon return to rescue her from imprisonment, only to be told that he has gone forever. Both *Mariana Pineda* and *Doña Rosita* are about the illusion of love and, even more importantly, its betrayal. Lorca, as we know, was only too aware of the bitterness of betrayal, feeling himself to have been abandoned by Dalí and Aladrén. Furthermore, although he did not complete *Doña Rosita* until 1935, it seems likely that he had been working on it as much as five years earlier, for during his stay in Cuba in 1930 he sang to Dulce María Loynaz some of the songs from Act One.[11] So Lorca's sense of betrayal would have been fresh in his mind and would, therefore, have acquired a much more poignant resonance in *Doña Rosita* than had been the case in *Mariana Pineda*. Undoubtedly, *Doña Rosita* is a much better and more mature play, and much of that maturity is surely due to Lorca's experience of life, both bitter and sweet, during the intervening years.[12]

Doña Rosita is also the only Lorca play in which the Granada middle class figures so strongly. During the 1920s and 1930s the bourgeoisie was, of course, a favourite target for the Surrealists for a variety of reasons. They considered, for example, that the combined influence of material wealth, education and religious indoctrination had had the effect of alienating many individuals from their true feelings by creating in them an impenetrable layer of pretentiousness, elegance and good manners. Furthermore, the bourgeoisie was characterized by a strong sense of self-satisfaction as well as a violent dislike of anyone who seemed to be a threat to their status or who did not conform to their standards. Consequently, the avant-garde movements and creative artists of the time – Surrealists, Futurists, Dadaists – launched the most ferocious attacks on all that they considered conventional and bourgeois. Buñuel, in particular, in films such as *Un Chien andalou* (1929) and *L'Age d'or* (1930) set out to expose bourgeois pretension and hypocrisy, and the bourgeoisie's incapacity for genuine feeling. As for Lorca, he was only too aware of the conservative and intolerant nature of the Granada middle class, conditioned by narrow-minded

Catholicism. Had they not, through their official representatives, made gypsies, Jews and Muslims their scapegoats over many years? Had they not looked with suspicion on the artists who met regularly at the Café Alameda in Granada, Lorca amongst them? Had they not vilified the members of La Barraca, characterizing them as homosexuals? Furthermore, by 1935 right-wing intolerance had become distinctly menacing throughout Spain, fanned by the spread of Fascism in Europe. In this regard *Doña Rosita* is, of course, a play set in the past, not the present – and it is not a direct comment on the Granada bourgeoisie of 1935 in the way that *Play Without a Title* would be a year later – but even though Lorca evoked in *Doña Rosita* a Granada of the past, the play was also in many respects a mirror to the present, for little had changed in a society and in a class whose survival depended on resistance to change.

As she grows older, Rosita, like so many spinsters in a society where marriage and children were regarded as a woman's main objective in life, becomes the object of people's mockery. In her long and impassioned speech in Act Three, she comments bitterly on the callous nature of public opinion: 'But everyone knew the truth and I'd find myself picked out by a pointing finger that ridiculed the modesty of a girl soon to be married and made grotesque the fan of a girl who was still single . . .' (p. 148). And just as she is the butt of adult scorn, so she is too of children who, parrot-fashion, imitate their parents: 'Girls and boys leave me behind because I can't keep up, and one of them says: "There's the old maid"; and another one, a good-looking boy with curly hair says: "No-one's going to fancy her again" ' (p. 149). In this way Rosita is little different from Yerma, singled out for her childlessness and branded with the name 'barren' – or, indeed, Lorca himself, persecuted for his homosexuality. Twenty-one years later, the film-director Juan Antonio Bardem portrayed a similar situation in his magnificent film *Calle Mayor* (*Main Street*). Set in a provincial town, *Calle Mayor* is the story of Isabel, a thirty-six-year-old spinster whose life revolves around her widowed mother, the family home and regular churchgoing. Marriage appears to be a possibility when Juan enters her life, but his courtship of Isabel is merely a trick designed to provide him and his bored friends with some amusement at the expense of a gullible spinster, and in the end, having proposed marriage, he cruelly abandons her, thereby ensuring that she will become the object of even greater mockery. Such attitudes towards spinsters and other 'abnormal' individuals were deeply ingrained in Spanish society, and continue to be so in the more remote and traditional areas of Spain.

Act Three of *Doña Rosita* also contains an account by the school-teacher, Don Martín, of the lack of respect shown to himself and his colleagues by the children of wealthy parents:

> They are all the children of rich parents, so they pay and you can't punish them . . . Believe me, the parents only laugh at the wicked pranks they play on us, because we are only assistant teachers and we don't examine the children. They think we have no feelings – for them we are people perched on the lowest rung of the social ladder . . .'
> (pp. 141–2)

Lorca, as a supporter of liberal ideas, felt very strongly about the exploitation of the poor and underprivileged by the rich. He was well aware, for example, of the extent to which the wealthy landowners exploited their workers, obliging them to work long hours in intolerable conditions for a few pesetas a day. The former's contempt for their employees is perfectly summed up by Bernarda Alba – even though her wealth is relatively limited – in Act One of the play which quickly followed on the heels of *Doña Rosita*: 'The poor are like animals. It's as if they are made of different stuff' (p. 13). And just as the landowners took advantage of their workers, so she has little compassion for her servants: 'You serve me and I pay you. Nothing more!' (p. 29). *The House of Bernarda Alba* is not primarily a political play, *Doña Rosita* even less so, but both reveal very clearly the lack of charity of a wealthy class which Lorca despised.

Lorca also lays bare bourgeois pretension and snobbery in Act Two of *Doña Rosita*. The Mother and her three unmarried daughters have, since the death of the father, fallen on hard times, but they still strive to keep up appearances, as the Mother explains:

> But even so, we've managed to keep our position in society. What agony I've gone through, madam, so that my girls shouldn't be deprived of hats! I've shed many a tear, sighed many a sigh on account of a ribbon or an arrangement of curls! Those feathers and wires have cost me many a sleepless night. (p. 125)

The great thing was, indeed, to be seen walking out in the evening and to be dressed for the occasion, which in the case of these three girls means sacrificing food. As the Mother notes: 'Many's the time I say to them: "Now what do you really want, dear girls? An egg for breakfast or a chair when you promenade"? They all reply together: "A chair"' (p. 125). Shortly afterwards, because it is Rosita's birthday, the Mother and the three daughters are joined by the two Ayola sisters, daughters of the photographer to the king. They, of course, have the money that the others lack, which doubtless explains why they are so silly and superficial, giggling and laughing at every opportunity. So, when they are offered a sweet: 'Oh, no! We ate just a little while ago. To tell the truth, I had four eggs with tomato sauce. I could hardly get up from the chair . . . *The AYOLAS begin an uncontrollable laughter . . .*' (p. 127). All these characters are, it is important to emphasize, presented from a comic perspective, and it is also true to say that Lorca laughs with them rather than at them. But this does not mean that the bourgeois vices of pretentiousness, snobbery and superficiality are in any way glossed over.

The play is a poem – as suggested by the subtitle – in the sense that, at times, it is highly lyrical and, above all, lays bare the inner life of Rosita herself, subjected to increasing pain and disillusionment. It is a comedy – as Lorca stated in his interview in *El Sol* – because it puts on stage a variety of characters, from Rosita's uncle to the Housekeeper,

Mr X, the Mother and her daughters, the Ayola sisters and Don Martín, all of whom make us laugh. The two elements – the poetic and the comic – appear to be contradictory, mutually exclusive, yet Lorca, in this play, weaves them together with the touch of a master, allowing the one to offset the other in a way which enhances both and which captures perfectly the contrasts of life itself.

The juxtaposition of laughter and tears was, in any case, part of Lorca's personality. On the one hand, he could be outgoing and extrovert, the centre of attention in any group of which he was a part, someone who could appreciate to the full the joys that life had to offer, while on the other, he often plumbed the depths of despair, as his depression in 1929 shows. The lighter side of his personality took pleasure in the long tradition of Spanish comic theatre from the sixteenth to the twentieth century. In the mid-sixteenth century, Lope de Rueda, regarded by many as the father of the Spanish theatre, had composed a number of short comic plays distinguished by boldly drawn comic characters and situations, while in 1615 Cervantes had published his collection of short comic plays known as *entremeses*, originally intended to be performed between the acts of full-length plays. That Lorca responded to these comic pieces is illustrated by the fact that three of the *entremeses* formed part of La Barraca's first tour in the summer of 1932, directed by Lorca himself. In addition, as we know, he had a great love of puppet-theatre, of which there was also a long Spanish tradition – Cervantes had introduced *Master Peter's Puppet Show* into the second part of *Don Quixote* (1615). In the Madrid of Lorca's time the puppet-show was an extremely popular entertainment, particularly in the Retiro Park where Lorca, Buñuel and another friend, Juan Chabas, helped the puppeteer, Mayeau, in the preparation of shows, which were also presented at the Residencia de Estudiantes. Furthermore, there were many examples both of puppet-plays and of broad farce in contemporary Spanish theatre. In *The Horns of Don Friolera*, written in 1921, Ramón del Valle-Inclán had introduced a puppet-show into the prologue to the play in which the

human characters take on the broad and often grotesque characteristics of the puppets themselves. In the same year, Jacinto Grau's *Mr
Pygmalion* appeared, in which the eponymous protagonist creates a
number of life-size puppets with human characteristics. And Carlos
Arniches, although not writing puppet-plays, produced a body of work
amongst which grotesque farces figure prominently.[13]

Lorca's work prior to *Doña Rosita* often drew heavily on these
Spanish traditions of farce and puppet-play. *The Tragicomedy of Don
Cristóbal and Señorita Rosita* and the much shorter *The Puppet-Play of
Don Cristóbal* are firmly in that tradition. Nevertheless, even in these
highly comic pieces there are suggestions of a seriousness, even of a
melancholy, which points to the synthesis of comic and dark elements
in Lorca's later work. This process is taken further, of course, in *The
Shoemaker's Wonderful Wife* and *The Love of Don Perlimplín*. In the
former, subtitled *A Violent Farce*, the broadly comic episodes in which
the characters stamp, storm about the stage and scream at each other
in a manner reminiscent of puppets, are interspersed with much more
serious moments, not least in the episode in which the Wife and the
Boy attempt to catch the butterfly, and, later, when she imagines her
ageing husband as a young and handsome lover. As for *The Love of
Don Perlimplín*, its farcical and grotesque elements are accompanied by
our awareness of the protagonist's sad plight – his discovery of his
impotence on his wedding-night – and his tragic realization that only
by disguising himself as a young man can he make the beautiful Belisa
love him. The three rural tragedies are by their very nature much
darker, but even in *Blood Wedding* there are flashes of humour, while in
The House of Bernarda Alba the Housekeeper's stories – of her relationship with her husband, for example – are as much a source of amusement
to the daughters as they are to the audience. Thus, the comic and the
serious run side by side throughout Lorca's work, reflecting the two sides
of his personality as well as a rich Spanish theatrical tradition. But
nowhere are they as finely or as consistently interwoven as in *Doña
Rosita*.

The comic note is probably at its most striking in relation to the presentation of the Mother and her three spinster daughters in Act Two. Their physical appearance, described in some detail in Lorca's stage direction, contains an element of caricature which places them firmly in the context of the earlier comic works:

> *The three pretentious girls enter with their mother. The* THREE SPINSTERS *wear huge hats with tasteless feathers, ridiculous dresses, gloves to the elbow with bracelets over them, and fans dangling from long chains. The* MOTHER *wears a faded black dress and a hat with old purple ribbons.* (p. 124)

Their conversation, furthermore, reveals both their pretentiousness and their lack of means, an incongruity which proves to be a rich source of humour:

> MOTHER: . . . We may have to eat potatoes or a bunch of grapes, but we've still got our Mongolian cape, or a painted parasol, or a poplinette blouse with all the trimmings . . . (p. 126)

And when the Ayola girls enter just afterwards, their appearance – 'They are richly dressed in the greatly exaggerated style of the period' (p. 127) – combines with their silly laughter to continue the comic effect. This is then sustained both in the spectacle of the Mother gradually becoming more drunk and in the song 'What the Flowers Say', which the assembled group sings around the piano, the song often comic in itself but potentially more comic still if the voices which sing the individual stanzas are not of the best.

The play also features a number of other comic characters and scenes. Although Mr X, who appears at the beginning of Act Two, is not described in physical terms, his statements pinpoint him as an incredibly pompous individual and a constant name-dropper. The Housekeeper, although not caricatured in the same way, frequently comments on characters and events going on around her in a highly comic manner, as in the case of the Uncle's watering of his plants and seeds: 'Yes, madam. But *I* don't say with all this spraying and all this water everywhere we'll soon have toads coming out of the sofa!' (p. 99). And there is humour too in her superstitious nature, as in the case of the curse which she places on the Nephew when he leaves Rosita:

> Let him have sleepless nights,
> Let the seed that he sows die,
> And by St Nicholas' well
> Let his salt turn to poison. (p. 107)

In Act Three Don Martín, although Lorca is entirely sympathetic towards him, strikes a comic note because his dreams of being a poet are totally at odds with his lack of poetic inspiration. Thus, the lines from his unperformed play, which he thinks have a 'fine ring' to them, could not be more bombastic:

> Oh, mother unequalled! Turn your eyes on
> Her who lies before you in wretched trance!
> Receive unto yourself these glittering jewels!
> Observe the terrible horror of death's advance! (pp. 142–3)

Given the above, one of the distinguishing notes about *Doña Rosita* is that the comic moments themselves have in many cases an underlying pathos. No sooner has Don Martín left because the children at his school 'have stuck a nail through the water-pipes', than the Housekeeper reveals his terrible circumstances: 'When he was ill, I took him some custard, and the sheets on his bed were as black as coal – and the walls, and the washbasin . . .' (p. 145). In Act Two, the ridiculous nature of the Mother's and the spinsters' appearance and the pretentiousness of their aspirations cannot conceal their straightened circumstances or their empty future. Similarly, in Act Three, the Housekeeper's comic attempts to cheer up the now widowed Aunt serve merely to emphasize their growing loneliness and isolation.

Many of the play's comic scenes either precede or follow episodes of high emotion. Thus, in Act One, the Uncle's fussing over his trampled seeds comes just before the nephew's announcement of his leaving Rosita for South America, the Aunt's angry exchanges with him and the highly lyrical scenes between Rosita and the three Manolas and then Rosita and the Nephew. And in Act Two, the comic interlude involving the Mother and her daughters follows on from the episode in which Rosita speaks with the Aunt of the anguish she feels at time's passing and her fiancé's failure to return. Throughout this play, then, laughter and tears walk hand in hand, sometimes juxtaposed, sometimes interwoven with each other. It is a balancing act of great delicacy, but Lorca handles it superbly.

True to Lorca's ideas on theatre, *Doña Rosita* is also highly stylized. His suggested settings for each act are as simple and as stripped of realistic detail as anything in his other plays. For Act One the setting is merely '*A room leading to a greenhouse*' (p. 99), for Act Two '*A room in DOÑA ROSITA's house. The garden in the background*' (p. 115) and for Act Three '*A small sitting room with green shutters opening on to the garden*' (p. 137). There is little indication here, therefore, that the three acts are set in specific periods, which suggests, in turn, that Lorca wished to use the settings merely as simple frames in which to place the characters. They, however, are dressed in period style. When Rosita first appears, she wears '*a rose-coloured dress, in the style of 1900, with leg-of-mutton sleeves and trimmed with braid*' (p. 100), in Act Two she '*is dressed in pink. The styles have changed from the leg-of-mutton sleeves of 1900. Her skirt is bell-shaped*' (p. 122) and in Act Three she '*wears a light pink dress in the style of 1910*' (p. 139), which finally becomes a white dress (p. 154). Costume itself is, therefore, used to denote period, but, in typical Lorca fashion, the dresses are bold and simple rather than fussily realistic. Furthermore, the colours of the various dresses – red, pink, light pink, white – are firmly linked to the cycle of mutable rose, and so they become important not for their realism – the dresses could equally have other colours – but for their significance as metaphor, as stylized symbols of the passage of time and of Rosita's fading beauty and hope. Similarly, the costumes of the Mother, her three daughters and the Ayola girls are vivid visual pointers to their characters.

In the same way, the directions for movement speak volumes. In the early part of the play 'ROSITA *rushes in*' (p. 100), demanding her hat, the Aunt and the Housekeeper look for it, find it, 'ROSITA *grabs the hat and rushes out*' (p. 101). The Housekeeper's comment that Rosita 'wants everything at top speed' (p. 101) suggests the excitement of youth and the love of life which the young woman's dashing in and out encapsulates, and it is repeated shortly afterwards when she rushes in in search of her parasol. In complete contrast, the scene in which the Nephew takes his leave of her is largely static, its lack of movement a pointer to the way in which Rosita's earlier high spirits have been transformed into despair. In Act Two the Mother and her daughters and the Ayola girls introduce a much more vigorous note, while Rosita's restless pacing of the room reveals her anxiety as she waits for the postman's arrival. When he is seen approaching, there is general excitement, which becomes a vigorous polka when it is revealed that Rosita is to be married by proxy. By the beginning of Act Three everything has changed: the Uncle is dead, time has moved on, the house must be sold, Rosita's hopes of marriage have finally vanished. The sombre mood is reflected in the Aunt who sits, in Don Martín's slow and laboured movement and, finally, in Rosita's stumble as she leaves the house for ever, supported by the Aunt and the Housekeeper. From beginning to end Lorca suggests the movement of the characters as precisely as he does in all his plays, as though he were a choreographer.

His directions for lighting correspond to Rosita's journey from optimism to despair. Initially, the stage is full of brightness, matching her vivid dress and animated mood. Act Two, which ends on a spirited note, repeats this pattern. But Act Three, marked by growing despair, is entirely different. It begins at six in the evening and ends as darkness is beginning to fall and storm clouds gather overhead. Here, as elsewhere, Lorca sees the lighting of the stage as an integral part of the play, a barometer for the changing moods and experiences of the characters.

The stylization evident in costume, movement and lighting is also present in the language, refuting any possibility that *Doña Rosita* could be a naturalistic play. In Act One in particular, and to a lesser extent later on, passages of formal verse disrupt and slow the momentum. First, there is the poem about the mutable rose (pp. 102–3), which appears again at the end of Act One, at the end of Act Two (in a somewhat different form) and again in an amended form near the end of Act Three. In Act One the whole of the episode involving Rosita and the Manolas is in verse, and this is followed almost immediately by another verse scene, when Rosita and her fiancé say goodbye. Consequently, in each case the emotional tone of the scene is heightened, for what we might call the ordinary day-to-day conversations of the characters suddenly become an episode in which the focus of attention narrows, emotion becomes more intense, and the language, now full of evocative simile and metaphor, underlines the emotion. These episodes are, as it were, peaks in the landscape of the play, but even so the surrounding prose dialogue is also far from being naturalistic. There are, indeed, a number of set-pieces in prose which have the repeated patterns, the insistent rhythm and the emotional intensity of poetry: Rosita's great speech in Act Three – 'I've become accustomed to living outside myself . . .' (p. 148) – is one example, but there are others, too: in the same act, the Housekeeper's speech about her dead husband and daughter (p. 140), as well as her vision of the Aunt, the Uncle, Rosita and herself together in heaven (p. 146); at the beginning of the play the Uncle's description of his roses (p. 102); and, in a rather different way, even Don Martín's account during Act Three of the tricks played by the children at school (pp. 141–2). Furthermore, even what we might call the 'ordinary' dialogue of the play is seen, on closer inspection, not only to be carefully structured around the principal themes of frustration, passing time and fading beauty, but also to be less ordinary than we might think. When, for example, the Aunt berates the Nephew in Act One for leaving Rosita, she does so in language that can hardly be described as naturalistic: 'You are going to pierce her heart with an arrow of purple ribbons. Now she's about to learn that a piece of linen's not just to embroider flowers. It's also to dry one's tears' (p. 105). Lorca rarely thought in terms of flat, unadorned prose.

Doña Rosita received its première on 12 December 1935 at the Teatro Principal Palace in Barcelona, where it was performed by the company of Margarita Xirgu, and directed by Cipriano Rivas Cherif, with the stage-design by Manuel Fontanals, the same team that had been involved in the staging of *Yerma* in Madrid one year earlier. As on that occasion, Lorca himself was once again involved in the production. Indeed, it seems that Lorca had written the part of Rosita with Xirgu in mind. Five months prior to the production he read the play to her, her husband and Rivas Cherif at a hotel in the mountains outside Madrid. Subsequently, he and Xirgu worked on it closely together, and, according to Antonina Rodrigo, spent hours discussing aspects of its staging.[14] In the production Lorca was himself responsible for the music. In short, as in the case of *Blood Wedding* and *Yerma*, Lorca was in no way a passive observer.

The opening night was an unqualified triumph. Writing in the Barcelona newspaper *La Vanguardia*, María Luz Morales suggested that

> this play affirms, without any question, his [Lorca's] vocation and direction as a dramatist . . . It is a play of fine literary quality, but its essence – I repeat – is theatrical. It can be favourably compared with the best productions in European theatre today . . .[15]

And Antonio Espina, the theatre critic of *El Sol*, shared this opinion:

Doña Rosita . . . is not just another good play amongst the few in contemporary Spanish theatre. It is an extraordinary play by a writer who
combines his great poetic gifts with the no less worthy talents of a
great dramatist.[16]

The earlier discussion of the play's stylization referred to the
simple, uncluttered nature of Lorca's ideas for sets, as suggested in the
published text. In the Barcelona production, however, that simplicity
seems to have disappeared in favour of a desire to create on stage a
realistic interior of a house, which, in that respect, was not very different from the sets of the comedies which flooded the commercial
theatre of Madrid and Barcelona. A photograph of the set for Act
One, for example, shows Rosita and the three Manolas against a background consisting of a large window flanked by heavy curtains. To
either side of the window, the walls of the room are decorated with
striped wallpaper along with portraits and paintings of traditional
landscapes, and the set is furnished with tables and velvet-backed
chairs. Nothing could be further removed from Fontanals' sets for
Yerma. On the other hand, the costumes corresponded closely to those
indicated in Lorca's stage-directions. In her review of the production,
Luz Morales noted for the first act that 'Rosita is an opening bud, in
colour the most brilliant red, like her friends the Manolas'. Although
there is no reference in either this or in Antonio Espina's review to the
colour of her dresses in Acts Two and Three, they would probably have
been pink and white, for both reviewers' descriptions of the Mother
and her daughters in Act Two suggest quite clearly that, in terms of
costume, Lorca's suggestions were faithfully carried out. Luz Morales
observed that their exaggerated clothes and jewellery introduced a
grotesque note to the second act, a point illustrated by a photograph
in which their exaggerated hats are evident.

The reviews also praised the character of the play and the acting,
in particular that of Margarita Xirgu. Antonio Espina was impressed
by the manner in which she succeeded in communicating the charac-

ter's changing emotions in the course of the three acts, and by how the actress suggested every emotional nuance by means of movement, gesture and, of course, speech. In her study of Margarita Xirgu's life and art, Antonina Rodrigo comments on the actress's skill in all these areas, and mentions in particular her use of her hands – an aspect of her acting previously praised by the Quintero brothers:

> Margarita's hands accompany very effectively her facial expressions, enlivening them, enhancing them, emphasizing them . . . It is a colour which reinforces another, a light which adds lustre, a silent music which completes a different melody: that from her lips . . .[17]

In photographs of the production, her hands are, indeed, much in evidence, and would have contributed as much to the portrayal of Rosita as they had done to the characterization of Yerma and the Mother in *Blood Wedding*. Of Xirgu's performance as a whole, Espina concluded: 'The character of Doña Rosita has become an unsurpass- able, unforgettable creation . . . in the career of our wonderful actress. Those present rewarded Margarita Xirgu with repeated curtain-calls.' But the company was praised, too, not so much individually but as a whole, pointing to the fact that, as had been the case in *Blood Wedding*, Margarita Xirgu led a true ensemble. Lorca, given his own experience with La Barraca, would have thoroughly approved.

For whatever reason, *Doña Rosita* did not have another major production in Spain until 1980, forty-five years after its initial staging. On this occasion the play was produced by the Centro Dramático Nacional, the Spanish National Theatre based in Madrid, and the role of Rosita was played by Nuria Espert, who, nine years earlier, had played Yerma in Victor García's famous trampoline production. The director was Jorge Lavelli, an Argentinian with great experience of both Spanish and European theatre in general. His production makes for an interesting comparison with the earlier one.[18]

Photographs of the set, designed by Max Bignens, immediately reveal a stylization which was absent from the stage design in 1935. The action of all three acts took place in a single room, but this was evoked simply and boldly, not by means of fussy realistic detail. Up-stage were two large wardrobes with mirrored doors, one on either side and at a slight angle. Across the back of the stage, at regular intervals, were a number of wooden frames that suggested doorways but which also, because they were open frames, revealed rows of shelves on which the Uncle kept his flower pots. Greenery suspended above accentuated the botanical flavour, but otherwise, apart from one or two chairs, the stage was totally bare. With the removal of the furniture in Act Three, the frames and shelves, now almost bare of flower-pots, suggested less a room than the skeleton of a room. When this production was presented at the Edinburgh International Festival in the summer of 1983, Robert Cushman noted in the *Observer* that the set was 'used to frame a production'.[19] That assessment is undoubtedly true, but it is also important to add that the uncluttered stage design, as well as evoking the essential elements of the play, allowed the attention to fall squarely on the acting area and on the actors themselves.

As for the costumes, B.A. Young, writing in the *Financial Times*, noted that in Act One Rosita appeared in a rose-pink dress, 'proudly displaying her enormous trousseau', while in Act Three she was, in Michael Billington's phrase in the *Guardian*, 'a tragic figure in white'.[20, 21] The dresses of the three Manolas in Act One, together with their black mantillas, created a much darker image, which, on the one hand, served to highlight Rosita's youthful optimism and, on the other, anticipated her ultimate sadness. As for the Mother and her daughters in Act Two, they were, as Lorca required, provided with huge feathered hats and extravagant full-length dresses with flounces and tassels, every item of clothing black in colour, reminiscent of great birds. In contrast, the two Ayola girls wore boaters on their heads, and were otherwise dressed in white blouses and trousers, suggesting not only their youth but, given their father's job, their desire to appear modern and fashionable. In Act Three, the Aunt, Don Martín and the

Housekeeper, all of them dressed in black, underlined the darkening mood, while at the very end, Rosita appeared in a long coat which opened at the bottom to reveal her dress, as white as the dying rose. The fact that she dragged her now useless wedding-dress behind her was a sad reminder of her empty future. In visual terms, then, nothing was wasted or out of place in this production.

In the reviews much space was, naturally, given to Espert's performance as Rosita, and they make it clear that she paid as much attention to movement as to the text. Francis King, reviewing the production in the *Sunday Telegraph*, noted that in Act One all is 'bustle as she radiates youth and hope dancing around the wide bare stage'. [22] Later on, however, she became 'a huddled ghost stalking the room, her mirror telling her that it is too late'. And John Barber in the *Daily Telegraph* commented on the way in which, through pure movement, the actress was able to suggest Rosita's growing despair: '. . . the sense of a wasted life is conveyed by a slight crouch, huddled arms, and a habit of walking heavily, as if caged in, around the walls of the room'. [23] Espert's particular skill in this respect was succinctly described by Mary Brennan in the *Glasgow Herald*: 'She has the ability to make every external action seem a spontaneous expression of an inner state.' [24] This emphasis on movement and gesture calls to mind the accounts of Margarita Xirgu's performance forty-five years earlier.

Although the reviewers devoted so much attention to Espert's performance, the acting as a whole received a good deal of praise. John Barber noted that 'the actress-manager is supported by her troupe of eighteen, directed by Jorge Lavelli with tender care', while Mary Brennan concluded that all the varying moods of the play were 'brilliantly conveyed by Julia Martínez, Carmen Bernardos, Carla Lucena and Joaquín Molín'. But the overall quality of this production was best summed up by Michael Billington: '. . . it is to be hoped that Edinburgh audiences won't . . . leave it to the last minute to discover they have a miracle in their midst'.

The first English-language production of *Doña Rosita* in Britain –

in my own translation – took place at the Theatre Royal, Bristol, in October 1989, directed by Phyllida Lloyd. The set, designed by Anthony Ward, evoked a conservatory with a sloping glass roof, covered by white cotton blinds and filled with flower-pots. Cleverly evoking the Uncle's greenhouse, it also implied the enclosed and claustrophobic nature of Rosita's life. When, at the end of the play, the blinds were drawn back to reveal storm clouds scudding across the sky, the effect perfectly underpinned Rosita's desolation. Her costumes – red, pink, white – mirrored throughout the changing nature of her life, and so followed Lorca's own directions. On the other hand, the costumes for the Mother and her daughters were over-exaggerated, as Nicholas de Jongh noted in the *Guardian*: 'The trio of visiting spinsters in livid black, eccentric feathered hats which look as though they would be shot in the countryside . . . are all on the verge of the preposterous.'[25] Quite clearly, they introduced a farcical note which dissipated their potential for pathos. As for the acting, Jeremy Brien, writing in *The Stage*, considered that Susan Curnow as Rosita, Eve Pearce as the Aunt and Sandra Voe as the Housekeeper, contributed 'three superb performances', a point echoed by Michael Schmidt in the *Daily Telegraph*, who concluded that 'Lorca has found unusually sympathetic interpreters at Bristol'.[26, 27]

Phyllida Lloyd was also the director of another production of *Doña Rosita*, which was staged, in the translation by Peter Oswald, at the Almeida Theatre, London, in the spring of 1997. The reviews in this case were rather mixed, and several reviewers, including Benedict Nightingale in *The Times*, felt that the production was 'too English': 'The final impression is of an honourable English stab at a tricky play but maybe too honourable. And certainly too English.'[28]

The conclusion to be drawn is, inevitably, that any director responsible for staging Lorca's work must have a thorough knowledge of it, as well as of the Spanish background that inspires it, a point well illustrated by Sue Lefton's 2001 production of *Blood Wedding* at Colchester.

6
The House of Bernarda Alba:
A Photographic Documentary

The House of Bernarda Alba is the story of a narrow-minded, intolerant and domineering mother, who rules her five spinster daughters with a rod of iron, imposing on them an eight-year period of mourning after the recent death of their father. An arranged marriage between one daughter, Angustias, and a much younger man, Pepe el Romano, inflames the envy and resentment of her sisters, not least because through marriage she will escape the prison-like existence which the other women have to endure. Another daughter, Martirio, who secretly loves Pepe, steals his photograph from Angustias's room. Adela, the youngest and most spirited of all the girls, has also been attracted to him for some time, and now begins to meet him late at night, after he has visited Angustias at her window. However, their illicit affair is exposed by the bitter and resentful Martirio after Adela has been with Pepe in the stable. Adela defies her mother's attempt to impose her authority, vowing that she will continue to see the young man. Bernarda, in response, attempts to shoot him as he escapes on horseback, and a triumphant Martirio informs Adela of his death. Distraught, Adela hangs herself. Bernarda imposes a further period of mourning on the four remaining daughters, and insists that everyone be told that Adela died a virgin.

Lorca completed this powerful story of intolerance and its consequences on 19 June 1936, exactly two months before his own death, itself the result in many ways of his resistance to the conservative values of the Spain in which he lived, and to that extent the play was highly prophetic, Adela being a projection of Lorca himself. The action of the play is set in one house, but that house has its counterpart in other houses in the unnamed village, a village which, precisely because it is unspecified, could be any village in any part of Spain. Indeed, the play's subtitle, *A Drama of Women in the Villages of Spain*, points to this broader meaning.[1] Furthermore, the attitudes and values that lie at the heart of the play were as true in 1936 of a substantial part of the urban Spanish population as they were of smaller communities. In other words, the house in the play, filled with intolerance and racked by internal differences, is the pressure-cooker that was Spain itself a month before the beginning of the Civil War.

By early 1933, the left-wing government that had come to power in 1931 had lost a great deal of support. A general election was set for November in which the Right triumphed, and over the next two years many of the previous administration's policies were overturned, causing serious political upheaval. In October 1934, the trade unions, fearful of the spread of Fascism, called for a general strike, the response to which was especially strong in the Basque region, Catalonia and Asturias, where the coal miners seized control of the capital, Oviedo, and formed a workers' army of thirty thousand armed men. The government immediately imposed martial law and sent in the troops. Towns were shelled, workers were killed or arrested and tortured, and in the course of three weeks of fighting more than a thousand Asturians died, at least three thousand were injured, and more than thirty thousand apprehended. In many ways Asturias proved to be a rehearsal for the brutality that lay ahead, of which Lorca became a well-known casualty. At the same time, the Catalans, led by President Lluís Companys, demanded an independent state. This, too, ended in failure, but both events convinced the Right that the country was on the point of a Moscow-inspired uprising.

By the end of 1935 the right-wing government was in total disarray. Parliament was dissolved at the beginning of 1936, and a general election took place one month later. On this occasion the parties of the Left, now grouped in a broad-based coalition known as the Popular Front, were triumphant, but this in turn hardened the resolve of the

Right. Reacting to the increasing violence perpetrated by right-wing supporters, the new government introduced a state of emergency, imprisoned leading members of the Falangist Party – the focal point of right-wing extremism – and outlawed the Party itself. Far from reducing tension, however, this merely served to fuel it, and between March and July the violence and assassinations increased, including the kidnap and murder of the leading right-wing member of Parliament, José Calvo Sotelo, in retaliation for the killing of José Castillo, a soldier and committed anti-Fascist. In Madrid, Lorca became terrified by such violence and resolved to join his parents in Granada, a decision which proved to be fatal. In Granada opposition to the Left was particularly strong. Right-wing groups disrupted teaching at the university, fought with opponents, and shot at groups of workers. In response, supporters of the Left wrecked and set fire to the offices of right-wing organizations. And, in the meantime, the Falangist Party was in the process of planning with the military an uprising against the Madrid government.

This rebellion was initiated on 17 July 1936, by army officers in Spanish Morocco. On the following day martial law was declared in the Canary Islands, and General Francisco Franco, who earlier in the year had been posted there after being removed by the government from his position as Chief of the General Staff, announced in a radio broadcast that war would be waged against those left-wing influences which were undermining his country. Simultaneously, army garrisons began to take control of towns and cities in the south of Spain: Cádiz, Córdoba, Jerez and Seville, with Granada falling to the military on 20 July. By late afternoon the main buildings had been seized, including Radio Granada, shops closed, public transport came to a standstill, and people stayed in the relative safety of their homes. The main resistance came from the Albaicín, the steep area of narrow and winding streets occupied by the working class, and much celebrated in Lorca's writing. But in three days machine-guns, cannon, mortars and even planes overcame the opposition, and the Nationalists took control of the whole of the city. In addition, the army began to recruit troops and to form local militias in order to take action against those who supported the Left. Lorca was a prime target.

Lorca's activities with La Barraca, closely associated with the left-wing government of 1931–3, had for a number of years provoked the hostility of the Right.[2] They frequently referred to the actors, and especially to Lorca, as homosexuals, and to the actresses in the company as prostitutes. Many of La Barraca's productions – *Fuenteovejuna*, with its story of peasants oppressed by their landlords, was a case in point – were seen as subversive, and right-wing sympathizers had attempted to disrupt the première of *Yerma*. During the last four years of his life Lorca also made a number of important gestures and statements. In 1933, for example, he joined the Association of Friends of the Soviet Union, and also signalled his opposition to the Fascist activities of Hitler's Germany. In a 1935 newspaper interview he spoke of his admiration for the USSR, its art, and its efforts to create a fair society. When the Popular Front was formed in preparation for the General Election of 1936, Lorca expressed his passionate support for it. After its victory he joined two organizations opposed to Fascism, the Friends of Latin America and the Committee of the Friends of Portugal. During the May Day parade he appeared at a window in the Ministry of Communications waving a red tie, and in an interview published in May in *El Sol*, he contrasted what he considered to be the admirable influence of the Moors on Granada in past centuries with the current city inhabited by 'The worst bourgeoisie in Spain'. It was a statement hardly calculated to endear him to his opponents. Quite clearly, Lorca's actions and statements, at a time when the Right was becoming increasingly bitter and dangerous, could only draw attention to himself. In the eyes of many, his homosexuality was an affront to Catholic values, and he was, of course, a famous writer – the ideal person of whom to make an example.

On 6 August a Falangist squad had arrived at the Lorca house in Granada, the Huerta de San Vicente, and searched the premises.

Three days later another group appeared there, apparently searching for the brothers of the caretaker, and in the process roughed up Lorca himself. Frightened by this incident, he went into hiding at the house of Luis Rosales, believing that he would be safe there, not least because two of the Rosales brothers were themselves leading Granada Falangists who would speak up for him. In the event, he was arrested on the afternoon of 16 August and taken for questioning to the nearby Civil Government building. Attempts by members of the Rosales family to secure Lorca's release proved to be in vain – as well as too late – for the order for his execution had already come from General Queipo de Llano, the supreme commander of the Nationalists in Andalusia, with the chilling words: 'Give him coffee, plenty of coffee!' Consequently, Lorca was taken by car, in the early hours of either 18 or 19 August, to a large house outside the village of Viznar, near Granada, which served as a holding post for Republican prisoners condemned to death. Hundreds of men and women were held there overnight, shot at dawn, and buried in the olive groves on the surrounding slopes.[3]

Although there is no precise account of Lorca's death, it has been imaginatively re-created by Juan Antonio Bardem in the 1987 film *Lorca: Death of a Poet* (*Lorca: Muerte de un Poeta*). A voice calls from the darkness: 'Federico García Lorca'. Lorca appears at once, dressed in a white suit, anxiety written all over his face. He is accompanied by Civil Guards and made to climb into the back of a waiting lorry where three other men, one of them on crutches, are guarded by soldiers and Falangists. The lorry moves off along a winding road. No one speaks. As the dawn light spreads across the sky, the lorry comes around a bend and stops. Lorca and his three companions, now seen from the front, climb down from the lorry and start to walk along the road. Behind the four advancing men, the soldiers and Falangists form a line in front of the lorry. Some of them kneel, aim their rifles, fire. In the sudden stillness a voice-over is heard: 'I want no weeping. One has to look death in the face. Silence! Be quiet, I said! We shall drown ourselves in a sea of mourning . . . Silence! Silence, I said! Silence!'

In this powerful and moving sequence, the terrible circumstances of Lorca's death are vividly suggested, and they are linked, too, by the voice-over, to Adela's suicide at the end of *The House of Bernarda Alba* – the dramatist and his character victims of a cold and heartless intolerance. The kind of hostility that Lorca inspired in his enemies, as well as one of its principal causes, may be gauged from the words of one of his killers, Juan Luis Trecastro, who boasted subsequently that he had put 'two bullets into his arse for being a queer'.[4] In the light of such hatred it is both appropriate and ironic that Lorca should have died in the vicinity of a spring known as Fuente Grande, which the Arabs, so admired by him, had called 'The Fountain of Tears'.

In conjunction with his increased, if sometimes naïve, political activities during the first half of the 1930s, Lorca also spoke of his desire to write plays which had to do with contemporary Spain. This was the gist of an interview published in *El Sol* in 1934:

> I wish to complete the trilogy of *Blood Wedding, Yerma,* and *The Drama of Lot's Daughters.* I still have to write the latter. Then I want to do something different, including a contemporary play about the times we live in, and put on stage themes and problems which people are afraid of confronting. The worrying thing here is that the people who go to the theatre do not want to be made to think about any moral issue.[5]

Many of Lorca's plays contain issues relevant to the time he lived in. For instance, *The Shoemaker's Wonderful Wife* highlights the destructive effect of malicious gossip, so common in small Spanish communities, on the individuals who are its victims, while *Blood Wedding* reveals the disastrous consequences of the common practice of arranged marriages, the characteristic Spanish obsession with good name, and the preoccupation with the ownership of land. Such issues are to be found, too, in *Yerma*, as well as the prejudice against childless women. But, although these were matters that Lorca found to be characteristic of contemporary Spanish society, they lay at the edge rather than at the centre of the more political attitudes that coloured his work in the last two years of his life. Prior to 1935, *Mariana Pineda*, written in 1923, was the only play that could be described as in any way political. Although it can be argued that Lorca was greatly interested in the potential of the love theme – that of Mariana's love for the leader of the Liberals – the play, in dramatizing the life and death of the eponymous Granada heroine (executed in 1831 for having embroidered a flag for conspirators who opposed the dictatorial rule of Ferdinand VII), inevitably mirrored in its depiction of right-wing attitudes the political situation in Spain in the 1920s, following General Miguel Primo de Rivera's 1923 *coup d'état*. Even so, the political thrust of *Mariana Pineda*, set as it is in the past, is never as telling or as relevant as that of the two plays written in 1935 and 1936: *Play Without a Title* and *The House of Bernarda Alba*.

Of the two plays, *Play Without a Title* is the most overtly political. By January 1936 Lorca had completed the first act of what was intended to be a three-act play but of which Acts Two and Three were never completed. The play begins with the appearance on stage of the Author – clearly Lorca himself – who at once confronts the largely middle-class audience and informs them that they are not going to see, as they expected, A *Midsummer Night's Dream*, but 'a tiny corner of reality', 'the things you do not wish to see . . . the simplest truths you do not wish to hear' (p. 107).[6] In the course of the act these truths are then revealed and the action becomes a confrontation between the audience and the Author. The theatre, the Author argues, should depict poverty, hunger, suffering, problems which in the 1930s plagued both rural and urban Spain and about which the bourgeoisie cared nothing. But the audience should also be made aware of the uncomfortable truths in their own lives, and an angry exchange takes place with the First Male Spectator, when the Author suggests that the former's wife, while seeing to his needs, may well be thinking about the handsome young man across the road. The increasingly hostile reaction of the audience then becomes not so much a process in which the Author unmasks its members, as one in which they unmask themselves. When, for example, a worker in the gallery protests that a workers' revolution will never harm defenceless people, the Second Male Spectator reveals himself to be a supporter of the Church and the army and an enemy of the workers, as well as of Jews. He proceeds to shoot the protesting worker, and, as he does so, boasts of having been trained in the use of arms by a German soldier. Here, then, is the Fascism which was on the march in early 1936, the intolerance which had crushed the miners of Asturias in 1934. Outside the theatre, meanwhile, the common people are rising up in protest. As the act ends, they break down the theatre doors and, encouraged by the Author, set fire to the building. In the people's revolution there is a clear anticipation of the triumph of the Popular Front in the General Election just one month later, while the destruction of the theatre building – evidently a traditional, proscenium-arch theatre – embodies Lorca's desire, expressed previously in *The Public*, to sweep away the old in all its forms and to create instead a form of theatre which speaks directly to its audience and places before it the unvarnished truth.

Although *The House of Bernarda Alba* is not as obviously political as *Play Without a Title*, it is in every respect a mirror of the reality of Spain at the time of its composition. As well as pointing to that reality in the play's subtitle, Lorca also stated, after the list of characters, that 'The poet points out that these three acts are intended to be a photographic documentary' (p. 3). They are, then, to be seen as a record of certain aspects of Spanish life, and consequently the background and the characters are much more grounded in contemporary reality than in any other Lorca play. Indeed, the unnamed village where Bernarda and her daughters live is closely based on Asquerosa, the village near Fuente Vaqueros, where the Lorca family lived between 1907 and 1909. Initially they lived in a house across the road from his aunt and cousins, later in a substantial house around the corner in Calle Iglesias, now open to the public.

In 1936 Lorca described a childhood experience in Asquerosa, which he claimed to be the inspiration for his play:

> There is, not very far from Granada, a small village where my parents owned a small property: Valderrubio. In the house adjoining ours lived 'Doña Bernarda', a very old widow who kept an inexorable and tyrannical watch over her unmarried daughters. They were prisoners deprived of all free will, so I never spoke to them; but I saw them pass like shadows, always silent and always dressed in black . . . at the edge of the yard there was a shared well, with no water, and I used to go down into it to watch that strange family whose enigmatic behaviour fascinated me. And I observed them. It was a silent and cold hell in the African sun, a tomb for the living under the harsh rule of a dark jailer. And so was born . . . *The House of Bernarda Alba* . . .[7]

The 'Doña Bernarda' referred to here was in fact Frasquita Alba Sierra, who in 1907 would have been almost fifty years of age. Her house, described in Lorca's account as 'adjoining ours', was in fact next door to that occupied by his aunt and cousins, and both houses shared a well, which meant that conversations conducted on one side of the dividing wall could be heard, via the well, on the other. There is no evidence that Lorca went down into the well as he later claimed he did, but one of his cousins, Mercedes Delgado García, certainly knew what was going on next door and kept her brothers and sisters – and Lorca, too – informed. As for Frasquita Alba, she was not a widow, as Lorca suggests, for she married her second husband in 1893, and died a year before him, in 1924. By reputation she was, though, somewhat domineering and doubtless strict towards her children, of which there were seven, five daughters and two sons. The names of three of the girls were used by Lorca in the play: Amelia, Magdalena and Pruden-cia – the first two for Bernarda's daughters, the third for a neighbour. Frasquita's daughter Amelia was married to José Benavides, whose surname Lorca gave to Bernarda's recently dead husband, Antonio

María Benavides. Again, José Benavides was known locally as 'Pepico el de Roma' because he came from the village of Romilla or Roma la Chica, and this was the source of Lorca's Pepe el Romano. Two more local characters were the inspiration for the play's Enrique Humanes (one-time suitor of Martirio) and Maximiliano – the real-life 'Maximiliano' lived on the other side of Calle Iglesias, down from the Lorca family house – the husband of the village-girl Paca la Roseta.[8] Two of Lorca's other female characters also had real-life sources, even though they were not women from Asquerosa itself: a distant relative, who apparently suffered from erotic hallucinations, was the inspiration for Bernarda's half-crazed mother; and Poncia, Bernarda's housekeeper, was undoubtedly based on servants in the Lorca household, and particularly on his favourite, Dolores Cuesta.

The house of the play's title is also firmly grounded in reality and allows us to form a very clear picture of its structure and lay-out. The opening stage direction immediately suggests its thick whitewashed walls. At the back of the house is the *patio* or courtyard, where the male mourners gather and where they are supplied with drinks. Behind this is the *corral* or stable-yard where, in Act Three, some of the daughters go to stretch their legs, and where they see the stallion, just released from the stable. Prior to this, the stallion has been kicking at the stable walls, the stables themselves being at the back of the house next to the *corral*. The whole area is surrounded by high walls in which is to be found the *portón*, the great door, through cracks in which Angustias, in Act One, eavesdrops on the men after they have left. The bedrooms, as was the custom in rural Spain, are not upstairs but downstairs, their windows facing the street. Thus, Angustias meets Pepe el Romano at her window at street level, and Adela likewise stands at her window almost naked so that he can see her when he passes by. Lorca, therefore, creates a vivid impression of the geography of the house and of the movements of the characters within it. But whose house was this in reality? In all probability it was not the house of Frasquita Alba, which Lorca had never entered. The house which he knew best in Asquerosa was the family house around the corner in Calle Iglesias, and a visit to it certainly suggests how the events that take place in the play could, by no great stretch of the imagination, have happened there. There is no more 'real' setting in the whole of Lorca's theatre.

This very strong sense of a real world is also created by many allusions to village customs and traditions, all of which were undoubtedly typical of Asquerosa. One such is the arrival of the mourners at Bernarda's house in Act One, the refreshments with which they are served, and the formal prayer which follows. Traditional, too, were long periods of mourning, even though they were generally shorter than the eight years imposed by Bernarda. The strict division between men and women was also a well-established fact of life: a woman's role was purely domestic, devoted to sewing and embroidery, and, if she were married, to seeing to her husband's needs and to producing children. Martirio's bitter remark in Act One rings very true indeed: 'All they want is land, oxen, and an obedient bitch to feed them' (p. 33). Men had the freedom to work outside, as well as other kinds of freedom, including sexual freedom. In Act Two Poncia observes of one of her sons: 'Years ago another of these women came and I myself gave money to my eldest son so he could go with her. Men need these things' (p. 63). Significantly, the wanton woman is condemned, but the man's behaviour is accepted. Again, the arrival of the harvesters from other places – prominent in Act Two – was an annual event. And then there is the emphasis in the play on local gossip and scandal, which must have been common enough in Asquerosa: Poncia spies on the neighbours through the cracks in the window-shutters (p. 7); Bernarda instructs the servants not to let her half-mad mother near the well so that the neighbours will not see her and have no cause for gossip (p. 23); Poncia knows all about the activities of the village-girl, Paca la Roseta, on the previous night and takes delight in informing Bernarda of it (p. 27); and Magdalena refers to the 'spiteful gossip', which seems to be a feature of the present day (p. 33).

This kind of malicious gossip, so characteristic of small communities,

was, of course, a constant threat both to individual and family repu-
tations. It is for this reason that Bernarda must have her house
spotlessly clean before the mourners arrive in Act One – otherwise she
might be accused of keeping an untidy house. Even so, the greater risk
lay, as it had done for centuries, in the vulnerability of women, married
or single, to male predators, for the slightest breath of scandal would
destroy a whole family's good name. At the end of Act Two, the
village-girl who has had an illegitimate child and buried it to avoid disgrace, is dragged through the streets, her offence made public, her
name and that of her family blackened forever. Such cases were obviously common enough. At the beginning of Act Three, the neighbour
Prudencia reveals that, because her husband's quarrel with his brothers is now public knowledge, he leaves the house by climbing the back
wall to avoid being seen, so conscious is he of wagging tongues.
Disputes over inheritance, as here, or over ownership of land were frequent and bitter in rural Spain, an ideal topic for common gossip and a
source of family dishonour. As for Bernarda, concern for her name lies
at the heart of her treatment of her daughters and of her insistence
that people be told that Adela died a virgin. The promulgation of a lie
immediately proves that honour and reputation was less to do with
truth than with what was perceived by others to be the truth. In short,
good name in small communities – and doubtless in large ones too –
was synonymous not with personal integrity but with public image. In
all these respects, then, Lorca created in *The House of Bernarda Alba* a
house, a group of characters and the sense of a community which are
rooted in reality. Indeed, while he was writing the play he would finish
a scene and run into the street, crying out excitedly: 'Not a drop of
poetry! Reality! Pure realism!'[9] In saying and believing this, he wanted
undoubtedly to distinguish between his new play and his previous
work – *Blood Wedding, Yerma, Doña Rosita the Spinster* – in which there
is a good deal of poetry. Like *Play Without a Title*, *The House of
Bernarda Alba* was, in his view, a play 'about the times we live in'.

This said, Bernarda Alba herself is not Frasquita Alba, even if the latter had the reputation in Asquerosa of being somewhat domineering. Rather, Lorca embodied in his main character the reality of the right-wing attitudes that he saw all around him between 1933 and 1936, fusing them into a single character, a single powerful image of tyranny and intolerance. Although the fact that she is dressed in black is normal enough for a widow in mourning – as it is for her daughters – the colour itself is at once evocative of black-shirted Fascists, and Bernarda's intolerance and authoritarianism are immediately evident in her very first appearance when she silences the weeping servant (p. 13). The word 'Silence!' is her first in the play and it is also, significantly, her last when, after Adela's death, she silences her weeping daughters. She is, then, the personification of repression, and the walking-stick with which she frequently asserts her authority – either banging it on the floor or hitting one of the girls – is the equivalent of an officer's staff, symbol of rank and military discipline. Indeed, she organizes the household, family and servants alike, in an almost military fashion, ordering here, commanding there, always in her sergeant-major manner. Having lived through the Primo de Rivera dictatorship of the 1920s and the harsh measures of a conservative government from 1933 to 1936, and with the extreme activities of the Right in 1936 itself, Lorca created in Bernarda Alba that cold and fanatical mentality. She is indeed the kind of person who would have had no hesitation in ordering the troops to crush the resistance of the Asturian miners in 1934.

She can also be identified with the rich, and especially with the wealthy landowners and prosperous farmers to be found in Andalusia in Lorca's lifetime. Gerald Brenan has written about Andalusia's 'landless proletariat':

> Three-quarters of the population consists in these men and their families, who are hired by the day, by the month, by the season – rarely for longer than that – by the overseers of the large estates or by the tenant farmers who rent from them. For more than half the year they are unemployed.[10]

The conditions in which these men and women worked were, needless to say, terrible. In 1930 their wages were 3 to 3.5 pesetas for an eight-hour day during four or five months of the year, rising to between 4 and 6 pesetas for a twelve-hour day for two or three months in the blazing heat of summer. Those who worked on remote farms earned even less, around 2.25 pesetas for men working a full day, and for women only half that amount. Although Bernarda is not the owner of a large estate, she is described by Poncia in Act Three as having 'the best stable in the whole region' (p. 89), she has a substantial house, and she employs people to work on her land, including Poncia's sons. Her treatment of her employees is, moreover, precisely that of the owners of larger estates: exploitative and heartless. Her dismissal of the weeping servant in Act One reveals her attitude to the proletariat: 'The poor are like animals. It's as if they are made of different stuff' (p. 13), and immediately before this the Servant has described just how poor she and others like her are when she refers to 'those of us who live in huts of mud, with a plate and a spoon' (p. 11). Her food consists of the scraps left over by Bernarda and her daughters, and, as far as her work in the house is concerned, it is long and arduous, as she says in Act Three: 'Bernarda keeps me at it all day long' (p. 103). The latter's lack of feeling for those who work for her, labourers and servants alike, is underlined by Poncia early in Act One: 'Tyrant of all she surveys. She could sit on your heart and watch you die for a whole year, and that cold smile would still be fixed on her damned face' (p. 7). Lorca himself had personal experience of the exploitation of the workers by their masters, for there were many such people in the region around Asquerosa, most of whom were resentful of Lorca's father's much more generous treatment of his own employees. It was, moreover, a situation which the left-wing government of 1931 to 1933 had attempted to address with a plan to nationalize and redistribute the land – a plan overturned by the Right two years later. Bernarda would certainly have been pleased by that.

If she speaks for the rich, Bernarda also voices the views of the

Church, the influence of which on Spanish life, in particular on the less well educated, is suggested in Act One by the continuous tolling of church bells, and just afterwards by the formal prayer in Bernarda's house. For many in the Roman Catholic Church, the sexual act, unless it served for procreation within marriage, was regarded as sinful, and sexual desire was therefore something to be kept in check. It is perfectly in character, then, that Bernarda should make every effort to control her girls, and also that she should condemn all those who do not meet her standards. When, in Act One, Poncia relates to her the story of Paca la Roseta and her escapade with a group of men in the olive-grove, Bernarda at once brands her a whore: 'She's the only loose woman in the village' (p. 27). In this instance she may be justified, but later on, in the case of the unmarried village-girl who has had a child and who is more victim than culprit, her accusations are even more vitriolic: 'Finish her off before the police arrive! A red-hot coal in the place of her sin!' (p. 85). And she is always ready to keep a rebellious Poncia in check by saying that her mother was a whore and that, by implication, Poncia herself is illegitimate (p. 77). Bernarda's views on sexual matters, reflecting those of the more narrow-minded in the Catholic Church and shared by many Spaniards, are, of course, marked by an intolerance and inflexibility, by a hardness of heart and a lack of charity which are distinctly at odds with true Christian values but which were, unfortunately, all too prevalent in the Spain of Lorca's time. In Bernarda, Lorca created a powerful image of those evils that he saw as typical of the Right and which brought about his own end just as effectively as the villagers in the play punish the young village-girl for her misdemeanours.

In all the ways described above, The House of Bernarda Alba is, then, firmly located in the reality of Lorca's life and times, from the house that Lorca knew to attitudes and prejudices which he encountered all around him. But if, as he suggested, the play is 'a photographic documentary', it is also much more than that, for Lorca's method was always to make the local and the particular a starting-point from

which he could move ever outwards, creating much broader reson-
ances. The particular setting of Bernarda's house is, in one sense, an
image of Spain in 1936, but, beyond this, it also becomes, as the action
of the play unfolds, an image of repression in general, regardless of
time and place, and Lorca's theme – as in *Blood Wedding* and *Yerma* – is
the timeless struggle between the individual's longing to be what he or
she is, and the forces ranged against that aspiration. In this respect
almost everything associated with Bernarda's house and household is
seen to be negative: the denial of joy, of hope, of liberty. Step by step,
Lorca evokes a powerful sense of confinement, of darkness, of death.
Act One is set in a room with shuttered windows; the walls may be
white but that whiteness is dulled and muted by the lack of sunlight.
Their surface broken only by some paintings of 'unrealistic landscapes'
(p. 5), these dull white walls suggest, too, the dead hand of monotony
and sterility, and point to lives in which nothing happens. The sense of
monotony is further emphasized by the whiteness of the sheets which
Bernarda's daughters sew at the beginning of Act Two and which link
one daughter to another, each of them condemned to a task as empty
of meaning for them as for a prisoner sewing sacks in a prison workshop. The women are, of course, dressed in the traditional black of
mourning, but the colour inevitably evokes lives darkened by despair
and even helplessness. Furthermore, if the house in which they live is
in half-light, this has, by the beginning of Act Three, become the darkness of night, which by this time has in emotional terms descended
upon the daughters as comprehensively as it has fallen upon the
house. And by the end of Act Three the darkness of Adela's despair at
the news of Pepe el Romano's fate becomes for her the permanent
darkness of death. As for the surviving daughters, they will continue
to live as they have lived thus far, but in ever-increasing hopelessness.

The image of this house as a prison is clear: the opening stage
direction specifies thick walls; when Angustias meets Pepe el Romano,
she does so at the barred window – a traditional feature of Spanish
houses but one which here deepens the impression of imprisonment;

in Act One Bernarda informs her daughters that they will live as if they had 'sealed the doors and the windows with bricks' (p. 21), and in Act Two she angrily tells them that she has five chains, one for each of them (p. 73). In addition, Bernarda's mother is often locked in her room, and when she escapes at the end of Act One she is locked up again (p. 45). Prior to this, Magdalena's comment that she has been 'walking through the rooms. To stretch my legs' (p. 33), brings to mind a prison exercise yard, and later in the same act Adela's protest against the nature of her life is equally suggestive: 'I don't want to be shut away!' (p. 39). The notion of confinement is expressed in a slightly different form by Poncia in Act Two: 'It's been my lot to serve in this convent' (p. 61). For Lorca the life of a nun, for the most part isolated from the outside world and dedicated to a strict routine, was also a form of imprisonment.[11]

So, from the starting-point of one particular situation, Lorca creates, through a network of visual and verbal images, a powerful impression of humanity trapped, of longings stifled, of all things positive denied. Bernarda's wretched, dark and depressing world exists wherever the human spirit is denied. But Lorca suggests too, of course, a different world from hers to which the human spirit eagerly aspires – a world which is far removed from confinement, darkness and death. At one point in Act One, Bernarda asks for a fan but angrily rejects the one Adela gives her, decorated as it is with red and green flowers: 'Is this the fan to give a widow? Give me a black one . . .' (p. 21). The colours used in the play are significant. Green occurs repeatedly throughout. Towards the end of Act One Adela suddenly appears in her green dress, rejecting the lifeless black of mourning. Green is, of course, so often associated with nature, and Adela is a child of nature, a young woman who responds to her natural instincts, who resists all efforts to deny them. It is no accident, therefore, that the setting for the love-making of Paca la Roseta and the men who take her with them should be the olive-grove (p. 27), or that one of the harvesters, whose work is in the fields, should be 'a boy with green eyes' (p. 63). On the other hand, red, an equally vibrant colour, is traditionally the colour of passion. It is appropriate, then, that it should be one of the colours that decorates Adela's fan, and also that it should figure in the harvesters' lively song, where the sexual implication of roses, often red, is perfectly clear:

> Open your doors and windows,
> You girls who live in the town.
> The reaper wants your roses
> To decorate his crown. (p. 65)

Yellow, suggestive of sunlight, evokes a world which is alive and which is well outside Bernarda's experience. The harvesters, vigorous and strong young men, work in the blazing sun and are described as reaping 'in tongues of fire' (p. 65) – it is an image which conjures up the vibrancy of a Van Gogh cornfield. From time to time shafts of sunlight penetrate the gloom of Bernarda's house, as in Act Two where the daughters watch the harvesters passing by: '*All the women listen in a silence pierced by the sunlight*' (p. 65). This merely emphasizes the extent to which Bernarda and her household are a world apart, and the irony inherent in Bernarda's surname, Alba – the Spanish word for 'dawn', with all its associations of brightness and optimism – is very clear. This was obviously the reason why Lorca's character was based on the real-life Frasquita Alba – not simply because this woman was strict but because her surname conjured up such ironic possibilities when applied to a dramatic character like Bernarda.

If the darkness of Bernarda's house has its counterpart in the world outside it, so its claustrophobia has its opposite in frequent allusions to open spaces. In Act One Adela's reaction to the news of Angustias's engagement to Pepe el Romano reveals her desire to escape: 'Tomorrow I'll put on my green dress and I'll go for a walk down the street! I want to go out!' (p. 39). Just after this, Angustias herself pleads with her mother: 'Mother, let me go out!' (p. 43). And at the end of the act,

Bernarda's half-mad mother voices the same aspiration: 'I want to leave here, Bernarda. To get married on the seashore, on the seashore' (p. 45).[12] The words become a kind of refrain, echoing through the prison-house. In Act Two, as we have seen, the harvesters work in the open air, and their song refers to open doors and windows, in marked contrast to those of Bernarda's house, closed and shuttered. In Act Three, Bernarda's mother, attempting to escape, repeats this idea: 'I want houses, but open houses . . .' (p. 197). And finally Adela herself makes a desperate effort to escape: 'No one will stop me!' (p. 115).

In this way, through key symbols and images, Lorca constructs two worlds, and in so doing creates a vital tension, not merely in the on-stage characters but also in ourselves, the audience, the observers of those characters. We are in our basic longings and instincts no different from them. We long for space, for freedom, for light, no less than we rebel against the notion of confinement, and so, in the course of the play, we are pulled in different directions, uplifted by allusions to green, to red, to yellow, to open spaces, cast down by visions of enclosure, of darkness, of escape thwarted. It is, of course, a response to the play in whatever language it is performed, and one which therefore proves its universal appeal. Once again Lorca uses a particular reality as the foundation on which he could construct stories and characters with which and with whom we can all identify.

The House of Bernarda Alba reflects Lorca's political and ideological stance, and embodied in Bernarda Alba herself is his opposition to the narrow-mindedness and intolerance of the Right. But Lorca's political views, which were all to do with freedom and the rights of the individual, cannot be seen in isolation from his sexual preoccupations, which were also to do with the right of the individual to be himself. During the last two years of his life, Lorca maintained a relationship with Rafael Rodríguez Rapún. Highly conscious of prevailing attitudes towards homosexuality, he had often striven to be discreet about personal relationships, but even so, he was frequently the victim of abuse. At the première of *Yerma* in December 1934, for example, shouts of 'Queer!'

had greeted him. Also, the supporters of the Right in Granada referred to him as 'The Queer with the Bow-Tie', and in 1935, both in the Casino and in the Café Hollywood in Granada, he was the object of vicious comments. During this period Lorca was working on the sonnets subsequently known as *Sonnets of Dark Love*, which may have been inspired by his relationship with Rodríguez Rapún, and which are clearly homosexual in nature. But, if he had come to terms with his homosexuality in a way he had not before his trip to New York, this did not mean that he was in any sense less bitter about the people who condemned it, nor indeed less conscious of his own 'outsider' status. Adela is thus his spokesperson, the equivalent of the Bride in *Blood Wedding*. When, in Act Two, Adela angrily asserts 'Leave me alone! Asleep or awake, it's my business, nothing to do with you! I'll do what I like with my body' (p. 55), she is the voice of Lorca himself. But, if Lorca was relatively careful and discreet, Adela is defiant and in the end reckless. In contrast to his desire to conceal his true sexual nature from his parents, Adela has no such reservations about her sexuality, as she tells Poncia in Act Two: '. . . I'd leap over my mother too . . . anything to put out this fire that rises up through my legs and my mouth' (p. 59). And in Act Three she does indeed attempt to leap over her mother, breaking the stick that represents her authority: 'You aren't my jailer any more! (*She seizes her mother's stick and breaks it in two.*) That's what I do with the tyrant's rod. Don't take another step. No one rules me but Pepe!' (pp. 113–15).[13] In all probability Adela is the rebel that Lorca would like to have been, defying convention and narrow-mindedness, breaking the bonds that sought to contain him. To an extent he did, of course, because he did have numerous homosexual affairs, but he became the openly defiant rebel only in the shape of a dramatic character who, in any case, is sexually conventional, not gay. By projecting his anguish on to a woman who loves a man, Lorca gave vent to his feelings but protected his sexual nature as effectively as he did in public by means of a wholly conventional appearance.

The questions which run through both *Blood Wedding* and *Yerma* –

'Why must this be?' 'Why is the world like this?' – also reverberate throughout *The House of Bernarda Alba*, and Lorca's tragic vision remains essentially the same. Adela's aspiration, her longing for Pepe el Romano, is as strong as the Bride's for Leonardo or Yerma's desire to have a child. Similarly, Bernarda's aspiration, which is also strong, is to pre-serve her family's good name. Both she and Adela pursue their objectives with ruthless determination, but they are, of course, objectives which are mutually exclusive, for Adela's pursuit of her passion involves the casting aside of the moral and social values that Bernarda would at all costs uphold. As well as this, their respective desires are ineradicable. In Act Three, for example, Poncia informs the Servant that Adela's passion for Pepe el Romano is nothing new: '. . . last year he was after Adela and she was mad about him' (p. 101). Neither the passage of time nor Angustias's engagement to Pepe has changed that attraction, for, as she informs Poncia in Act Two: 'Looking into his eyes is just like slowly drinking his blood!' (p. 59). The union of Adela and Pepe is, then, the 'marriage of blood' that is also the Bride's and Leonardo's. But Bernarda's obsession with name and reputation is just as powerful, deeply ingrained in her for many years. In short, mother and daughter's paths are mapped out, their clash inevitable and disastrous. This sense of inevitability is underlined, in particular, in Act Three, during the conversation between Poncia and the Servant. The former observes: 'When you can't control the tide, the easiest thing is to turn your back so as not to see it' (p. 101). And again: 'I can't do anything. I tried to head things off, but now they frighten me too much' (p. 101). In the final confrontation with Martirio, Adela, too, underlines the powerlessness of human beings to change the course of things: 'There's no solution here. Whoever must drown, must drown' (p. 111). The presence of fate, as in *Blood Wedding*, creates a final terrible bleakness as Adela hangs herself and her sisters face a future devoid of hope. The feeling of pity awakened by our awareness of Adela's earlier predicament becomes with her death and her sisters' fate that same sense of terror aroused by Greek tragedy.

If the influence of classical tragedy is very evident in *Blood Wedding* and *Yerma*, it is equally so in *The House of Bernarda Alba*. As we have seen, the company of Margarita Xirgu and Enrique Borrás had presented Seneca's *Medea* and Hugo von Hofmannsthal's *Elektra* on several occasions and in different locations throughout 1933 and 1934, and in August 1934 the great actress also presented *Iphigenia* in the Greek Theatre in Ampurias.[14] As for *The House of Bernarda Alba*, the very title of the play suggests a dynasty of the kind to be found in classical tragedy – a point reinforced when, for example, Bernarda draws attention to her own family line: 'That's how it was in my father's house, in my grandfather's too' (p. 21). Again, the emphasis on a female protagonist cannot but call to mind the powerful female characters of Greek and Roman plays: Medea, Elektra, Phaedra, Antigone. And, in the characters of Poncia and the Servant, Lorca creates a modern equivalent of the classical chorus, whose purpose it was both to give out information and to establish the mood. In Act One, the dialogue between the two women tells us all we need to know about Bernarda, and in Act Three it effectively prepares us for the dark events that lie ahead. The chorus in classical drama was, of course, sung or chanted. Lorca's lines are not, but they do have a marked rhythmic quality which places them firmly in that tradition.

Lorca's work with La Barraca had come to an end in the autumn of 1935, largely because of the increasing demands of his own creative writing, but the lessons learned from directing the company cannot be underestimated. In this respect *The House of Bernarda Alba* is the work of a dramatist whose touch is absolutely sure and who knows exactly what will work on stage. His suggestions for the sets again have that simplicity that marked his work with La Barraca, for the sustained effect of women in black against walls painted white is more stark and concentrated than in any other play. The process is one of paring down, of eliminating fussy, realistic detail, and of thereby creating striking visual images which universalize their meaning. When in Act Two, for example, Martirio '*remains seated on the low chair, with her head in her hands*' (p. 65), she is both a particular woman and a more general image of despair, just as in Act One Adela's entry in her green dress suggests both a lively individual and an image of spirited youth every-where. These two extremes – Martirio static, Adela entering quickly – also point to the importance of contrast and movement in the play, and to Lorca's sure control of both these elements. At the beginning of Act Two, for instance, the daughters, Adela apart, are seated, engaged in sewing the sheets. From time to time they get up, go out or argue amongst themselves, but the rhythm of the action is relatively slow, reflecting the tedious nature of their lives. But then there are sudden flurries of activity: when, as the harvesters depart, three of the girls rush out to catch a glimpse of them (p. 65); when Angustias enters furiously (p. 69), demanding to know who has stolen her photograph; or when, at the end of Act Two, the daughter of Librada is dragged through the streets (p. 85). Lorca beautifully controls the pace of the action. The movement is very different from that of *Blood Wedding*. There is no element of dance, but, throughout, the relative inactivity of the people in the house erupts into violent action that reflects their frustrations and pent-up emotions, as well as keeping the audience permanently on its toes. In terms of movement the play is highly styl-ized but seems perfectly natural and realistic. It is Lorca's particular triumph to have fused two opposites with such conviction.

The same can be said of the play's language. It seems realistic but is in reality carefully shaped and honed, eliminating needless clutter. Bernarda's words are verbal blows, assaulting the ears of those around her, instructing, commanding, wounding, not a word wasted, her language in every sense reflecting her unbending nature. Very often the conversations of her daughters have a dragging rhythm which, as in Magdalena's case, encapsulates her despair: 'I know I'll never get married. I'd rather carry sacks to the mill' (p. 21). Or else, as in the case of Adela, the language exposes her defiance and resolve: 'This is just the beginning. I've had the strength to take what I want. The spirit and the looks that you don't have . . .' (p. 109). There is no irrelevant exchange in the play: language and character are one, the whole tightly structured and therefore stylized. As Francisco García Lorca has pointed out:

> *The House of Bernarda Alba*, of these plays, is the one which has the most direct inspiration in reality . . . And in spite of this basic reality, I would say that this is his most artful play and the one which is most disciplined in technique . . .[15]

The first production of *The House of Bernarda Alba* took place not in Spain – the circumstances of Lorca's death made this impossible – but in Buenos Aires where it opened at the Teatro Avenida on 8 March 1945, almost nine years after Lorca's death, and so it was the first time that the dramatist was not present at the première of one of his major plays.[16] However, the production, once again by Margarita Xirgu's company, was steeped in the spirit of Lorca, the part of Bernarda Alba having been written for Xirgu. Also, the stage-designer was Santiago Ontañón, who had worked with Lorca on *Blood Wedding* and *The Love of Don Perlimplín,* and several of the actresses had also appeared in productions of other Lorca plays. In short, the involvement of these people ensured that the play would be staged in the way that Lorca would have wanted.

Ontañón's design remained faithful to Lorca's suggestions, as had his sets for *Blood Wedding* in 1933. Years later he observed that, in accordance with Lorca's own stage directions, he emphasized the whiteness of the walls in Acts One and Two, something which many future directors of the play would ignore. Furthermore, he preserved the three separate locations specified by the dramatist: an inner room for Act One; a different inner room for Act Two; an inner patio or courtyard for Act Three. To keep costs down a single set is nowadays much more common, but Lorca's intention was clearly to take the action of the play further and deeper into the house, thereby showing the growing isolation of Bernarda's daughters from the outside world. In addition, Ontañón's design reflected the simple austerity and stylization demanded by Lorca, for photographs from all three acts reveal plain uncluttered walls against which the characters stand out in bold relief.

Margarita Xirgu chose her actors with great care, always conscious of the importance that Lorca attached not only to the psychological depth of his characters but also to the way in which gesture, movement and speech brought his characters to life. Poncia, experienced in the ways of the world, was played by María Gámez, Adela by Isabel Pradas and Martirio by Pilar Muñoz. Carlos H. Faig, reviewing the production in *El Hogar*, concluded that Margarita Xirgu had 'taken her actresses along sure pathways', while the theatre reviewer of *La Nación* drew attention to the 'psychological insight' displayed by María Gámez, the 'spirit' in the performance of Isabel Pradas, and the 'steely sharpness' portrayed by Pilar Muñoz. [17, 18] As for Margarita Xirgu as Bernarda, the critic for *La Nación* drew attention to her 'manner and . . . her voice', while Faig praised 'the enormous force of her gestures . . . the quality of her delivery'. But, if her own performance was a triumph, the production was in general a fine example of the ensemble acting to which Lorca himself aspired in his work as a director. At the end of the performance, the audience went wild, overwhelmed by what they had seen. Margarita Xirgu addressed them, her voice trembling with emotion: 'He [Federico] wanted this play to be premièred here, and so it has been, but he wanted to be present and fate has prevented it. A fate which has made many people weep. A curse on war!'[19] It was indeed an emotional and an unforgettable occasion, as well as a fitting tribute.

The House of Bernarda Alba did not receive its first Spanish production until 1964, when it opened on 10 January at the Teatro Goya in Madrid, directed by the distinguished film-director Juan Antonio Bardem, and designed by the painter Antonio Saura. Once more, Lorca's original vision was achieved. The sets, for example, contained the black and white contrast suggested by the dramatist, and were described by the theatre critic of the *Heraldo de Aragón* – when the play was performed in Zaragoza in 1965 – as constituting a 'stylized realism'.[20] Indeed, the production team went further than Lorca in this process of stylization, for in his production notes Bardem spoke of stripping away unnecessary detail, and so, in Act One, the dramatist's 'jute curtains' and the paintings on the walls were dispensed with.[21] In addition, the walls in all three acts were considerably heightened so that the impression of women trapped in a kind of well was made much stronger. Production photographs reveal the inhabitants of the house dwarfed by the walls, the women's smallness and helplessness very clear indeed. But if Bardem went rather further than Lorca in this aspect of stylization, he also insisted on keeping the three separate sets.

> It is essential that Acts One and Two take place in different rooms. The location of the action becomes more enclosed by the walls of the house. In Act One the outside world is still near. In Act Two *every-thing* has moved inwards.[22]

The impression of a closed world from which there is no escape was also created by lighting effects. Bardem considered that the lighting of the stage should change only when a door was opened, allowing light in from an outer area. In Act One, for example, Poncia, the Beggar Woman and the mourners enter from the street. For a few moments, then, the inner room would be flooded with sunlight. Similarly, in Act Two, the door to the patio is opened to let in some air, and at the end of the act Poncia goes out to see what is happening in the street. In all these instances Bardem believed that the sudden illumination of the stage would both suggest the world outside, for which Bernarda's daughters long so much, and, by way of sudden contrast, emphasize the prison-like darkness of the world to which they are condemned.

Bardem's production notes also contain extremely interesting observations on the characters. He felt, for instance, that, because Bernarda is completely confident of her power, she has no need to prove the point. She should raise her voice, therefore, only when her authority is threatened. Even at the end of the play, when she is made aware of Adela's suicide, she loses her self-control only for a moment before reasserting her iron grip. As for Poncia, Bardem made the point that, although she is a servant, she is by no means servile. Interestingly, he noted that village or peasant women rarely use excessive gestures even at moments of joy or sadness. Their emotions are expressed in the tone of their voice, although here, too, excess should be avoided. In Bardem's production, the role of Bernarda was played by Cándida Losada, an actress of great experience, whose performance was highly praised for its control by Felipe Bernardos in the newspaper *Amanecer*:

> It is not necessary to play the part of Bernarda with lots of shouting . . . She [Cándida Losada] has succeeded in reaching the heart of the drama by exercising complete control of her voice and delivery. Her acting is wonderful, her approach measured, her gestures concentrated . . .[23]

And, as for María Bassó in the role of Poncia, Cistue de Castro drew attention to the way in which she succeeded in capturing all the different moods of the character. In the opinion of the critics the other characters were also interpreted to great effect, and Bardem's production was considered a great success, as D. Martínez Benavente noted in *El Sol*:

> In my opinion, the theatrical qualities of *The House of Bernarda Alba* have been realized in an exceptional production by Juan Antonio Bardem . . . At the end of each act and at the final curtain, the audience applauded long and enthusiastically, and the actors were obliged to advance to the edge of the stage to take their bow . . .[24]

Twenty years later, a major production of the play, directed by José

Carlos Plaza and designed by Andrea D. Odorico, opened on 16 November 1984 at the Teatro Español in Madrid, a theatre with which Lorca himself had been closely associated. One of the interesting features of this production was the director's desire to move away from the style of previous stagings by emphasizing not the play's symbolism but its naturalism, and, in addition, the reduction of the three different sets to one – the various rooms at different points of the stage and opening out at the back onto an inner patio. Plaza's insistence on naturalism meant that the uniform whiteness of the walls was abandoned in favour of realistic detail, with skirting-boards, cupboards and floors of baked clay. This approach also meant that light entered the rooms of the house through the windows and from the inner patio. In his production notes, Plaza suggests that the events of Act One occur around midday when the sun is already strong, while Act Two is set around three o'clock, when the light is glaring and the heat suffocating.[25] Clearly, the director's aim was to create on stage a world which was more specific, more precise than that of earlier productions, and this also applied to the costumes. Instead of the black favoured by Xirgu and Bardem, Plaza opted for 'dark colours'. In the privacy of the house, therefore, the women wore clothes which, although still dark in colour, were more varied and less austere. But if the overall effect of sets, lighting and costume was to anchor the action in a very real world, was it in any way counterproductive? Lorca's technique – despite his assertions of the realism of this play – was not to dwell on detail but to pare away, to simplify and stylize reality in a way which transformed the specific into something much more general, more universal. Plaza thus ran the risk of creating a naturalism that ran contrary to Lorca's instincts.

Plaza also rejected the idea that the characters are in any way symbolic, and in an interview in *El País*, he stressed the fact that his interest lay in the psychology of each individual and in attempting to 'understand the reasons for the way they behave'.[26] Bernarda, he suggested, had been married initially by arrangement to an older man, and, after his death, had fallen in love with Antonio María Benavides, a man of lesser social status. He, however, had subsequently indulged in a number of affairs, and her disappointment had then been further exacerbated by the fact that in two marriages she had borne five daughters and no son to inherit the estate. Her bitterness lies at the heart of her desire to protect her daughters from a similar fate, although this also goes hand in hand with her determination to avoid village gossip. In general, Plaza saw Bernarda as a woman who, for personal and social reasons, acts in the way she does, her harshness a form of self-defence.

As for Bernarda's daughters, Angustias is a constant reminder of her mother's first marriage, and for that reason has been marginalized, as well as been made to feel something of an outsider by her four half-sisters. Magdalena, the eldest of the children of her mother's second marriage and her father's favourite, is a disappointed woman, at thirty years of age resigned to her fate, and further embittered by the fact that Angustias inherits much of her stepfather's money. Amelia is the most withdrawn and reticent of the girls, someone who would rather avoid problems, and who, despite her seeming closeness to Martirio, is not really close to any of her sisters. Martirio is, for Plaza, the most intelligent of the five sisters, but her physical defects – her limp and her hump back – mean that she, like Angustias, feels marginalized, and this in turn fuels her resentment of others, not least in matters of love, for which she longs but has never enjoyed. Adela, at twenty the youngest of the daughters, is the most bored by her way of life, and, in attempting to escape that boredom, the most self-centred and unthinking. But, for all their different personal histories, Plaza also saw the sisters as largely uneducated women who, despite their complaints, find a certain comfort in their material well-being and, in the end, are fearful of change, other than in an equally comfortable marriage. The exceptions to this are María Josefa, who is in any case oblivious to reality, and Poncia, so experienced in the ways of the world. But even she, materially dependent upon Bernarda, is far from anxious to seek employment elsewhere.

As with his approaches to staging, lighting and costume, Plaza's view of the characters as individuals with a history is rooted in naturalism, a point which the critics picked up in their reviews of the production. E. Haro Tecglen spoke in *El País* of 'a theatrical naturalism', and José Monleón in *Diario 16* of 'Plaza's realistic staging'.[27, 28] For Monleón, the performances of some of the actresses were more convincing than others within the naturalistic framework, while Haro Tecglen felt that the daughters, far from being individualized, were more a uniform group – rather strange in the light of Plaza's insistence on their personal histories. In general, it seems fair to say that Plaza's approach to Lorca's play was less successful than that of Xirgu and Bardem, but it also suggests that, as in the case of all great works, it lends itself to very different interpretations.

Strangely enough, there seem to have been more major productions of *The House of Bernarda Alba* in English translation than in the original language – proof enough of the play's lasting and widespread appeal. Six years after its Buenos Aires première, it was staged in New York at the American National Theater and Academy; in 1963 the Actors' Workshop staged a very successful production at the Encore Theater in San Francisco; in 1972 it was performed at the ADAL Theater in New York; and two years later at Nuestro Teatro in the same city. In 1979 and 1989, again in New York, it was presented to considerable acclaim – performed in Spanish with English translation provided – by the Repertorio Español.

The first major British production took place at the Greenwich Theatre, London, in 1973, in which the film actress Mia Farrow played Adela and the translation was by the dramatist Tom Stoppard. In 1986 a second production began a run at the Lyric Theatre, Hammersmith, London, and in January 1987 transferred to the Globe Theatre (now the Gielgud) in the West End, directed by the acclaimed Spanish actress Nuria Espert, and with Glenda Jackson as Bernarda and Joan Plowright as Poncia. Four years later there was a production at the Playhouse, Nottingham, in which Adela was played by Helena

Bonham-Carter, soon to make her name in film. In late 1992 the play was presented at the small but highly acclaimed Gate Theatre in Notting Hill, London, and in May 1999 at the Young Vic Theatre, London. In addition, there have been very many productions by amateur theatre groups.

The most publicized British production by far was that directed by Nuria Espert, which ran in the West End for several months. The involvement of a Spanish director who was familiar with Lorca's theatre and who had recently performed both as Yerma and as Doña Rosita in major Spanish productions promised much, but, in the event, the production divided the critics and failed to resolve many of the issues which confront English-language productions of Lorca's plays. The major problem, evident not only in this but in other productions too, is one of accent. In his review of the Greenwich Theatre production of 1973, J.W. Lambert suggested in *Drama* that, as Adela, Mia Farrow was 'too home counties'.[29] Twenty-six years later, in the production at the Young Vic, the problem was exactly the same. And this too was a prominent feature of the West End staging, as Eric Shorter noted in the *Daily Telegraph*: '. . . the voices remain those of an English theatrical drawing-room – well bred, beautifully enunciated, highly intelligent, but stuck, so to say, in Professor Higgins' territory rather than Lorca's'.[30] The mistake was, and still is, to confuse Bernarda and her family, because they are prosperous, with the English middle class, when in reality they are, as Carlos Plaza pointed out, uneducated and living in a village in rural Spain. In this respect a production in English is much better served by a regional accent which is down-to-earth and robust, and which in particular avoids the vowel-sounds of southern English. To hear Poncia speak in such a manner is quite absurd.

The stage-design by Ezio Frigerio for Espert's production consisted of a towering back wall, in front of which the action of the whole play took place, Lorca's three settings reduced to one. Despite the fact that the wall featured barred windows, the set as a whole failed to create that sense of enclosure and growing isolation from the outside world so strongly suggested by earlier Spanish productions. Indeed, it was described by Paul Preston, writing in the *Times Literary Supplement*, as 'monumentally operatic. Suitable for *Fidelio* . . .'[31] It can certainly be said, without fear of contradiction, that the grandeur of the set had nothing to do with a village like Asquerosa, and little to do, therefore, with Lorca's intentions. And again, the sense of heat, suggested so well by Lorca's dialogue, was not particularly strong, and neither was the stage suddenly flooded with sunlight as doors are momentarily opened.

As for the interpretations of the characters by the actors, the observations of Spanish directors such as Juan Antonio Bardem are extremely important. As we have seen, he made the particular point that Bernarda, conscious of her power, has no need to raise her voice except at certain moments, or indeed to use excessive gesture. In order to appreciate this point one only has to see the performance by Irene Gutiérrez Caba in the film version of the play, directed by Mario Camus and released in 1987. What, then, of Glenda Jackson in this crucial role? In general her performance was exaggerated. Martin Hoyle in the *Financial Times* commented: 'Ramrod-rigid, her voice harsh, the most passionately committed of our actresses tries to compensate with sheer intensity.'[32] And in the *Guardian* Michael Billington concluded: 'Glenda Jackson's tyrannical matriarch . . . rules over her brood like a female leopard . . . and howls with sadistic relish as an errant village woman is dragged through the street'.[33] Clearly, howling has no place in Lorca's character. There is a telling contrast, moreover, at the play's conclusion between Jackson's reaction to the sight of Adela's dead body and that of Irene Gutiérrez Caba in the Spanish film. Jackson fell to her knees in a kind of convulsion – a moment described by Jim Hiley in the *Listener* as 'her peculiarly unmoving final agonies'.[34] Gutiérrez Caba, on the other hand, reveals her feelings only for a moment, stands stock still, and in a flash recovers her self-control. The difference in interpretation could not be greater.

And as for the other performances, Joan Plowright was far too superior and plummy-accented as Poncia, and the actresses who played the daughters too public school.

For many people *The House of Bernarda Alba* represents Lorca's greatest theatrical achievement. In terms of structure it is certainly his tightest, most concentrated play, for the whole of the action takes place in the rooms of one house and the pace and movement is wonderfully controlled throughout. In addition, Lorca has created here some marvellously rounded and convincing characters. Bernarda herself is one of the most memorable creations in world drama – she sticks in the mind long after the play's conclusion – Poncia is in many ways her equal, fleshed out in rich detail, and, of the daughters, Angustias, Martirio and Adela are striking in how very different from each other they are. It is a play full of highly theatrical moments: Bernarda's first entry; María Josefa's sudden appearances; Adela's arrival in her green dress; the singing of the harvesters; the punishment of the village-girl; Adela's breaking of her mother's stick; Bernarda's attempt to shoot Pepe el Romano; and Adela's suicide. Given that the action occurs within one house, the variety of incident is quite remarkable.

To state that *The House of Bernarda Alba* is Lorca's best play is, perhaps, not to do justice to his other works. His plays are great in different ways, and, in their differences, show that Lorca was essentially an innovative dramatist, one who always sought new ways of expressing issues which were both personal and constant.

Conclusion

This study of Lorca's plays reveals him to be a dramatist whose work has as its mainspring the preoccupations and dilemmas of his personal life, yet is at the same time consistently fresh and innovative. There is throughout his theatre a cluster of themes which, deeply rooted in the events of his emotional experience, give his work a remarkable coherence and a powerful charge. On the other hand, each play is different from its predecessor, be it in the way in which the themes are presented or in the dramatic form adopted by Lorca, ever eager to experiment. In either case, he reveals himself to be a writer who is rarely satisfied with what he has achieved, one who constantly attempts to revitalize dramatic form. The combination of issues felt and dramatic technique and style revisited explains in large measure the vitality and appeal of his plays over such a long period of time.

Amongst Lorca's themes, love and passion are, of course, preeminent. Initially unsure, perhaps, of his own sexual orientation, love takes the form in his first play, *The Butterfly's Evil Spell*, of a rather naïve and dreamy aspiration on the part of Boybeetle, dazzled by the beauty of Butterfly. By the time he wrote *Blood Wedding*, a dozen years later, there was no such hesitation, for in the relationship of the Bride and Leonardo passion is intensely physical – 'Her body for him, his body for her' (p. 75) – as it is in his last play, *The House of Bernarda Alba*, where, for Adela, passion is 'this fire that rises up through my legs and my mouth' (p. 59). The expression of the theme of passion, of its nature and power, grew ever stronger in the light of Lorca's own experience, and yet in all but one of his plays, *The Public*, his homosexuality was replayed in heterosexual relationships. The explanation lies quite clearly in Lorca's awareness of the homophobia of the society in which he lived, as well as in the realization of what was acceptable on stage. *The Public* was, in his own words, 'for the theatre years from now', to be performed for a more open-minded society. In the 1920s and 1930s it was more prudent and practical to dress personal feelings in the conventional trappings of male–female relationships, which was little different, after all, from the way in which Lorca, throughout his adult life, presented himself to the public at large as a conventional man. But the façade does not, of course, conceal or minimize the force of the passion itself. On the contrary, Lorca's identification with the Girlfriend, the Bride and Adela is complete, the authenticity of their feelings drawn from his own anguish.

Frustration, inextricably linked to passion and intensely felt by characters as different as Boybeetle, Mariana Pineda, Don Perlimplín and Doña Rosita, was also something with which, in consequence of failed and broken homosexual relationships, Lorca was also all too familiar. In *The Public* in particular he vividly portrayed the rejections and betrayals which in reality he doubtless experienced at the hands of individuals such as Salvador Dalí and Emilio Aladrén. And if in, say, *The Love of Don Perlimplín* or *Doña Rosita the Spinster*, frustration seems less brutal and violent than in the world of many gay men, the fact is that it is just as real and painful, and has merely been shaped to the situation and the character by Lorca's sure touch. His vision and imagination also allowed him to project personal experience into situations in which love, passion and frustration took on a different form, or existed in a different context. So Yerma's passion is not for her husband but for the child she longs to have; her frustration the reaction to her failure to conceive, not to a disappointment in love. And in *The Love of Don Perlimplín*, as in *When Five Years Pass*, male impotence – the failure of a man to respond to a woman – and the related theme of childlessness, is subtly explored. What cannot be denied is that these were preoccupations which Lorca felt intensely, and their vibrancy in his plays would not be what it is without that connection.

To some extent the theme of passing time was also linked to Lorca's sexual relationships, for the men to whom he was attracted – Salvador Dalí, Emilio Aladrén, Rafael Rodríguez Rapún – were invariably younger than himself. Second Friend's fear of growing old, expressed so powerfully in *When Five Years Pass* – '. . . this face is mine and they're stealing it from me' (p. 142) – and Adela's protest in *The House of Bernarda Alba* – 'I don't want to lose my whiteness in these rooms!' (p. 39) – are surely the voice of Lorca himself as he moved into middle age and became less confident of his powers of physical attraction. But, in a more general sense, as the characters of his plays constantly remind us, he seems to have been keenly aware of the way in which passing time brings change, disillusionment and the destruction of dreams. Doña Rosita is, of course, the perfect example of this awareness as time passes her by, but so is Yerma, her hopes of a child diminished as the years go by, and the daughters of Bernarda Alba, their future more depressing than their past.

Lorca was also, as we have seen, morbidly preoccupied with death, observing on one occasion that 'A dead man is more dead in Spain than in any other part of the world', and also given to acting out his own death. At all events, death occurs in the majority of his plays and is frequently associated with terror, both at the prospect of its coming and at the sense of the joy of life lost forever. Thus in *When Five Years Pass* the Child pleads 'I don't want to be buried!' (p. 136) while the Old Man remorselessly observes: 'But in front of us, in four or five years' time, there's a black pit, and we'll all fall into it!' (p. 142). We can only imagine what Lorca's feelings must have been when in August 1936, at the age of thirty-eight, he was faced with his own execution.

If the network of themes which underpin the plays were shaped by personal experience, so in the end was Lorca's concept of tragedy. Other things played their part, no doubt, in particular the tradition of classical tragedy, as well as his familiarity with the world of the Andalusian gypsies and their history of misfortune. But Lorca responded to these things precisely because they were one with his own experience; because they evoked a world in which the individual was the plaything of forces outside his control, helpless to shape his own destiny. What, after all, could be more difficult than to be homosexual in a society which was at once narrow-minded, traditional, intolerant and homophobic? Why was his nature such? Why had the dice so fallen? From the first to the last, Lorca's plays place individuals in situations in which their dreams and desires run counter to the demands of others: Boybeetle, Mariana Pineda, the Bride and Leonardo, Yerma, Adela. The outcome is, of course, catastrophe – in Yerma's words: 'I looked for carnations and only found a wall . . . a wall to beat my head against!' How often Lorca must have shared those feelings, that dark despair! The power and consistency of the tragic vision that informs his work would not be so were it not the bitter fruit of his personal experience.

Stylistically, Lorca's theatre is both consistent and enormously varied. Its consistency lies in the fact that it is essentially stylized and anti-naturalistic, *The Butterfly's Evil Spell* as true to that principle as *The House of Bernarda Alba*. The effect of stylization is, needless to say, the opposite of the effect of naturalism, for the latter involves precise location, local colour, specific placement in time, and realistic detail, while the former implies the broader stroke, the stripping away of detail, timelessness and universality. Many of Lorca's plays are set in the world he knew so well, especially the towns and villages of Andalusia, yet Lorca's dramatic technique is one which transforms the local and particular into the universal, an effect largely achieved through the creation of images of different kinds, which are at once specific and more general. In terms of settings, the '*Room painted yellow*' (p. 33) and the Mother dressed in black of *Blood Wedding* are, on the one hand, characteristically Spanish, but the simple, pared-down nature of the image is one that also evokes a bitterness, a harshness and a grief which are universal, while the knife, an ordinary household implement, becomes, by the end of the play, the equivalent of the sword of Damocles. It is significant, too, in relation to the broader resonance of Lorca's theatre, that so many of his characters possess generic names: in *Blood Wedding* the Bride, the Bridegroom, the Mother, the Father; in *When Five Years Pass* the Young Man, the Girl-friend, the Old Man, the Friend. And even when the names are real, they are often symbolic: in *The House of Bernarda Alba* Martirio and Angustias (martyrdom and anguish); in *Blood Wedding* Leonardo (the burning lion); and in *Doña Rosita* the protagonist herself (the little rose). All these are truly universal characters, placed in situations and experiencing emotions familiar to us all.

The process of universalization is one important reason for the enduring appeal of Lorca's theatre; another is his constant experimentation. Although all the plays explore the same themes, no play is a mere repetition of another. The three rural tragedies may have a certain similarity in terms of background and community, but in other ways they are significantly different from each other. *Blood Wedding* is, of the three, the most expansive, for its action is set in a number of locations and involves three families in a complex series of relationships. *Yerma*, although it, too, has various locations, is much more introspective, focusing on the inner life of its protagonist, and *The House of Bernarda Alba*, narrowing the action even further to the setting of a single house, is physically and emotionally the most claustrophobic. Furthermore, the poetic passages that distinguish *Blood Wedding* are pared down in *Yerma* and almost eliminated in *The House of Bernarda Alba*. While the three plays belong to the same family, as it were, they suggest quite clearly that Lorca always sought to achieve something new in his work – to dress familiar preoccupations in new theatrical clothing.

The point is made even more forcibly in the case of the other plays. Commencing his theatrical career with a play about insects, Lorca moved on to *Mariana Pineda*, a historical subject, and experimented, too, with the traditions of the puppet-play and farce in three works – *The Tragicomedy of Don Cristóbal and Señorita Rosita*, *The Shoemaker's Wonderful Wife* and *The Love of Don Perlimplín* – achieving in each more subtle and moving effects. In complete contrast, *The Public* and *When Five Years Pass*, two enormously ambitious plays, draw upon the avant-garde and, in particular, on Surrealism in its various aspects. *Buster Keaton's Spin*, although a theatre piece, owes something to cinematic techniques. *Doña Rosita the Spinster*, coming between *Yerma* and *The House of Bernarda Alba*, could not be more different from either, a bitter-sweet mixture of laughter and tears reminiscent of Chekhov. And Lorca's penultimate play, *Play Without a Title*, more politically driven than any other work, involves stage and audience in a manner suggestive of Pirandello. But if all this suggests that Lorca was something of a magpie, the various sources on which he drew were transformed by his genius into plays of great originality and power. What is quite astonishing, too, is that he was able to work on very different plays at the same time, one overlapping with another. This undoubtedly points to a dramatist of energy, flexibility and ever-changing moods. It was a restless energy which, combined with powerful themes and dramatic subjects, explains the vitality and continuing appeal of Lorca's theatre.

Notes

INTRODUCTION

1. For an English translation of the letter, see Ian Gibson, *Federico García Lorca: A Life*, London: Faber and Faber, 1989, pp. 74–5. Gibson's book contains the most detailed account of Lorca's life, but see also Leslie Stainton, *Lorca: A Dream of Life*, London: Bloomsbury, 1998.

2. There are detailed studies of the work of this theatre group by Suzanne Byrd, *'La Barraca' and the Spanish National Theatre*, New York: Ediciones Abra, 1975, and by Luis Sáenz de la Calzada, *'La Barraca': Teatro Universitario*, Madrid: Biblioteca de la Revista de Occidente, 1976.

3. See Gibson, pp. 446–70.

4. All references, indicated by page numbers, are to my own translations in *Lorca Plays: One*, *Lorca Plays: Two* and *Lorca Plays: Three*, published by Methuen in 1987, 1990 and 1994 respectively. *Lorca Plays: One* contains *Blood Wedding*, *Doña Rosita the Spinster*, and *Yerma* (translated by Peter Luke). *Lorca Plays: Two* consists of *The Shoemaker's Wonderful Wife*, *The Love of Don Perlimplín*, *The Puppet-Play of Don Cristóbal*, *The Butterfly's Evil Spell*, and *When Five Years Pass*. *Lorca Plays: Three* has *Mariana Pineda*, *The Public* (translated by Henry Livings) and *Play Without a Title*.

5. On the influence of European avant-garde theatre on Spanish dramatists, see Gwynne Edwards, *Dramatists in Perspective: Spanish Theatre in the Twentieth Century*, Cardiff: University of Wales Press, 1985.

6. Ibid., pp. 84–7.

7. The translation into English is my own, unpublished.

8. See Gibson, pp. 137–8.

9. Ibid., p. 147.

10. The works of Freud, which were available in Spanish translation in the

1920s, were much discussed at the Residencia de Estudiantes and proved a source of fascination to the Surrealists, budding or otherwise.

11. See in particular Antonina Rodrigo, *Margarita Xirgu y su teatro*, Barcelona: Editorial Planeta, 1974.

12. The translation is my own, unpublished.

CHAPTER 1

1. Unless otherwise stated, all translations into English in this chapter are my own, unpublished.

2. The translated letter can be found in Gibson, pp. 74–5.

3. See Luis Buñuel, *Mon dernier soupir*, Paris: Robert Laffont, 1982, pp. 75–6.

4. From *The Secret Life of Salvador Dalí*, London: Vision Press, 1968, p. 176.

5. Ibid., p. 203.

6. See Stainton, p. 134.

7. See Meryle Secrest, *Salvador Dalí: The Surrealist Jester*, London: Weidenfeld and Nicolson, 1986, p. 122.

8. Ibid., p. 76.

9. See Gibson, pp. 209–12.

10. In a letter to Carlos Morla Lynch. See the collection of Lorca's letters, *Federico García Lorca: Epistolario*, Christopher Maura (ed.), Madrid: Alianza, 1983, Vol. 2, p. 128.

11. See Gibson, p. 268.

12. Federico García Lorca, *Trip to the Moon: A Filmscript*, Bernice G. Duncan (tr.), New York: New Directions, 1964, Vol. 18, pp. 33–41.

13. See Luis Cardoza y Aragón, *El río. Novelas de caballería*, Ciudad México: Fondo de Cultura Económica, 1986, p. 351.

14. An English translation of the play by Henry Livings can be found in *Lorca Plays: Three*, London: Methuen, 1994.

15. *Lorca Plays: One*, Gwynne Edwards (tr.), London: Methuen, 1987. Page references are to this text.

16. See the bilingual edition, *The House of Bernarda Alba/La casa de Bernarda Alba*, Gwynne Edwards (tr.), London: Methuen, 1998.

17. See Mildred Adams, *García Lorca: Playwright and Poet*, New York: George

Braziller, 1977, p. 196.

18. For a detailed account see Edwards, *Dramatists in Perspective*.

19. For an informative study of the Surrealist movement in Spain, see C.B. Morris, *Surrealism and Spain 1920–1936*, Cambridge: Cambridge University Press, 1972.

20. Buñuel, *Mon dernier soupir*, pp. 122–3, and, on *Gypsy Ballads*, in a letter of 14 September 1928 to José Bello. See Agustín Sánchez Vidal, *Luis Buñuel: Obra literaria*, Zaragoza: Heraldo de Aragón, 1982, p. 30. The translation into English is my own.

21. The letter was to Sebastián Gasch. See *Federico García Lorca: Epistolario*, Vol. 2, Maura (ed.), p. 114.

22. The lecture, 'La imagen poética de Don Luis de Góngora', can be found in Federico García Lorca, *Obras completas*, Arturo del Hoyo (ed.), Madrid: Aguilar, 11th edition, 1966, pp. 62–85.

23. See Gibson, p. 107.

24. On this topic, see C.B. Morris, *This Loving Darkness: The Cinema and Spanish Writers 1920–1936*, Oxford: Oxford University Press, 1980.

25. See Lorca, *Obras completas*, pp. 1762–7.

26. Ibid., pp. 1810–11.

27. In an interview published in *La Nación*, Buenos Aires, 14 October 1933, p. 9.

28. For a full account, see Maria Delgado and Gwynne Edwards, 'From Madrid to Stratford East: *The Public* in Performance', *Estreno*, 16, no. 2, 1990, pp. 11–17.

29. January 1988.

30. January 1988.

31. See Delgado and Edwards, pp. 11–17.

32. 13 October 1988.

33. 13 October 1988.

34. 12 October 1988.

35. 13 October 1988.

CHAPTER 2

1. See Rafael Martínez Nadal, *Lorca's The Public: A Study of His Unfinished Play* (El público) *and of Love and Death in the Work of Federico García*

Lorca, London: Calder and Boyars, 1974, p. 98.

2. Carlos Morla Lynch, *En España con Federico García Lorca: Páginas de un diario íntimo, 1928–36*, Madrid: Aguilar, 1958, pp. 105–12.

3. The interview is published in Lorca, *Obras completas*, del Hoyo (ed.), p. 1811.

4. See *Lorca Plays: Two*, Edwards (ed. and tr.).

5. See Gibson, pp. 157, 220.

6. Ibid., p. 229.

7. Ibid., pp. 275–6.

8. See Lorca, *Trip to the Moon*, Duncan (tr.), pp. 35–41.

9. Photographs of Lorca from childhood up to the year of his death, including several of him in a white suit, may be found in José Luis Cano, *García Lorca, biografía ilustrada*, Barcelona: Ediciones Destino, 1962.

10. See Lorca, *Obras completas*, del Hoyo (ed.), p. 1754.

11. See Gibson, p. 146.

12. See *Lorca Plays: Two*, Edwards (ed. and tr.).

13. See Chapter 1, note 22.

14. There is a very useful study of Expressionism by J.L. Styan, *Modern Drama in Theory and Practice, 3, Expressionism and Epic Theatre*, Cambridge: Cambridge University Press, 1981.

15. See David George, 'Commedia dell'arte and Mask in Lorca', in *Lorca: Poet and Playwright*, Robert Havard (ed.), Cardiff: University of Wales Press, 1992.

16. Rafael Alberti, *La arboleda perdida*, Buenos Aires, 1959, p. 130. The translation is my own.

17. See Gibson, pp. 431, 434.

18. See Francisco Alvaro, *El espectador y la crítica: el teatro en España en 1978*, Valladolid: Gráficos Andrés Martín, 1979, p. 83.

19. *Ya*, September 1978.

20. 30 April 1989.

21. 30 April 1989.

22. 22 August 1989.

23. 7 September 1989.

24. August 1989.

25. 26 August 1989.

26. August 1989.

27. 19 February 1997.

CHAPTER 3

1. On the history of the company see Byrd, '*La Barraca*', and Sáenz de la Calzada, '*La Barraca*'.

2. Quoted by Alardo Prats in 'Los artistas en el ambiente de nuestro tiempo', *El Sol*, Madrid, 15 December 1934.

3. See Edward Gordon Craig, *The Art of the Theatre*, London: Heinemann, 1980, p. 138. (The original edition of Craig's book had appeared in 1905.)

4. See Byrd, '*La Barraca*', p. 47.

5. The Spanish text of the lecture, 'Las nanas infantiles', is given in Lorca, *Obras completas*, del Hoyo (ed.), pp. 91–108. There is an English translation in Federico García Lorca, *Deep Song and Other Prose*, Christopher Maurer (ed. and tr.), London and Boston: Marion Boyars, 1980, pp. 7–22.

6. For the Spanish text, see Lorca, *Obras completas*, del Hoyo (ed.), pp. 39–61; for an English translation, see Lorca, *Deep Song*, Maurer (ed. and tr.), pp. 23–41.

7. For the Spanish text see Lorca, *Obras completas*, del Hoyo (ed.), p. 304.

8. For an English translation, see Lorca, *Deep Song*, Maurer (ed. and tr.), pp. 104–22. See also Federico García Lorca, *Gypsy Ballads*, Robert G. Havard (ed. and tr.), Warminster: Aris and Phillips, 1990. This volume contains all the poems in translation, with introduction and commentary.

9. For more information on Margarita Xirgu's theatre work, see Rodrigo, *Margarita Xirgu y su teatro*.

10. On the original story, see Gibson, pp. 335–9. A detailed account also appeared in the *Sunday Times Magazine*, 29 June 1986, pp. 34–9, in connection with the fiftieth anniversary of Lorca's death.

11. See Jean J. Smoot, *A Comparison of Plays by John Millington Synge and Federico García Lorca: The Poets and Time*, Madrid: Ediciones José Porrúa Turanzas, 1978.

12. For the Spanish text, see 'Canción de jinete' ('The Rider's Song'), in Lorca, *Obras completas*, del Hoyo (ed.), pp. 376–7.

13. Ibid., 'La Luna y La Muerte' ('The Moon and Death'), pp. 264–5.

14. Ibid., pp. 430–32. The poem 'Romance sonámbulo' ('Somnambular Ballad') is in Lorca, *Gypsy Ballads*, Robert G. Havard (tr.), pp. 52–7.

15. See Gibson, p. 378.

16. In his lecture on 'deep song'. See Lorca, *Obras completas*, del Hoyo (ed.), p. 46.

17. For a more detailed consideration of the subject, see Gwynne Edwards, 'The Way Things Are: Towards a Definition of Lorcan Tragedy', in *Anales de la literatura española contemporánea*, 21, 1996, pp. 271–90.

18. Quoted in the Spanish edition of the play, introduced and edited by José Monleón, Barcelona: Aymá Editora, 1971, p. 31.

19. See Morla Lynch, pp. 329–35.

20. See Francisco García Lorca, *Federico y su mundo*, Madrid: Editorial Alianza, 1980, p. 335.

21. See Christopher Maurer, 'Bach and *Bodas de sangre*', in *Lorca's Legacy: Essays on Lorca's Life, Poetry and Theatre*, Manuel Durán and Francesca Colecchia (eds), New York: Peter Lang, 1991, pp. 103–14.

22. See Marcelle Auclaire, *Vida y muerte de García Lorca*, Aitana Alberti (tr.), Ciudad México: Era, 1972, p. 275.

23. *El Sol*, Madrid, 9 March 1933, p. 8.

24. *La Vanguardia*, Barcelona, 24 November, 1935.

25. 11 June 2001.

26. 6 June 2001.

CHAPTER 4

1. See Gibson, p. 289.

2. See Morla Lynch, pp. 426–9.

3. For the Spanish text, see Lorca, *Obras completas*, del Hoyo (ed.), pp. 201–3.

4. Ibid., pp. 433–4.

5. The pilgrimage to Moclín is described in Gibson, pp. 289–90, and in Stainton, p. 332.

6. See Sáenz de la Calzada, pp. 123–72. The author, a member of the company, provides a detailed account of the itinerary.

7. All translations from *Yerma* are my own, unpublished.

8. For the English text, see *Calderón Plays: One*, Gwynne Edwards (tr.),

London: Methuen, 1991.

9. Gibson, p. 439. Lorca had originally made this statement in an interview published in the newspaper *El Sol* on 10 June 1936, just over a month before his murder.

10. For the Spanish text, see Lorca, *Obras completas*, del Hoyo (ed.), pp. 1754–5.

11. The adjective *yermo* means 'barren', used in particular to describe unproductive land. The feminine form, *yerma*, has presumably been applied to Juan's childless wife by the villagers in a typically cruel and unfeeling manner, and is, in effect, a nickname.

12. For an account of Spanish theatre at this time, see Edwards, *Dramatists in Perspective*.

13. In *Blood Wedding* the Bride's mother, anticipating her daughter's actions, has been unfaithful to her husband, while the father and the brother of the Bridegroom, both murdered, are pointers to his own fate.

14. See Byrd, p. 71.

15. Ezio Levy, 'La Barraca di García Lorca', *Scenario*, Vol. 10, 1934, p. 530.

16. See the introduction to Federico García Lorca, *Three Tragedies*, James Graham Luján and Richard O'Connell (tr.), Harmondsworth: Penguin, 1961, p. 25.

17. See Chapter 3, note 3.

18. For an account of the première, see Morla Lynch, pp. 432–6.

19. See the edition of the play edited by Mario Hernández, Madrid: Alianza Editorial, 1980, pp. 135–6.

20. 31 December 1934.

21. 30 December 1934.

22. 30 December 1934.

23. 4 October 1961.

24. García's and Monleón's views may be found in the edition of the play edited by Monleón, Barcelona: Aymá Editoria, 1973, pp. 26–9.

25. 20 August 1986.

26. 20 August 1986.

27. 24 August 1986.

28. 28 March 1987.

29. 27 March 1987.

CHAPTER 5

1. Lorca himself said that Act One took place in 1890, Act Two in 1900, and Act Three in 1910. The subtitle – *A poem of 1900 Granada* – refers therefore to the turn of the century rather than to 1900 itself.

2. If fifteen years have passed since the Nephew's departure, and the action of Act Two takes place in 1900, this means that Act One is set not in 1890 but in 1885.

3. The interview took place on 15 December 1934.

4. See Gibson, p. 400.

5. The factual background to the play is well documented by Gibson, pp. 404–7.

6. The argument does not quite hold if Act One takes place in 1885.

7. Lorca wrote an evocative description of the Albaicín in *Impresiones y paisajes*, Granada: Paulino Ventura, 1918. The text is available in Lorca, *Obras completas*, del Hoyo (ed.), pp. 1535–92.

8. See Robert Lima, *The Theater of García Lorca*, New York: Las Americas Publishing Co., 1963, p. 243.

9. See the introduction to Lorca, *Three Tragedies*, Luján and O'Connell (tr.), p. 22.

10. Karl Czerny (1791–1857) was an Austrian composer and pianist. Since Lorca was himself an outstanding pianist and chose the music for the first production of *Doña Rosita*, he clearly felt that Czerny's *étude* underpinned the mood of this scene.

11. See Gibson, p. 290.

12. See Francisco García Lorca's observation in the introduction to Lorca, *Three Tragedies*, Luján and O'Connell (tr.), pp. 22–3.

13. On the theatrical background, see Edwards, *Dramatists in Perspective*.

14. See Rodrigo, pp. 227–30.

15. 14 December 1935.

16. 15 December 1935.

17. See Rodrigo, p. 229.

18. For details on this production, see the book produced by the Centro Dramático Nacional: Federico García Lorca, *Doña Rosita la Soltera*,

Madrid: Colección Libro – Documento Centro Dramático Nacional, 3, 1981, chapter 3.
19. August 1983.
20. August 1983.
21. August 1983.
22. August 1983.
23. August 1983.
24. August 1983.
25. 16 October 1989.
26. October 1989.
27. 19 October 1989.
28. 1 May 1997.

CHAPTER 6

1. All references and translations into English are from the bilingual edition of the play, Edwards (tr.).
2. See Gwynne Edwards, '"Comedia corriente de los tiempos actuales" : Lorca's *Comedia sin título*', *Journal of the Institute of Romance Studies*, 2, 1993, p. 334.
3. For details on the last weeks of Lorca's life, see Gibson, Chapter 12.
4. Ibid., p. 468.
5. An interview with Alardo Prats, *El Sol*, 15 December 1934. See Lorca, *Obras completas*, del Hoyo (ed.), p. 1767.
6. See *Lorca Plays: Three*, Edwards (ed. and tr.).
7. See Morla Lynch, pp. 488–9. The translation is my own.
8. For background, see Gibson, pp. 436–7.
9. Described by Adolfo Salazar in '*La casa de Bernarda Alba*', *Carteles*, Havana, 10 April 1938, p. 50.
10. Gerald Brenan, *The Spanish Labyrinth*, Cambridge: Cambridge University Press, 1943, pp. 114–26.
11. 'The Gypsy Nun', one of the poems in *Gypsy Ballads*, describes the frustration of a young woman sent to a convent.
12. Although Lorca's love of Granada was deep and constant, he frequently

referred to it as a land-locked town. Geographically it is, of course, cut off from the sea by the Sierra Nevada and is very different in that respect from Seville, which is on the River Guadalquivir and offers easy access to the ocean. For Lorca the sea represented open spaces, freedom and escape.

13. On the other hand, Lorca would not have wished to react to his mother as Adela does to hers.

14. See Byrd, p. 77.

15. See Lorca, *Three Tragedies*, Luján and O'Connell (tr.), p. 28.

16. See Rodrigo, pp. 268–73.

17. *El Hogar*, Buenos Aires, March 1945.

18. *La Nación*, Buenos Aires, 9 March 1945.

19. See Rodrigo, p. 271.

20. Cistue de Castro, 29 January 1965.

21. Bardem's production notes are published in Federico García Lorca, *La casa de Bernarda Alba*, Barcelona: Aymá Editora, 1964, pp. 109–22.

22. Ibid., p. 110.

23. 29 January 1965.

24. 29 January 1965.

25. Plaza's production notes can be found in Federico García Lorca, *La casa de Bernarda Alba*, Madrid: Los libros del Teatro Español, 1984.

26. 16 November 1984.

27. 18 November 1984.

28. 16–18 November 1984.

29. 'Plays in Performance', *Drama*, 73, No. 109, 1973, pp. 27–8.

30. 19 January 1987.

31. 26 September 1986.

32. 19 January 1987.

33. 10 September 1986.

34. 21 January 1987.

Select Bibliography

Lorca's Plays in English Translation

Lorca Plays: One, Gwynne Edwards (with Peter Luke) (tr. and ed.), London: Methuen, 1987

Lorca Plays: Two, Gwynne Edwards (tr. and ed.), London: Methuen, 1990

Lorca Plays: Three, Gwynne Edwards (with Henry Livings) (tr. and ed.), London: Methuen, 1994

Blood Wedding, Gwynne Edwards (tr. and ed.), London: Methuen, 1997

The House of Bernarda Alba / La casa de Bernarda Alba, Gwynne Edwards (tr. and ed.), London: Methuen, 1998

Background and Criticism

Adams, Mildred, *García Lorca: Playwright and Poet*, New York: George Braziller, 1977

Allen, Rupert, *Psyche and Symbol in the Theater of Federico García Lorca*, Austin and London: University of Texas Press, 1974

Anderson, Andrew A., *García Lorca: La zapatera prodigiosa*, Critical Guides to Spanish Texts, London: Grant and Cutler, in association with Tamesis Books, 1991

Auclair, Marcelle, *Vida y muerte de García Lorca*, Ciudad México: Era, 1972

Babín, María Teresa, *García Lorca, vida y obra*, New York: Las Américas, 1955

— *Estudios lorquianos*, Puerto Rico: Editorial Universitaria, 1976

Binding, Paul, *Lorca: The Gay Imagination*, London: GMP Publishers, 1985

Buñuel, Luis, *Mon dernier soupir*, Paris: Robert Laffont, 1982

Byrd, Suzanne, *'La Barraca' and the Spanish National Theatre*, New York: Ediciones Abra, 1975

Cano, José Luis, *García Lorca: Biografía ilustrada*, Barcelona: Destino, 1962

Correa, Gustavo, *La poesía mítica de Federico García Lorca*, 2nd edn, Madrid: Gredos, 1975

Dalí, Salvador, *The Secret Life of Salvador Dalí*, London: Vision Press, 1968

Delgado, Maria, and Gwynne Edwards, 'From Madrid to Stratford East: *The Public* in Performance', *Estreno*, 16, 1990, pp. 11–18

Doggart, Sebastian, and Michael Thompson, *Fire, Blood and the Alphabet: One Hundred Years of Lorca*, Durham: University of Durham, 1999

Edwards, Gwynne, '*Bodas de sangre* in Performance', *Anales de la literatura española contemporánea*, 22, 1997, pp. 469–91

— '"Comedia corriente de los tiempos actuales", Lorca's *Comedia sin título*', *Journal of the Institute of Romance Studies*, 11, 1993, pp. 337–50

— *Dramatists in Perspective: Spanish Theatre in the Twentieth Century*, Cardiff: University of Wales Press, 1985

— 'Federico García Lorca: "Para el teatro dentro de muchos años"', *Anales de la literatura española contemporánea*, 17, 1992, pp. 125–44

— 'Lorca in the United Kingdom', *Donaire*, 10, 1998, pp. 23–30

— 'Lorca on the English Stage: Problems of Production and Translation', *New Theatre Quarterly*, 4, 1988, pp. 344–55

— *Lorca: The Theatre Beneath the Sand*, London: Marion Boyars, 1980

— 'Productions of *La casa de Bernarda Alba*', *Anales de la literatura española contemporánea*, 25, 2000, pp. 699–728

— 'Translating Lorca for the Theatre: *Blood Wedding, Yerma* and *The House of Bernarda Alba*', *Donaire*, 11, 1998, pp. 15–23

— 'The Way Things Are: Towards a Definition of Lorcan Tragedy', *Anales de la literatura española contemporánea*, 21, 1996, pp. 271–90

— '*Yerma* on Stage', *Anales de la literatura española contemporánea*, 24, 1999, pp. 433–51

Fernández Cifuentes, Luis, *García Lorca en el teatro: la norma y la diferencia*, Zaragoza: University of Zaragoza, 1986

Flys, Jonathan M., *El lenguaje poético de Federico García Lorca*, Madrid: Gredos, 1955

Frazier, Brenda, *La mujer en el teatro de Federico García Lorca*, Madrid: Plaza Mayor, 1973

García Lorca, Federico, *Gypsy Ballads*, Robert G. Havard (ed. and tr.),
Warminster: Aris and Phillips, 1990

— *Bodas de sangre*, H. Ramsden (ed.), Manchester: Manchester University
Press, 1980

— *La casa de Bernarda Alba*, H. Ramsden (ed.), Manchester University Press,
1983

Río, Angel del, *Vida y obras de Federico García Lorca*, Zaragoza: Heraldo de
Aragón, 1952

García Lorca, Francisco, *Federico y su mundo*, Mario Hernández (ed.), Madrid:
Alianza, 1981

— *In the Green Morning: Memories of Federico*, Christopher Maurer (tr.),
London: Peter Owen, 1989

Gibson, Ian, *The Assassination of Federico García Lorca*, New York: Penguin, 1983

— *Federico García Lorca I: de Fuente Vaqueros a Nueva York, 1898–1929*,
Barcelona: Grijalbo, 1985

— *Federico García Lorca II: de Nueva York a Fuente Grande, 1929–1936*,
Barcelona: Grijalbo, 1987

— *Federico García Lorca: A Life*, London: Faber and Faber, 1989

— *Lorca's Granada: A Practical Guide*, London: Faber and Faber, 1992

Havard, Robert, G. (ed.), *Lorca: Poet and Playwright*, Cardiff: University of
Wales Press, 1992

Higginbotham, Virginia, *The Comic Spirit of Federico García Lorca*, Austin and
London: University of Texas Press, 1976

Higuera Rojas, Eulalia-Dolores de la, *Mujeres en la vida de García Lorca*, Madrid:
Editora Nacional y Excma Diputación Provincial de Granada, 1980

Honig, Edwin, *García Lorca*, New York: New Directions, 1963

Hooper, John, *The New Spaniards*, revised edn, London: Penguin, 1995

Laffranque, Marie, *Les Idées esthétiques de Federico García Lorca*, Bordeaux:
Institut d'Études Hispaniques, 1967

Lima, Robert, *The Theater of García Lorca*, New York: Las Américas, 1963

Marinello, Juan, *García Lorca en Cuba*, Havana: Belic, 1965

Martín Martín, Jacinto, *Los años de aprendizaje de Federico y Francisco García
Lorca*, Granada: Excmo Ayuntamiento de Granada, 1984

Martínez Nadal, Rafael, *Lorca's* The Public: *A Study of His Unfinished Play* (El público) *and of Love and Death in the Work of Federico García Lorca*, London: Calder and Boyars, 1974

Mora Guarnido, José, *Federico García Lorca y su mundo*, Buenos Aires: Losada, 1958

Morla Lynch, Carlos, *En España con Federico García Lorca: Páginas de un diario íntimo, 1928–1936*, Madrid: Aguilar, 1957

Morris, C.B., *García Lorca, Bodas de sangre*, Critical Guides to Spanish Texts, London: Grant and Cutler, in association with Tamesis Books, 1980

Morris, C.B., *García Lorca, La casa de Bernarda Alba*, Critical Guides to Spanish Texts, London: Grant and Cutler, in association with Tamesis Books, 1990

Rodrigo, Antonina, *Margarita Xirgu y su teatro*, Barcelona: Editorial Planeta, 1974

— *Lorca–Dalí, Una amistad traicionada*, Barcelona: Editorial Planeta, 1981

Sánchez, Roberto G., *García Lorca: Estudio sobre su teatro*, Madrid: Editorial Jura, 1950

Sánchez Vidal, Agustín, *Buñuel, Lorca, Dalí: El enigma sin fin*, Barcelona: Editorial Planeta, 1988

— *Luis Buñuel: Obra literaria*, Zaragoza, Heraldo de Aragón, 1982

Sáenz de la Calzada, Luis, *'La Barraca': Teatro Universitario*, Madrid: Biblioteca de la Revista de Occidente, 1976

Schönberg, Jean-Louis, *A la recherche de Lorca*, Neuchâtel: Baconnière, 1966

— *Federico García Lorca: l'homme, l'œuvre*, Paris: Plon, 1956

Smoot, Jean J., *A Comparison of Plays by John Millington Synge and Federico García Lorca: The Poets and Time*, Madrid: Ediciones José Porrúa Turanzas, 1978

Stainton, Leslie, *Lorca: A Dream of Life*, London: Bloomsbury, 1998

Trend, J.B., *Lorca and the Spanish Poetic Tradition*, Oxford: Basil Blackwell, 1956

Umbral, Francisco, *Lorca, poeta maldito*, Madrid: Biblioteca Nueva, 1968

Valle, Luis González del, *La tragedia en el teatro de Unamuno, Valle-Inclán y García Lorca*, New York: Eliseo Torres and Sons, 1975

Vilches de Frutos, María Francisca and Dru Dougherty (eds.), *Los estrenos teatrales de Federico García Lorca*, Madrid: Tabapress, 1992

Warner, Robin (ed.), *Yerma*, Manchester: Manchester University Press, 1994

Index